PERSPECTIVES ON PAUL

PERSPECTIVES ON PAUL

Ernst Käsemann

SIGLER PRESS

MIFFLINTOWN, PA

FIRST SIGLER PRESS EDITION 1996

This book is a translation by Margaret Kohl of *Paulinische Perspektiven*
copyright © 1969 by J. C. B. Mohr (Paul Siebeck) in Tübingen,
Germany.

This limited edition licensed by special permission of
Augsburg Fortress.

Library of Congress Card Number 96–6426

ISBN 1–888961–00–7

Dedicated with gratitude
to the theological faculties in Durham and Edinburgh,
which universities have conferred on me
the honour of a Doctorate in Divinity

CONTENTS

PREFACE

The basis of this book is four lectures which I delivered a number of times in America during 1965 and 1966 and which I have since revised. I have added three articles which are related to the main theme. The one on 'The Saving Significance of the Death of Jesus in Paul' has already appeared in a slightly different form in the collection edited by F. Viering, *Zur Bedeutung des Todes Jesu*, 1967, pp. 11–34. That on 'The Cry for Liberty in the Worship of the Church' is taken from *Apophoreta*, the Festschrift for E. Haenchen, 1964, pp. 142–55; the Verlag De Gruyter, Berlin, have kindly given me permission to include it here. The article on 'The Spirit and the Letter' was to have been given as a lecture to the Societas Novi Testamenti Studiorum in 1967, but I was prevented by illness.

I have no intention of presenting an outline of Pauline theology in this book. Nevertheless, I hope that I have succeeded in drawing out important aspects of it. Once again, both friends and opponents will find that I have not taken a party line. An incidental description of me by a reviewer as 'a man who disagrees with everybody about everything' goes rather too far; were that the case, I would have to be put away. Nevertheless, as one who is fond of keeping out of step, I regard it as a compliment that others are aware of the results earlier than the ways that lead to them. We can never get away from prejudices, but we must keep trying to become more independent and at least to penetrate more deeply into the problems with which we are faced. It is probably more difficult for theologians to be converted than for other people. Perhaps one is on the way when one has decided not to howl with the wolves or to bray with the asses.

The fact that a Briton protected me against the criticism of his fellow countryman that I mentioned above gives me courage to dedicate these articles to two theological faculties of whose recognition I am proud.

Tübingen
August 15 1969

I

ON PAUL'S ANTHROPOLOGY

Few themes have so enduringly influenced the whole of theology during the last generation as the theme of Paul's anthropology. An analysis of this anthropology was, indeed, one of the essential presuppositions and catalysts of what is known as the 'theology of existence'. It was from this starting-point that Rudolf Bultmann formulated his programmatic statement: 'Every assertion about God is simultaneously an assertion about man and vice versa. For this reason and in this sense Paul's theology is, at the same time, anthropology. . . . Thus, every assertion about Christ is also an assertion about man and vice versa; and Paul's christology is simultaneously soteriology.'[1] Bultmann is working from the insight that Paul neither talks about God and Christ nor about the world and man in isolation; for him each is related to the other.[2] But Bultmann goes far beyond the generally recognized[3] relation of creator and creature as the basis of Paul's anthropology, because this is to miss its specific and unique character. In the whole of the New Testament it is only Paul who expounds what we should call a thoroughly thought-out doctrine of man, although, oddly enough, it already became superficial in the hands of his disciples or was even abandoned by them altogether. This fact has to be explained before we venture on what Paul includes in the rest of his biblical proclamation. Neither exegesis nor

---

[1] *Theology of the New Testament* I, 1952, p. 191.

[2] *Ibid.*, pp. 190f.

[3] Cf. W. Gutbrod, *Die paulinische Anthropologie*, 1934, pp. 5f., 19f.; C. H. Dodd, 'Man in God's Design according to the New Testament', *Man in God's Design*, 1952, p. 10; P. I. Bratsiotis, 'Das Menschenverständnis des Neuen Testamentes', *ibid.*, p. 21 : H. Mehl-Koehnlein, *L'homme selon l'Apôtre Paul*, 1951, p. 6; W. D. Stacey, *The Pauline View of Man*, 1956, p. 238, where the writer even goes so far as to deny that Paul was interested in anthropology *per se*.

theology benefits by harmonization, for both have to aim at particu-
larization if they are not to end up in the obvious or in the prejudices of the moment.

Bultmann rightly draws attention to the importance which Paul
assigns to the individual. The other New Testament writers view a
person more or less as the representative of a group – Judaism or the
Gentile world, the chosen people, the disciples, the church. For Paul,
too, this aspect has its relevance, and he always has it in mind. But at
the same time, with unusual emphasis and by no means merely
paraenetically, he brings the individual, as believer or unbeliever,
into prominence. This can hardly be by chance: the faith in the God
who justifies the ungodly which Paul proclaimed so passionately does
not merely burst apart the bonds of the law; it also breaks through
the religious regulations and social ties or limits which had obtained
before. In so far as these are still retained and recognized, they are
merely the sphere in which the Christian has to prove his liberation
from the forces which had once enslaved him, and with it the sole
sovereignty of Jesus. Even within the church he must not fall back
under the pressure of similar dependencies; even in the community
of the body of Christ he is more than a dispensable member of a cor-
poration, for he is the irreplaceable representative of his Lord.

Paul here differs from the Gnostics who, as far as we can see, were
the only other people who possessed a fully worked-out anthropology.
No doubt, under the pressure of its enthusiasm, the church began to
dissolve into a multiplicity of groups and individuals. Interpreting
their divinely conferred gifts as heavenly privileges, they ecstatically
demonstrated, each in his own way, the gospel of liberated man.
Both his historical milieu and his personal experience brought the
apostle close to these people, so that it was not by chance that he was
able to adopt their language and to concede that, up to a certain
point, they were right. At the same time, there was a basic difference
between them. True, both speak in antitheses of the old things of
earth and the new things of heaven. Both say that only the miracle of
rebirth can turn the fleshly man into the pneumatic. But Paul is
aware of the potential relapse into fleshly existence with which the
Corinthians evidently do not reckon. He is not content with ecstatic
manifestations, but asks what use they are to the Christian community.
For him the Christian is not yet removed from temptation, but must
prove himself in the face of that temptation. In his view the divine
Spirit also demonstrates its presence, astonishingly enough, in the

capacity for self-criticism, although that fact was all too often forgotten or suppressed in the church. Paul, in fact, saw this Spirit as being more than the manifestation of a supernatural power which disseminates, with explosive force, its manifold gifts on earth in the end-time; and in consequence he did not understand even the pneumatic as being merely the demonstrator of this power. The man who believes himself to be immune from temptation knows that he is no longer responsible. He has in principle severed himself from all earthly things, even if he pays tribute to them in practice; he is laying claim to heavenly status. This may be exemplified, as he thinks, in speaking with tongues (the language of the angels) or in other ecstasies and in miraculous deeds. The manifold character of the gifts of the Spirit are certainly praised. But they only reveal different aspects of the self-manifestations of the transcendent. The difference in the gifts is therefore no longer of decisive importance, since all radiate the same heavenly splendour. Consequently the bearers of the gifts are not ultimately differentiated either, although the world sees them as different. They themselves know that 'there is neither slave nor free, there is neither male nor female'. Circumcision and uncircumcision, Greek or barbarian origin – all are unimportant. Earthly individuation is a delusion. Supernatural unity joins together what appears on earth to be individual and differentiated. The truth within and behind such reality is the uniformity of heavenly being.[4] This uniformity is consequently postulated by slaves and women in worship and is aimed at in everyday life. This is the Christian root of the secularized demand for equality made by the revolutions of the western world.

Of course, Paul cannot uphold this anthropological scheme, although he shares many of its premises. He, too, speaks about the transformation of earthly life, but in his view this shows itself only in a new life lived to the praise of God and for the service of one's neighbour. For Paul, unity in the body of Christ does not mean the sameness of all the members; it means the solidarity which can endure the strain of the differences – the different gifts and different weaknesses of the different members. Faith confers a sense of responsibility, though it does so in a freedom which cannot be qualified either by the models and programmes of a systematic doctrine or by casuistry. It rather gives concrete form to the phrase 'worthy of the Lord' in

[4] Gutbrod, *op. cit.*, pp. 29f., speaks of 'uniformity in differentiation', which would be applicable to the enthusiasts rather than to Paul.

varying situations and according to the partner involved, discovering this form out of love and hope, with imagination and sympathetic understanding – that is to say with an open-mindedness which cannot be tied down by legalistic or even moral prescriptions. The individual existence which develops in a framework of this kind can hardly be conceived of in more radical terms. Here the individual is the representative, not of an idea or an organization, but of the crucified Lord whose unmistakable characteristics can never be appropriated by ideologies or organizations without friction or anomaly. They must be constantly recognized afresh and transferred to new data. For them, there is no cultic centre which permits of continual repetition. Their purpose is to permeate everyday life and to determine a historical path which no one knows in advance. A member of the Christian community does not represent a static order, although most Christians assume that this is the case. He is constantly representing others and is in confrontation with them. Everyone has his own gifts and his own duty; everyone is irreplaceable in the service assigned to him and unmistakable in his particular capacities and weaknesses. That is why the apostle is always repeating the watchword, 'Everyone according to the gifts which God has given him, everyone according to his calling.' In redemption, as in creation, everything is differentiated because otherwise no mutual service is possible. God does not want stereotypes. He challenges the individual not to let himself be fitted into a pattern or a programme, even in his natural, political and spiritual ties; he challenges him to resist uniformity, to discover and use the talents given to him, not to think himself useless because of his faults and failings, but to be in his own station in life a banner of victory uplifted for Christ. To overlook this is to misunderstand Paul's teaching about the Word of God. As Bultmann rightly points out, the primary concern of this teaching is not to convey dogmatic information, nor even to give an elevating account of salvation history, although both these things are necessary and have their proper place. Paul's real concern is with address. It may occasionally be useful – indeed, it may even be fundamentally necessary – to put this still more strongly: his concern is with challenge, by virtue of which the creator calls from chaos into being and the redeemer from destruction to salvation. Prophecy is challenge when it is aligned to promise, exodus and the first commandment. The word of the cross is challenge when it teaches us that the glory of the church is that it can be the earthly image of its exalted Lord and can take up the cross after him. Finally, the message of the resurrection of the dead is also challenge, because it does not only mean victory over the grave but also the reality of the *basileia*, in which the demonic world is conquered and left behind, and complete liberty is won.

I think it is important to put this in as sharp a form as possible, because it also throws light on Paul's anthropology. According to the apostle, whatever else may determine man, he is a challengeable and a continually challenged being. This is a constitutive part of his existence, and it is not only his ontic being which is thereby determined on each particular occasion. From this starting point it is also possible to trace the ontology which is so much talked about today.[5] Man is always faced with a call – a call to which he must respond in his thinking, his speaking, his acting and his suffering. He is a created being in that he experiences the divine address, which compels him to earthly pilgrimage. This fact makes him a historical being: he stands beneath the sign of exodus and his horizon is hope. This is reflected in his history, inasmuch as he understands creation as the first and redemption as the last call to himself and his world, in that he is continuously claimed or blessed by neighbour and stranger, is assailed by fears and demons and is faced with the compulsion of dying. The believer fits into this pattern, too: in the shadow of the cross of Christ he breaks through already existing, fixed systems and camps, grasping the Gospel as *promissio*, no longer measuring life and death by what is to hand but interpreting them as spheres in which, hearing the divine call, a man can obey or close his ears to it, for a time or for eternity. For salvation does not simply mean a state; it is an endless path which has been thrown open to us, a path which is ceaselessly characterized by a forgetting of that which lies behind and a straining forward to that which lies ahead. The romantic may deem this a journey into adventure, the nihilist may call it a march into no-man's land. Both descriptions would be a misunderstanding – a misunderstanding justified in one respect by Gen. 12 and Heb. 12, in so far as even salvation contains the unplumbed depths of its future and, in imitation of the Nazarene, presents itself on earth paradoxically *sub contrario*, in this, too, challenging the world and its forces. Ultimately, however, the path is a path overshadowed by the promise of the first commandment, in which all the challenges of the Gospel

---

[5] Paul always speaks of man in his specific reality and his anthropological ontology must be deduced from this. The present article is particularly concerned with this theme, and is thus a reply to E. Güttgemanns' criticisms in *Der leidende Apostel und sein Herr*, 1966, pp. 207ff.

are summed up and from which the Christian life itself acquires the
hall-mark of challenge – the challenge of being called to be a new
creation and a new man. This, then, is the horizon which makes the
radicalism with which Kierkegaard spoke of the individual possible
and meaningful. It is also, it seems to me, the dimension out of which
Pauline anthropology grew and developed – an anthropology which
is unique among the New Testament writings in its searching
intensity.

Astonishingly enough, it is only for about the last hundred years
that this anthropology has been a separate subject of research. F. C.
Baur, the pioneer of radical historical criticism, assigned problems of
detail to lower criticism, which had not yet recognized the necessity
of fitting every epoch into the universal movement of mind in its
gradual acquiring of consciousness. With his eyes turned towards the
meaning of history, he only extracted from anthropology a self-
understanding which pointed beyond itself to the meaning of cosmic
happening. Anthropology could only take on central significance after
the idealistic conception had been lost in the multiplicity of separate
questions (to whose fundamental problems it had given access), thus
giving way to positivism.

In 1872 Lüdemann published his book on Paul's anthropology.[6]
This book determined the period which followed, not only because
scholars could never again lose sight of its theme but because Lüdemann laid bare what was an apparently insoluble dilemma. For those
who had not yet abandoned idealism, something like a Pauline
schizophrenia resulted. In the history of religion this manifested itself
in a syncretistic combination of Jewish and Hellenistic traditions. It
meant the parallelism of a juridical-ethical and a sacramental-
mystical way of thinking. Man – at least redeemed man – became
the point of intersection between nature and the supernatural,
which were dualistically split apart. To be alive to this, and to
allow oneself to be drawn more and more by the divine Spirit into
the supernatural sphere, seemed to be the specifically Christian
characteristic, although that remained an awkward and only partly
acceptable view in the environment of Protestant culture. Things
became even more difficult, since from the end of the nineteenth
century onwards it was recognized with increasing clarity that the
eschatological expectation of the end of the world determined the

---

[6] Hermann Lüdemann, *Die Anthropologie des Apostels Paulus und ihre Stellung
innerhalb seiner Heilslehre*, Kiel, 1872.

whole of the New Testament, and Paul especially. Cultic and mystical piety on the one hand and ethical demands on the other were clung to; everything else was a matter of perplexity. The key notion of 'organism' offered a solution and a refuge. From this standpoint earthly life was conceived of as a maturing process, in which the transition from the natural to the transcendental sphere is accomplished, the Christian community, like the world itself, being the testing place of inner growth and earthly creativity. Interruptions, relapses, and breaches in the development could be acknowledged. What hovered before the mind of the individual as an endlessly approaching, far-off goal was objectively guaranteed, so to speak, in the church, so that the remaining dualism of ideal and empirical reality could be, if not removed, at least intellectually spanned.[7]

It was into this situation that Bultmann's interpretation irrupted in 1925,[8] illuminating the whole of Paul's theology from the perspective of his anthropology. Bultmann's view has fallen under the catchword of demythologizing, although this only takes the preliminary historical work into consideration, not the systematic goal. The basic insight of Bultmann's interpretation was that the apostle's anthropological termini do not, as in the Greek world, characterize the component parts of the human organism; they apply to existence as a whole, while taking account of its varying orientation and capacity in any given case.[9] That this called in question the whole idea of organism in Pauline theology is seldom clearly recognized, important though this is. Of course, key words and images from the organic sphere can be found. They become important, however, only in ecclesiology, or, to be exact, in the theme of the world-wide body of Christ with its many members. It would seem that the idea of organism was not primary even here, because the *motif* first describes in mythological terms the breaking in of the lordship of Christ as transcendent reality into the earthly sphere. Probably it was Paul himself who, for paraenetic purposes, first rationalized the *mythologoumenon* with the help of the idea of the *polis* or the cosmos as a community of many members – a notion taken from popular philosophy.

---

[7] An approach to the overcoming of this dualism in the history of religion can now be found in Egon Brandenburger's book, *Fleisch und Geist*, 1968.

[8] It first appeared in his article on Paul in RGG² IV, cols. 1019ff.

[9] Cf. also E. Schweizer, *TWNT* VII, 1028ff., 1045f.; J. A. T. Robinson, *The Body*, 1952, p. 12; Mehl-Koehnlein, *op. cit.*, p. 26; Stacey, *op. cit.*, pp. 222ff. For another view see T. W. Manson, *On Paul and John*, 1963, pp. 37f.; Bratsiotis, *op. cit.*, p. 29.

The organic therefore serves here as the point of contact with the ethical demand. In I Cor. 15.35ff. the relation between the earthly and the risen body is described in terms of the image of the seed and the fruit, but the point of the analogy is not the growth through change but the breach which dying makes between the old and the new. Only miracle can bridge the two. So it is not by chance that the apostle comes to grief in his attempt to depict pictorially the connection of earthly and heavenly corporeality, or has to resort to a number of doubtful analogies.[10]

The problem which is involved here must not be considered in isolation, though this is common practice. For it reveals a logical dilemma which is generally obscured, not exposed, by the catchword about the historicity of existence and the world. The notion of an inherent continuity of life is alien to Paul's thinking.[11] In places where we would speak of development, the idea of miracle takes hold in Paul, the miracle which bridges the gap between different things. Thus baptism marks the death of the old man and the miraculous beginning of a new life under the banner of the resurrection. That is why in Gal. 2.20 he declares: 'It is no longer I who live, but Christ who lives in me.' In the same way, in Rom. 7.10 the fall is described as being the death of the original creature. Adam is a different person before and after the fall. The apostle therefore does not adhere to the Jewish view which – completely consistently and understandably in the light of their understanding of the Law – maintained that a divine likeness still remained. For him, only Christ has and is *imago dei*, an image which is only given back to us with faith. Just as the Christian is divided from Jew and Gentile through the sacramental event, so also the epochs of salvation history are contrasted with one another, Adam, Abraham, Moses, Christ and the world of the resurrection being sharply distinguished. This is the point where the notorious dilemma in I. Cor. 15.35ff. is to be found. It is possible to talk about the transfigured body; but this means the glorified body which is in crass contrast to the 'base' one – it is not the heavenly transformation of the latter. According to II Cor. 5.2ff. the two phases are divided by a stage of nakedness, before which Paul feels a positively metaphysical shrinking, because the earthly is left behind and the heavenly is not yet attained. When, however, he assumes that those who experience the *parousia* will be 'further clothed', he evi-

---

[10] It was different in Jewish circles; cf. Brandenburger, *op. cit.*, pp. 6off.
[11] Cf. F. Neugebauer, *In Christus*, 1961, p. 112.

dently means a complete transformation. This corresponds to the fact that in II Cor. 4.7ff. he talks paraenetically of transfiguration as being a participation in the suffering and death of Jesus. At the present time the power of the resurrection expresses itself in the actual shattering of the earthly vessel, in being crucified with Christ, in obscurity, in lowliness and obedience. The conclusion to which all these statements leads is that according to Paul discontinuity is the mark of both existence and history, not only in what is to hand in them but also in their encounters with salvation. It is only God who gives continuity, the God who, as creator, does not abandon his creatures, not even after the fall and far less under the token of promise and grace. In the whole of history, continuity only results from the divine faithfulness; and hence it manifests itself in miracle.

Because this is the case, the notion of organism, which is derived from earthly things, cannot play the part here which is frequently assigned to it. For Paul the world is not, as it is for the middle Stoa, the sphere of general sympathy. Without grace, which makes mutual service possible, it remains what it was at the beginning – a chaos of conflicting powers warring against one another, even, or especially, in the religious sphere. The all-embracing community breaks down where the law fences off its devotees from the Gentiles, or where enthusiasts take over the kingdom of freedom. The apostle does not make the cosmic order one of his themes, as in Luke's Areopagus discourse. When he talks about the cosmic order he merely stresses the duty of the citizen, of women and slaves, to conform to their station in life. The true and universal 'order' which he proclaims manifests itself in the eschatological 'peace', in the *treuga Dei* as a state of salvation and return to a lost creatureliness. It does not join on to and restore what is already in existence; it revolutionizes the world and the hearts of men through a new birth.

This forces us to a conclusion which has constantly been evaded at the cost not only of a better understanding but also of an appropriate approach to the question. It is always assumed as a complete matter of course that Paul shared our current view that the ultimate essence of the self – something like 'existence' itself – remains the same in all phases of life and salvation history. Even insight into the historical nature of man does not affect this ineffaceable continuity of the self, which survives all alterations and ruptures, and which Bultmann calls authentic existence. Now, it is impossible to overlook the fact that Paul does speak of a 'self' of this kind, which (according to Rom.

7.22) is, as inmost self, subject to the power of sin and yet has delight
in the will of God, or which will be called beyond the gates of death
before the judgment seat of Christ. But we must not make things too
easy for ourselves by forgetting the other side of the shield; for in Rom.
7.9 we find the exact opposite: 'I died'; and in Rom. 7.14, 'But I am
carnal, sold under sin'. This leads on to the problem of Rom. 7.16ff.,
according to which man is divided and in hopeless conflict with himself. This problem cannot be solved here. It serves us primarily as
evidence that our idea of identity is alien to the apostle's thinking.
The same thing emerges if we look at what he has to say about baptism, where he declares that the old man truly and radically dies; the
new man is therefore not to be understood as something like a metamorphosis of the old. Finally, we must enquire what we can and
should understand by the naked self which is not yet further clothed
but, being withdrawn from the earthly body, has to appear before the
seat of the final judge before becoming a partaker in the glory of the
resurrection. It is only in I Cor. 5.5 that Paul has given an answer to this,
when he says that the spirit of the incestuous man is to be preserved
through and beyond the judgment. But what this spirit actually is
remains as cloudy and undefined as the 'inmost self' of Rom. 7.[12]

We shall come back to this question again at the end. For the
moment it is enough if we establish the dilemma, because this takes
the interpretation of Pauline anthropology beyond even Bultmann's
analysis. By abandoning the question of the meaning of history or,
rather, by narrowing it down to the question of the meaning of the
historical nature of existence, Bultmann was inevitably bound to
maintain that Pauline theology takes its bearings from the individual.[13]
His presentation of New Testament theology is determined by this
thesis. Personal relations colour the total picture and allow even
Christian service to be described within the framework of an individual ethic. The fruitfulness of this approach is as indisputable as the
fascination of its systematic consistency. Yet the claim of this interpretation to exclusive truth must be deemed untenable. The fact that
it only corresponds to the self-understanding of 'modern' man (who
is in any case talked about in highly general and abstract terms)
belongs to the nineteenth century rather than to the second half of

---

[12] Cf. Brandenburger, *op. cit.* p. 83.
[13] *History and Eschatology* (Gifford Lectures), 1957, p. 42. For the contrary view
cf., for example, Dodd, *op. cit.*, pp. 17ff.; Mehl-Koehnlein, *op. cit.*, pp. 44ff.;
Robinson, *op. cit.*, pp. 7f.; O. Cullmann, *Salvation in History*, 1967, p. 67.

the twentieth. Contemporary literature and the visual arts do not testify greatly to man as the vehicle of history, even when they depict entirely secular man. To an increasing degree we feel ourselves to be manipulated, and biology, sociology and research into behaviour disclose that this is not merely a characteristic of our particular period; it is an essential aspect of humanity. That does not mean that we must give absolute, or even primary, importance to this way of looking at man. But we must stop pushing it aside altogether. Contemporary theology is still having to pay for the fact that it is still a victim of the heritage or curse of idealism to a greater degree than it cares to admit. It could have learned as much from Marxism as it did from Kierkegaard and would then have been unable to go on assigning the absolutely decisive role to the individual.

This is a wide field, and I only mention it here in order to draw theology's attention to the change in our horizon which it must recognize if it does not mean to cling to positions which are hardly still defensible today and to fly from the challenge of a present which took shape long ago. We must at least question the correctness of the dogmatic-philosophical postulate which presupposes the basic self-same identity of man throughout the differing phases of his life and in all the various epochs of history, declaring that in the temporal world fashions change but that our inmost selves endure. Variations can be typified and the individual can be classified under a certain pattern. But a particular man is always more or less than his image. The troubled history of the church shows that even the call of the same religion does not guarantee the same understanding of existence, and structures are not reflections of reality; they are at most a condensation of reality; normally they are an abridgment of it, and at worst they may be its caricature. Every ontology must prove itself against ontic experience, although ontologies can undoubtedly help us to deepen that experience. It is apparent, however, that our range of experience has considerably expanded in the last generation, owing to scientific and technical progress as well as the horrors and catastrophes we have experienced. The interdependence of mankind in all sectors of life and the nightmares of a future which we can foresee and plan to a greater degree than ever before are bound to determine our anthropology as well. The palpable and fundamental crisis in all branches of learning, including philosophy, has to do with the fact that we have too uncritical an attitude towards the idealistic heritage of the 'Christian' West.

Little can be said against Bultmann's attempt to present theology in the light of anthropology and Christology in the light of soteriology as such, especially when it proves to be so fruitful. But, though Bultmann talks about the theological horizon of anthropology and the Christological root of soteriology 'and vice versa', he does not explain why this 'and vice versa' never receives due attention.[14] How far is this 'and vice versa' reconcilable with his other statement[15] that the anthropological and soteriological orientation of Pauline theology can best be treated in a doctrine of man? Does this judgment not detract from the weight of the preceding 'and vice versa', in so far as it in fact establishes that there is an irreversible descent? Is this not a postulate which, in its approach at least, cannot be maintained as a basic principle? If the dialectic of 'and vice versa' is seriously meant, neither theology nor anthropology can 'properly' be conceded priority. Yet it might be possible to develop the connection of the two in the light of Pauline Christology, thus avoiding the danger both of a Christian metaphysic and of a Christian humanism. This is all the more true since soteriology has all too frequently been developed in an ecclesiological sense, Christology then becoming a mere peg on which to hang this particular type of soteriology. It is even a question – and one which demands the most careful examination – whether a theology presented as a doctrine of man can ever be anything other than a special form of a soteriology which takes its bearings from ecclesiology. The widespread agreement which Bultmann's outline has met with, particularly in the Catholic church and (on the basis of different presuppositions) in certain theological quarters in America, might even be considered evidence that this is so. It is certainly the case when Hans Conzelmann lays down the principle that: 'Theology is anthropology, as this message does not speak about this and that, about God, the world and man, but concerns me.'[16] It is not the final phrase which is in dispute but the alternative implied, for this would reduce the New Testament considerably. Moreover, Paul undoubtedly talked 'about this and that, about God, the world and man' as well. No doubt he had his reasons. For him the world is simply not the 'sphere of being'[17] of the individual, and even the key word 'historicity' loses its meaning if it is related to private existence in this way.

[14] Güttgemanns correctly points this out (p. 210).
[15] Bultmann, *Theology* I, p. 191.
[16] *Outline of the Theology of the New Testament*, 1968, p. 159.   [17] *Ibid.*, p. 206.

Now this is, of course, the danger when faith is conceived of primarily in terms of self-understanding. It has obviously to do with an understanding both of being as a whole and of existence, and is not adjusted to take over a compendium of Christian dogmatics or a collection of religious and philosophical opinions. One cannot fail to notice that Bultmann is passionately opposed to an identification of self-understanding with what the idealist tradition calls self-consciousness. He is not concerned with the illumination of being which is acquired through meditation and experience, but with that illumination conferred by the preached Word, which continually leads to a new decision – an illumination of being, that is, which is inseparable from the obedience of faith. Nevertheless, the distinction can hardly be made completely or preserved intact. For even in the hearing of the gospel, experience and tradition are verified. On the other hand, experience can never be acquired unless I am addressed from outside myself, unless, that is to say, I become aware of a *kerygma*, which can be passed on and can even form the basis of a dogmatic.[18] The terminological distinction therefore bears witness to an intention which it does not adequately safeguard. On the contrary, possible misunderstandings are almost unavoidable when the catchwords of 'authentic existence' and 'detachment from the world' are associated with the key word 'self-understanding'. For Bultmann, 'authentic' man is man who gives up all his securities and is called back to creatureliness. 'Detachment from the world' does not aim at spiritualization and pious introspection; it characterizes the believer as being no longer determined by what is at hand in this world but as being eschatologically liberated for his future, to use theological terminology. This undoubtedly takes over aspects of the biblical proclamation. But it shows the theological problem which arises when the content of that proclamation is clothed in formulae belonging to the idealist tradition. This also shows itself in the fact that man continues to be thrown into relief against nature and the history which could be more than the stage for his personal acting and suffering. The self-understanding of the believer, in which he discovers his 'authentic existence' and 'detachment from the world', divides him both from traditional dogmatics and '*Weltanschauung*' and from what is at hand in the realm of nature, of society and of mankind

---

[18] Historical criticism undoubtedly exposes dogmatic prejudices and fallacies, but it remains sterile if it does not also make a person willing and able to form dogmatic judgments.

as a whole. Can we escape the conclusion that man is here again being interpreted as a constitutively spiritual being – the interpretation which the Greeks passed on to the Western world and which was transmitted to us through idealism?

But the findings of Pauline anthropology are against this conclusion. Not enough attention has been given to the generally admitted fact that in Paul's anthropology man is relatively seldom described as 'soul' or 'spirit';[19] and that even then the terms have no great significance. He is a 'soul' according to Old Testament tradition in so far as he acts and suffers, prompted by an inward impetus, capable of acts of will[20] and dependent on ideas and inclinations. As 'spirit' he can reflect, and is in this superior to other created things, without, however, transcending either them or himself.[21] Except in one passage, a direct relationship or correlation to the divine Spirit is never asserted.[22] Though man may be described terminologically as spiritual, he is identified with the fleshly, and counts as possessed and as rebelling against the heavenly world.

The one exception is I Cor. 2.11: 'For what person knows a man's thoughts except the spirit of the man which is in him? So also no one comprehends the thoughts of God except the Spirit of God.' Clearly this is reasoning from analogy, with its accent on the second clause. It gives the criterion for a right Christian knowledge and proclamation. Real truth is only available to the man who is led by the spirit of God. In order to win acceptance for the argument of the second clause, the first clause reminds the reader of the Stoic and popular philosophical view according to which man arrives at true self-understanding by means of the spirit which participates in the divine pneuma. Under the influence of its own tradition, the idealist interpretation misunderstood the trend of the verse and put the stress on the analogy. The spirit was thus fundamentally defined – in God and man alike – as self-understanding, and this determined the interpretation of Pauline anthropology as a whole: as a spiritual being man is called to knowledge of himself. Moreover, divine enlightenment

[19] Cf. Gutbrod, op. cit., pp. 79ff.; G. Bornkamm, Paulus, 1969, pp. 142f.

[20] The conclusion that in the New Testament man is determined more by his will and actions than by his knowledge is basic to Adolf Schlatter's theology; but it has seldom been adopted.

[21] W. G. Kümmel points out in Das Bild des Menschen im Neuen Testament, 1948, p. 24, that the word 'body' in II Cor. 7.5 means the same thing as 'mind' in II Cor. 2.13.

[22] For another view cf. T. W. Manson, op. cit., p. 36; Robinson, The Body, p. 19; Bratsiotis, op. cit., p. 33; Stacey, op. cit., p. 145.

comes to his aid in his struggle with the powers of this world. We are bound to ask whether nineteenth-century New Testament exegesis was not the victim of a disastrous mistake, and that on the basis of a single verse. In view of the insights we have since acquired, we must at least subject the passage to the closest criticism. The apostle is seldom fortunate in his analogies because his impetuous temperament always made him argue from the point at which he was aiming, without always considering sufficiently the appropriateness of the material he drew on for evidence. The analogy used in I Cor. 2.11 will not hold water because in Hellenistic Christianity the divine pneuma means the power of ecstasy and miracle, and Paul, though varying and deepening this interpretation, will not surrender it altogether. Moreover, it is highly doubtful, not only in the light of our own experience but also in the context of Pauline anthropology, whether the spirit of man possesses an adequate self-understanding apart from the revelation in Christ. Generally speaking, we know ourselves least of all. Even probable theories usually break down if I have to apply them to myself. In Pauline theology this fact plays a role which cannot be overlooked. Human gifts and capabilities are by no means denied in this theology. It is characteristic of it to be seldom concerned with our deficiencies and weaknesses; and guilt, at least, is not associated with them. If Paul speaks of our 'weakness', he nearly always means the temptation which assails us from outside and which limits our freedom of movement. Unlike the usual sermon, the apostle is exceptionally unconcerned with our deficiencies; his attacks are directed against the strong. The Jews and the enthusiasts are the targets for Paul's criticism, because they feel strong and because the apostle recognizes their strength. For him the strong man is always the representative of the world and its religiosity, where these are at their most interesting and are at the same time most deeply compromised. For gifts and capacities – though Paul does not deny that they *are* gifts and capacities – can be perverted and then conceal from the person thus drawn into the vortex of perversion not only salvation but also a true understanding of his existence.

This finds its clearest expression in Rom. 1.20f. and I Cor. 1.21 with their terminological borrowings from popular philosophy; here Paul basically acknowledges the creature's capacity to recognize himself as creature by virtue of divine revelation, but he considers this capacity to have been, in actual fact, lost. Religiosity especially, according to Paul, demonstrates both this potentiality and its negation, so that it again and again introduces a process of degeneracy which ruins both man's understanding and his morality, and transforms the world into a chaos. It is only under the lordship of Christ that the devout man ceases to make his worship a means of self-justification and self-praise. Thus he embodies most clearly the nature of this world. The world sacrilegiously violates the truth of its Lord, who desires to remain its creator at all times, and at the same time surrenders the reasonableness which could and should recognize neediness as being the ineffaceable stamp of created being. In this way he arrives at the cleavage described in Rom. 7.14ff.: man has a presentient knowledge of what is good and necessary, i.e. a life aligned with the will of God. Yet it is this very presentient knowledge which constantly drives him into the delusion that, whether by his religious observances or by his misdeeds, he has to assert and justify himself – that he has to seize by violence what only the child can receive as a gift. He is unable to escape into the open, to freedom and the peace of those who are reconciled with their Lord. He remains in conflict with himself and, because he is self-ensnared, subject to the forces of this world.[23] Fear and defiance close the way to the gladness of those who are willing to take and who can therefore meet others in the act of giving, free from anxiety and presumption. The tortured cry of Rom. 7.24 is therefore what the apostle hears from the lips of all natural life: 'Wretched man that I am! Who will deliver me from this body of death?' It is the same cry which, Rom. 8.19ff. tells us, the rest of creation takes up as if in echo when it longs for the glorious liberty of the children of God; even Christians join with it, in so far as they are still subject to earthly temptation and look for perfection, i.e., still have to wait in hope.

All this shows that Paul undoubtedly has and formulates an understanding of human existence. But, characteristically, he has no fixed term for it. He helps himself out with borrowings from Greek, sometimes using 'reason', sometimes 'the inner man', thus coming close, at least, to a dualistic way of looking at things.[24] What else can an understanding of existence be called if it sees man as being in conflict with himself? It is not by chance that this usage deviates from what the apostle elsewhere describes as 'reason' and 'conscience', i.e., the

[23] Cf. Bultmann, 'Romans 7 and the Anthropology of Paul', *Existence and Faith* (ed. Schubert M. Ogden), 1960, pp. 147–57.

[24] Cf. Gutbrod, *op. cit.*, pp. 86f.; Bultmann, *Theology* I, p. 199; for another view see Kümmel, *op. cit.*, p. 23; but Kümmel is too quick to deny a dualism within the world. The anthropological dissension can hardly be overlooked.

capacity to form critical judgments and to practise self-criticism.[25] Here he is thinking of potential acts or acts already performed. Reason in this sense controls or adjusts the possibilities which present themselves to us in life or which we have to reject; but this does not mean that it has already grasped the truth about ourselves. Through conscience we show that we are subject to transcendent demands and (since we are forced to reflect about our actions) that we have been transposed into the field of tension between guilt and innocence. This is splendidly evaluated in Rom. 2.15f. as evidence that man lives in the shadow of the last judgment; that is to say, he is always standing before a tribunal whose seat of justice is not yet clearly occupied. There is also the mistaken, the weak, the violated and even the slain conscience. The truth about ourselves is plain here only in so far as we do not arrive at peace with ourselves by ourselves, as long as we remain, against our wills, restless beings, irritated by a mysterious counterpart within ourselves. We cease to be human when we withdraw ourselves from this counterpart or when we are withdrawn from our self-conflict by an alien power. It is man's secret nobility to have to reflect about himself in this way, to be compelled to criticize himself, to be forced to confront himself with the question of the right and the true. But this does not mean that we are already translated to the sphere of clarity in which everything is simple and we ourselves are plain and undivided. Our path has not as yet a fixed goal which would lead us on beyond the particular situation of the moment. Our self-understanding does not give us the possibility of transcending ourselves. On the contrary, according to the apostle the natural man demonstrates what is open to created being at its peak and what remains closed to him. He is in very truth a spiritual being and to that degree the crown of creation. But he is as entangled spiritually as he is in the things of the flesh, exposed to longing and torment, still his own enemy in his thinking and striving, even in his piety, and yet in his desirous watching for freedom proof of the fact that he has been addressed and challenged. As questionable and questioning existence in him the cry of all creation is articulate.

Consequently it is not permissible to interpret man as an individual, resting within himself and fundamentally separable from the rest of the world.[26] This can be shown most clearly from the most important

---

[25] Cf. Gutbrod, *op. cit.*, pp. 49–68; Bultmann, *Theology* I, p. 217.
[26] Cf. E. Schweizer, *TWNT* VII, p. 1079.

and controversial[27] of Paul's anthropological concepts, the body.
Here, too, one must first of all get away from the Greek tradition,
where it originally meant the corpse and was eventually used in the
sense in which we speak of 'hands' or 'souls', to denote a certain
number of people. We have already established that the idea of organism involved was not taken over by Paul. It is impossible to decide
without examination whether it is admissible to assume the meaning
of 'physical form', at least in I Cor. 15.35ff.; this must be made
dependent on the total interpretation. The apostle may undoubtedly
have taken over current phrases from time to time; such a phrase,
for example, is probably to be found in the formula 'absent in the
body'. The curious trichotomy 'spirit, soul and body' in I Thess. 5.23
shows this clearly. Thus the alternation between 'body' and 'self' is
not surprising either, especially if all Paul's anthropological terms
describe the whole man. We ought therefore to be at least conscious
of the important consequences which follow if we almost everywhere
deduce from this alternation the basic meaning of 'person' or even
'personality' for the Pauline concept of 'body'. It still seems to me by
no means certain that the expression can mean this in Greek.[28] At all
events, for the apostle the heart is the centre of human life and is the
dominating term for personal existence. On the other hand, the
extensive parallelism of 'body' and 'flesh' in his writings suggests that
the 'physical' aspect of earthly existence was of decisive importance
for him and must certainly not be belittled. When, in a deliberate
paradox and moved by an anti-cultic tendency, Paul demands the
sacrifice of our bodies as our spiritual worship (Rom. 12.1 and I Cor.
6.20), this is not by chance. According to Rom. 6.12ff. the new
obedience to be offered in the body is the mark of Christian status,
being the fruit of baptism and the anticipation of the bodily resurrection of the dead, which Paul emphatically upholds. The co-
herence of Pauline soteriology is destroyed once we modify in the
slightest degree the fact that for Paul all God's ways with his creation
begin and end in corporeality. For him there is no divine act which
is not directed towards this or which does not desire so to manifest
itself. This fundamental interest displays itself again in the fact that
Paul ascribes to corporeality not only anthropological but also
eucharistic, ecclesiological and even Christological relevance: the

[27] Cf. Bultmann, *Theology* I, p. 192; J. A. T. Robinson, *The Body*, p. 9.
[28] For the latest expression of the contrary view, see E. Schweizer, 'Die Leiblichkeit des Menschen. Leben-Tod-Auferstehung', *EvTh* 29, 1969, p. 41.

exalted Lord manifests himself on earth in the physical food through which we can participate in him and which binds together the members of the church in his body. It may well be that these last statements take over pre-Pauline views and that it is therefore inadmissible simply to co-ordinate them with the anthropological statements about corporeality. On the other hand, one can make the interpretation too easy for oneself by passing over possible connotations and beginning with the reduction. It is at least worth considering whether these connotations have a heuristic significance.

Bultmann's interpretation certainly tends in the opposite direction. In the interpretation of I Cor. 6.13ff. it becomes involved in inextricable contradictions, because it is forced to understand 'body' sometimes as the seat of sexual life, sometimes as the physical organism, sometimes as the self, or person;[29] and Bultmann is obviously bothered because this last meaning is not adhered to throughout. But the interpretation has itself imported these difficulties into the text because, contrary to the text itself, it would like to distinguish and divide the human person from its corporeality. It is not even put out by the tremendous statement that not only is the body meant for the Lord but that the Lord is meant for the body. If this is not viewed as a reckless overstatement, it shows that the apostle intends man to be understood entirely in the light of his corporeality and that that is why he relates even Christology and soteriology to it.[30] This relationship is also the root of his eschatology of the physical resurrection, which must not be set aside as being merely mythological unless the same is done for the Christology and soteriology as well.[31] To confine the problems involved here to the field of exegesis, however, would be to make them unduly innocuous. It is significant for both hermeneutics and systematic theology that Bultmann (under Heidegger's influence) conceives human reality primarily as possibility, whereas Paul at most sees possibility as a manifestation of reality and always assigns to the body the reality of creatureliness, the reality of the fall, of redemption, of the resurrection of the dead, with all of which the appropriate functions are associated. It can therefore hardly be

---

[29] Bultmann, *Theology* I, pp. 194f.

[30] As Güttgemanns correctly sees, *op. cit.*, pp. 230f.

[31] For Bultmann's view see *Theology* I, p. 198. The mythology of Pauline eschatology and the 'unfortunate consequence' of thinking in terms of substance are not disputed. But the question is whether corporeality in Paul's sense can be primarily determined in terms of substance.

maintained that the body is treated as being 'neutral in itself'.[32] Man
can never be 'neutral in himself' and is certainly not so in his corporeality, which is always already modified. An ontology which
deprives him of this already-existing modification in order to observe
him *per se*, falls a victim to abstraction and no longer allows him the
humanity of creatureliness.[33] Of course, this is not Bultmann's intention. Corporeality is for him the possibility of a relationship with God,
i.e., the possibility of being good or evil.[34] This goes beyond the sphere
of mere morality. In this context, good and evil are paraphrases for
an appropriate or a perverted relationship to oneself, i.e., the 'authen-
ticity' of existence which is to be attained or thrown away, in which
man 'can be under his own control' or can 'lose his grip on himself'.[35]
This interpretation rests on the fact that it is only in Rom. 8.13 that
the body appears as the subject of our actions, though at the same
time the phrase about the *praxeis* of the body which must be put to
death manifests a curious separation between them and the acting
human subject. The 'object of his conduct' has become so independent that man 'is under the sway of an outside power, which has
seized from the self the power of control over itself'. To this extent,
corporeality means the experience of being at odds with oneself,
which at the same time challenges the authentic self to separate
itself from its own acts.[36] This leads us inescapably to the definition
that man is body 'when he is objectivized in relation to himself by
becoming the object of his own thought, attitude or conduct; he is
[body] in that he can separate from himself and come under the
domination of outside powers'.[37]

It is surely hardly by chance that Bultmann here falls back into
the terminology of the subject-object contrast which he otherwise
rejects so emphatically. If the body is defined as the instrument of our
acts, or at least as the subject of our acting and suffering, it is clear
that – contrary to the intention which otherwise determines his interpretation of Pauline anthropology – the term is no longer understood

---

[32] For another view see Conzelmann, *Outline*, pp. 173f.

[33] This danger becomes obvious when Güttgemanns (p. 230) calls the body 'a
permanent ontological structure of human existence'. On the other hand, Gutbrod
(pp. 32f.) rightly speaks of the concreteness, factualness and reality of human
existence, though he simplifies this on pp. 36, 39, where the body is regarded as
being the organ of activity.

[34] Bultmann, *Theology* I, p. 198.

[35] *Ibid.*, pp. 197f.

[36] *Ibid.*, p. 197.

[37] *Ibid.*, pp. 199, 202f.

ON PAUL'S ANTHROPOLOGY 21

as covering the whole man; and there is then good reason for distinguishing the authentic person from the body. It is no counter argument to say that what characterizes human existence ontologically, in the structure of man's relationship to himself, only falls apart ontically.[38] Ontology (whose highly doubtful force for Paul has still to be established) would then be merely the conjectural justification of a system which does not want to hand over reality to schizophrenia, which remains orientated towards the spiritual being of man, clinging to it at least as 'possibility' and structure, and which therefore continues to concede to man transcendence over nature. It is revealing to use expressions which describe the self as being at least potentially one with itself, under its own control, at its own disposal. For it is precisely this that is never true of the creature; nor is it conferred upon the believer either, even though he lives and dies to his Lord; he remains estranged from himself no less than the sinner under the rule of outside forces. Finally, what is not taken into account in all this is that our soul and conscience may perhaps constitute a relationship to ourselves, but we stand bodily in a sphere which can by no means be summed up under the individual aspect. Ontological speculation cannot remove corporeality from the realm of nature. It is related, not to existence in isolation, but to the world in which forces and persons and things clash violently – a world of love and hate, blessing and curse, service and destruction, in which man is largely determined by sexuality and death and where nobody, fundamentally speaking, belongs to himself alone.

To define this in ontological terms: corporeality is the nature of man in his need to participate in creatureliness and in his capacity for communication in the widest sense, that is to say, in his relationship to a world with which he is confronted on each several occasion.[39] We are always what we are in the mode of belongingness and participation, whether as friend or foe, whether in thinking, acting, or suffering. In so far the anthropological statement about the body really is linked with the eucharistic and ecclesiological assertions according to which we participate in the *Kyrios* through the elements of the Lord's Supper, which are the means of communication with him, and become part of his body as of the new creation – the world

---

[38] It is characteristic of Bultmann's interpretation that he adheres to the idea of continuity as a matter of course (*Theology* I, p. 198). For the contrary view see Conzelmann, *Outline*, p. 189.

[39] My dissertation *Leib und Leib Christi*, 1933, p. 125, already makes this point.

as it is transformed through the Lordship of Christ. It may well be that these latter views are pre-Pauline. The apostle was at least able to find his own meaning in them in the light of his basic understanding of corporeality. The statement that our body belongs to Christ, but that Christ also belongs to our body, is also understandable: our corporeality is the relationship to the world and the creatureliness of our existence to which the appointed cosmocrator must lay claim if he is to establish the *basileia* in the universe, as I Cor. 15.25ff. promises. Finally, we can understand why Paul does not share our interest in the permanent identity of man with himself and in the continuity of history in its manifold phases. It is hiatus which is the mark of that historicity in which the world of creation is divided from the world of sin, from the world under the lordship of Christ and from the world in the reality of the resurrection; and the breaches are so deep that only the fall of man and miracle can bridge them. The apostle – unlike Judaism in general – never expressed the view that man remained in the image of God, even after the fall. *Imago dei* is for him Christ and Christ alone; it is he who, with the membership of his body, restores to believers, and to them only, the lost divine image which was once the stamp of created being.

The ontological statement of Pauline anthropology is crystallized in its ontic conclusions: man is always himself in his particular world; his being is open towards all sides[40] and is always set in a structure of solidarity.[41] Just as he can only be this corporeally,[42] so the power of the resurrection also encroaches on the individuality and orders us within the communion of the *basileia*, which Paul therefore only allows to be physical. It is only death which isolates. In I Cor. 7.14 the apostle felt able to call children holy because of their physical relationship to their Christian parents. He did not oppose, at least, the Corinthian practice of vicarious baptism; I Thess. 4.13ff. shows that he took the congregation's concern about the fate of their dead seriously; conversely, he felt that union with a prostitute (I Cor. 6.15) was a blasphemous rivalry to communion with Christ; and according to II Cor. 5.2ff. he shrank in metaphysical horror from the nakedness of the transitional state. All this only becomes comprehensible if solidarity is the stamp and function of corporeality. When (according to I Cor. 5.5) the body of the incestuous man is delivered over to

---

[40] E. Schweizer, *Die Leiblichkeit des Menschen*, p. 48.
[41] J. A. T. Robinson, *The Body*, pp. 8f., 79.
[42] E. Schweizer, *TWNT* VII, pp. 1071, 1079; Conzelmann, *Outline*, p. 189.

Satan, the church is through this excommunication abolishing the solidarity effected by baptism and is thrusting the man out of the new creation into the isolation of those dedicated to death. If 'body' primarily meant the personality, II Cor. 12.2 would be meaningless. Even 'being caught up' is not a withdrawal from the body, though it means transference to another world, so that from this aspect the problem of identity with the earthly being arises once more. The idea of creatureliness is narrowed down if it is applied to the individual from the outset, and it remains abstract if 'authentic' man is permitted to transcend nature, society and history, and is set apart from created being as a whole.

Admittedly, it is bound to come to this if existence is contrasted with a world which for its part can only be related as a closed and indivisible whole to the earthly sphere, with its natural data and laws. According to Paul, since Adam man has wandered through many worlds, as he does in his personal life – worlds divided by the frontiers of fall, law, promise, gospel, and resurrection or judgment, worlds which in each case set their stamp on their members. Man is a mutable being; his possibilities run the gamut from human beast through those who belong to the established upper or lower orders – the barbarians and Greeks, the Gentiles and the Jews – to those who fall under the lordship of Christ and to those who are already perfect. To put it in dangerously epigrammatic form, man is all this as projection of a world which is distinguished from other simultaneously-existing or successive worlds, without there being any ultimate and all-transcending harmony, as in the Middle Stoa. The world is not neutral ground; it is a battlefield, and everyone is a combatant.

Anthropology must then *eo ipso* be cosmology just as certainly as, conversely,[43] the cosmos is primarily viewed by Paul under an anthropological aspect, because the fate of the world is in fact decided in the human sphere. But neither the exegetical nor the theological findings allow what the apostle calls the universe to be reduced to the world of men alone. He can quite well talk about the sphere of non-human created being, which becomes his own arena, and the three-storeyed structure of his world picture cannot be overlooked, with its division between heaven, earth and the nether regions.

Above all, we must not overlook Pauline demonology, with its associated metaphysical dualism. This is, of course, generally denied, because it is thought to be irreconcilable with belief in creation.

[43] Bultmann, *Theology* I, pp. 254ff.

There is no need to quarrel about words. Recognition of God as creator of the world as well as of one's own existence need not at all exclude the observation that since the fall of Adam man's heart and will and thinking have been corrupted and have fallen into the power of demonic forces. Such a view is indeed inescapable if redemption is to be understood as eschatological *creatio ex nihilo*. Only a theory which postulates free will can have any interest in weakening this metaphysical dualism into an ethical one. And Pauline theology contradicts this on every side. Man, entangled in self-conflict, practically speaking always subject to evil, is not free. The earth is a battle open to all comers; it is no longer cosmos but a chaos of rebellion. To this extent, as Rom. 1.18–3.20 brings out, it is subject to the divine judgment, from which only grace in Christ saves. Only someone who does not know or share the nightmares of contemporary man can fail to sympathize with those of Paul, or can maintain – as if we were still the last custodians of the ethical idealism of a liberal world – that Paul was entirely lacking in interest in apocalyptic schemes, because he was not conscious of any plan in history[44] and only preserved a rudimentary hope in the resurrection of believers.[45] But according to I Cor. 15.25ff. the apostle's hope was directed towards the time when Christ would rule and place all his enemies under his feet, when God would be all in all. In this context our own resurrection means no more and no less than participation in a world set free by the *basileia*. What is apocalyptic here is not merely the historical outline which is inevitably involved, with its divisions into separate epochs – Adam, Abraham, Moses, Christ and the kingdom of freedom. The idea that (according to Rom. 1.20ff.; 5.12ff.; 7.13ff.) Adam's fate is repeated and confirmed in every individual is also an apocalyptic one. Just as each person is both himself and his world, so he is also himself and Adam on the path which he follows. The view of Rom. 8.19ff. is also apocalyptic in its assertion that the whole creation waits with groaning for the glorious liberty of the sons of God and that the church in its worship even declares itself at one with creation in this expectation. The apostle's self-understanding is apocalyptic when (according to Rom. 11.11ff.) he sees his task to be to convert the Gentiles, as a step towards inciting unbelieving Israel to conversion – his mission thus being a preparation for the parousia. Aocalyptic, finally, is the disquieting question which not only moves the apostle but apparently faces every Christian, a question bound up with his task and his existence: who owns the earth?

It is more than an uncalled-for understatement to say that all this is rudimentary. To leave it out of consideration is not even an essential consequence of the demand to demythologize – a demand which I would by no means reject. It is resignation, not faith and reason, if we are content with a private self-understanding, which turns the Christian practically speaking into a non-political being and confines his responsibility to personal human relationships. The apostle was more exacting than his interpreters today, in so far as these content themselves with a Christian humanism in which Christology possesses at most an awakening and a controlling function. Where the *Kyrios* is turned into an example and a model, Pauline anthropology also becomes unbearably stunted and falsely orientated.

This becomes clear if we consider the contrast of spirit and flesh in which Paul thinks the whole world and even the Christian community has been entangled since Christ (Gal. 5.16ff. is especially characteristic). It has always been felt to be a problem that the expressions 'body' and 'flesh' in Paul run parallel for part of the time, or are even synonymous. This is in the first place explicable in the light of the fact that the word 'flesh' takes up the traditional Old Testament and Jewish usage. Here creature is divided from creator, so that the word is also applicable to man in his physical aspect. At the same time, however, it is important to differentiate at this point. The 'body', though belonging to and sympathetic to the rest of creation, is yet as concreteness contrasted with it; whereas 'flesh' rather designates creation's exponent. The word 'flesh' is therefore appropriate to bring out the community of married partners, for example, or the community of a nation, or of mankind as a whole in its earthly circumstances. Conversely, it is not pure chance that Paul expects the resurrection of the body, not the resurrection of the flesh. What is to hand on earth is always the evanescent circumstance which is shattered in death.[46] Even more important perhaps: man's body can be contrasted with his soul, mind or reason, whereas flesh, where it relates to our existence, includes all this because, even in these latter possibilities, we are still nothing more than creatures. This, then, provides the bridge to the technical use of 'flesh' in dualistic antithesis to the divine Spirit, a usage which derives neither from Greek

[46] E. Brandenburger, *Fleisch und Geist*, pp. 44, 53, therefore opposes the assumption of a 'neutral' usage, in the sense in which we use 'natural'.

thought nor from pre-Qumran and pre-Philonic Judaism.[47] For in Greek, flesh is a substance which one can *have* but not *be*, let alone be possessed by; whereas in the Old Testament and pre-Philonic Judaism flesh denotes the creature that perishes, but it is not a hostile active power, opposed *per se* to the divine Spirit and struggling against it for mastery of the world.[48] We meet this radicalization in Gal. 5.16ff., however, and it determines the whole of Pauline anthropology.

This admittedly brings us up against an apparently insoluble problem, because the question is now how far the same word can be used to describe human existence and universal power. But this is a fictitious problem, if we take account of our previous analysis, whose cogency now becomes apparent. The terms used in Pauline anthropology all undoubtedly refer to the whole man in the varying bearings and capacities of his existence; but they do not apply to what we call the individual at all. Here existence is always fundamentally conceived from the angle of the world to which one belongs. Existence is 'flesh' in so far as it has given itself over to the world of the flesh, serves that world and allows itself to be determined by it. But since confrontation with the creator is characteristic of this world, and since this confrontation has in fact always meant the isolation and rebellion of the creature, 'flesh' is also the sphere of the demonic. But this situation is ambivalent: the fall of man allowed the demonic cosmic scope. Conversely, the demonic reaches out for man objectively from cosmic breadths and depths (in Hellenistic terms, it reaches out from the stars, with the force of *ananke*) in order to enslave him and even continues to threaten the Christian community. It perverts law, reason, history, existence and even the charismata and thus compels man to sin and death. Without Christ, men experienced this as the estrangement and self-contradiction of existence which cries out for redemption; in the church it is felt as constantly threatening and ever-present temptation. For even believers are not withdrawn from the flesh while they are on earth. But they are no longer forfeit to the flesh and can fight against its demonic power. They can only do this, however, if they are ruled by the other world and the power of the divine Spirit. For even the believer has neither

---

[47] Cf. Brandenburger, *op. cit.*, pp. 178ff.
[48] On this point see Bultmann, *Theology* I, p. 201; he declares that in view of the ruling character of the flesh, 'according to the flesh' does not correspond to 'according to the body'.

being, existence nor power in himself. His continuity and identity also rest outside himself, in his participation in the heavenly world and in his communication with the Word of his creator, which is always challenging him anew to leave his own past behind and which drives him forward into the future of his Lord. Man can only have the Spirit when he denies the flesh. This is not merely, or not primarily, an individual matter, however; it means being involved in the world-wide conflict between *civitas dei* and *civitas terrena*. Anthropology is cosmology *in concreto*, even in the sphere of faith.

The truth inherent in the theology of existence must certainly not be overlooked. Paul really did in a decisive sense develop this cosmology as anthropology. The question to whom the earth belongs can only receive its legitimation and its answer when it is clear to whom *we* belong. That explains Bultmann's apposite observation that the cosmos is primarily observed from an anthropological perspective, namely as the world of men; and that even the powers who dominated man before Christ no longer appear as mythical cosmocrators, as they did before the apostle, but are primarily identified, in anthropological relevance, with law, error, sin and death. Present redemption can only be maintained when individual people, joined together in a visible community, uphold it in its corporeality, uphold it scandalously and credibly, making clear with their existence the kind of pressures to which they are no longer ultimately subject. Salvation which does not manifest itself in lived discipleship becomes a religious postulate and an incomprehensible ideology. Even the Christian faith can become superstition. We must certainly demythologize if we are to translate the message of early Christianity into our own time. But it would be a fatal mistake if we attempted to make this the pivot of theology. This could only lead to a new dispute about pure doctrine and to another kind of dogmatism. The mythical form of the biblical *kerygma* is a barrier on the road to faith. Its real enemy is and remains superstition, which may express itself in a hundred different kinds of practice and theory, but ultimately manifests itself in neglected, corrupted discipleship which fails to press forward into fresh worlds.

We can sum up what we have said in ontological terms: there is no such thing as man without his particular and respective world. But world means more than the mere sphere of living in, let us say, co-humanity. The world is always a sphere of sovereignty whether under the insignia of creation, the insignia of sin, or the insignia of the redemption which can be experienced today as well as that which is still to come. It is in this that it reveals its unfathomable depths. According to Paul, it is the constitutive character of the world in which we live to break up a multiplicity of sovereign spheres, which mutually penetrate one another, are superimposed on one another, fight against one another and are in constant flux. This affects each separate existence.[49] As created being, man does not only belong to his respective, already existing world. Thus far we are forced to the paradoxical definition that, according to the apostle, man is a being who cannot be determined solely in the light of his own self. His existence stems from outside himself. But since this is true of all created being, we must be more precise: man is the creature who, radically and representatively for all others, submits to his Lord, becoming the instrument which manifests his power and his universal claim. It is precisely this which is brought out in Gal. 2.20 in Paul's description of Christian existence: 'It is no longer I who live, but Christ who lives in me.' But that is not only true of Christians.[50] This is shown by the fact that Paul is apparently able to disregard the human person when he speaks of the power of sin which is in our members and which works through them.[51] This corresponds to the fact that Christ takes possession of our members for his service, making us part of his body. We ourselves do not determine what we are. It is delusion to imagine that this is the case and presumption to rely on it. Consequently, the deluded and presumptuous attempt to take our destiny into our own hands is again and again superseded by the experience of our limitations and self-alienation, an experience which drives us to defiant or helpless despair. From this angle Paul is bound to be interested in the interruptions in existence and history, not in continuity and identity. From this point of view, too, it is understandable that, unlike the Stoics or Philo, he pays no tribute to the ideal of character-building, even in the life of the believer. Man is not under his own control. His salvation and his ruin depend on the Lord whom he serves. The world is in constant flux and man is a pilgrim; in the

---

[49] Contrary to Bultmann's view in 'Man between the Times according to the New Testament', *Existence and Faith*, 1960, pp. 248–66, the task of anthropology is therefore more than to expound the dialectic of man's paradoxical existence.

[50] Güttgemanns, *op. cit.*, pp. 207ff., seems to have seen this.

[51] Bultmann, *Theology* I, p. 194, says that the members as the individual faculties of our existence are comprised in the body as a whole; but he does not perceive the problem touched on above. For an opposing view, see G. Bornkamm, *Paulus*, p. 141.

same way there is mutation in existence. It manifests itself in change of lordship and life in another world. These ontological observations characterize the horizon under which Paul develops not only his anthropology and cosmology, but his Christology, soteriology, ecclesiology and eschatology as well.

We cannot go into this further here, for to do so would mean outlining the whole of the apostle's theology. In particular we should have to show that forfeiture to the demonic powers is fundamentally contrasted with the service of the crucified Lord; it is he and he alone who leads us from slavery to sonship and into the liberty which is only comprehensible in the light of that sonship; and it is he and he alone who leads back perverted creation from delusion, presumption and despair into the light of truth. The point here was simply to show that the various aspects of Pauline theology are thematically linked and have a mutual bearing. This theology possesses systematic power and completeness, with which we must not interfere (for example, by reducing it to anthropology and soteriology) unless we are prepared to imperil the whole.

One final question, however, must not remain unanswered. The beginning and the end of our analysis seem to be irreconcilably contradictory. We started from the position that Paul, more than any other New Testament writer, viewed man as an individual. We went on from this to call anthropology crystallized cosmology and to term every person the projection of his respective world and that world's Lord. How is this antithesis to be bridged?

The first thing to notice is that the apostle does not speculate about human possibilities. Our ontological analysis has been filtered out of the statements which Paul made about human reality in the light of his Christian understanding. It thereby emerges that although certain facts can certainly be fitted into an ontological framework, they cannot, on the other hand, be logically deduced from a comprehensive ontology. Where dying and death separate the new Adam from the old, modern ideas about development, the individual and existence are not much help in reconciling what for the apostle is irreconcilable. Basic premises are not enough to reduce everything to a common denominator. Here, if anywhere, we should have to consider and demonstrate what redemption through Christ as Lord means for Paul and what the nature of Christian freedom (the reverse side of the obedience of sons) is in his view. In the course of this discussion it would emerge that sanctification must not be interpreted as a process of inner maturing which leads up step by step to ever-increasing perfection. It is true that Paul can compare the disciple of Jesus with the runner who struggles for a prize in the arena. But his efforts are not for himself. Christ has freed us of concern for our own salvation. We have to concentrate on our task: to be found faithful and to serve God in the profane things of everyday life. II Cor. 13.4 tells us that in this way we become the earthly representatives of the exalted Lord and, by bearing the marks of the one who was crucified, reflect his imitation as the way of salvation; we thereby experience the basic divine law of II Cor. 12.9, however, according to which the power of grace works through those assailed by temptation. This power remains an alien force which must not be used for one's own purposes and which sweeps those possessed by it into death, if by this means they can make way for the kingdom of the resurrection. Man before Christ and without him is marked by the self-contradiction of being unable to reach the life he strives for; and the Christian is marked by the paradox of being offered up on the triumphal altar of his Lord. Here, too, the mysteriousness of existence remains. Only the gospel has the clue to the hieroglyph man – the clue to his past and present as well as to his future. But since the gospel finds this clue in the light of the cross and *sub contrario* of truth and appearance, it preserves the question and the offence which surrounded the Nazarene.

This brings us to a second question. Where we no longer have to strive for our own salvation and no longer need to fear external powers, we become free for other people, for whom we otherwise at most only find time and attention as allies or opponents. The man who is liberated from himself and from the fascination or the horror of this world in its structures perceives his neighbour. His life becomes, like the life of his Lord, vicarious service for all fallen, perverted and subjugated creatures. The bearer of the charismata takes upon himself in love the burden of others in order to make them free. The important thing is that this love knows no limit. The community of the church may give us courage, equipment and a direction for the urgent task of the moment, but our mission does not derive from the church, nor is it restricted by it. Our mission breaks through the church's territory as it does through every other camp and follows its Lord into the no-man's-land between the fronts in order to call men to reconciliation.

These two characteristics form the unmistakable signature of

Christ and his disciples; they cannot be replaced by anything else at all and stand out from all forms of organization as the ultimate ties. It is only when we are clear about this that we can understand why Paul only applies the category of the individual to the believer. Participation in the lordship of Christ keeps the image of the Nazarene alive by setting us at the point where (in the words of Gal. 6.14f.), being crucified to the world and the world being crucified to us, light breaks out of the shadow upon the new creation. There even religious uniforms are finished and done with, there even the community of the church only exists in mutual representation, each in his own particular place, each with his own particular service, each with his own particular blessing. Paul, at least, allowed the church to be made up of nonconformists who are and remain useful members of the whole simply by virtue of their particular gifts and functions. For him man under the rule of sin could never be an 'individual' but was, as representative of his world, a victim of its powers. For him, the 'individual' is not the premise of an anthropological theory but the result of the grace which takes people into its service. It differentiates in the Christian community especially, so that every earthly sphere is opened to its challenge. According to the apostle, individuation does not follow from already existing individualities; it is a crystallization of our calling, in which the point at issue is the universal lordship of Christ.

Here, then, we also find the theme of process. When Rom. 8.19ff. takes up the Jewish idea of the birth pangs of the Messiah, from which the new man and the new world are to emerge, it is not the notion of moral perfection that is under consideration; it is apocalyptic expectation. The same is true when in Gal. 4.19 Paul talks about his community as little children to whom he has to give birth so that Christ can be formed in them. This is not the description of a programme; it depicts the need for a setting forth into a not yet realized future. Man's position is still open. The only thing that gives it contour at present is that the Christ who was crucified and obedient is named as both the judge of the world and the criterion of the new creation. Man cannot be defined from within his own limits, but he is eschatologically defined in the light of the name of Christ, just as Adam once received his name from God, thereby acquiring a definition as creature. It is true of both that they are unable to give themselves being and existence, but remain dependent on grace, which is new every morning and never finds an end.

II

THE SAVING SIGNIFICANCE OF THE
DEATH OF JESUS IN PAUL

The Reformers were indisputably right when they appealed to Paul for their understanding of evangelical theology as a theology of the cross. But this view is no longer generally recognized today, even in the Protestant churches. Generally speaking, and in the Anglo-Saxon countries especially, it is considered to be a narrowly denominational interpretation or misinterpretation – an attitude which has an unhappy effect on ecumenical conversations. It must be asserted with the greatest possible emphasis that both historically and theologically Paul has to be understood in the light of the Reformation's insight. Any other perspective at most covers part of his thinking; it does not grasp the heart of it.

Admittedly we can no longer maintain this on the basis of an unbroken confessional tradition, or out of the inherent logic of a dogmatic system. Anyone who knows anything about the history of modern Pauline research knows that exegetical scholarship has here, too, confronted the confessional traditions with hard problems and has shaken them severely. This was necessary, since no tradition can merely be preserved in a glass case. Every generation alters the heritage of its fathers when it tries to take over that heritage in its own historical situation. That was how orthodoxy, pietism and the Enlightenment came to make the theology of the cross shallow, narrow and rigid. This was bound to provoke exegesis, for its part, to examine the basic material afresh. In reaction against ruling ecclesiastical doctrine and the popular piety of the churches, it then arrived at different – and sometimes even contrary – interpretative possibilities. Exegesis has both the right and the duty to experiment, because otherwise thinking is not possible. Thus the relation between the life of the church and theological scholarship is, like all true companionship, only fruitful if it remains in a state of tension. The dialogue has to lead the parties involved away from traditional horizons into paths till then untrodden; and the unavoidable conflicts must not be shunned. Here, as in the rest of life, sacrifice, error and guilt are unavoidable. An obstinate defence of the status quo is death to life and thought. It makes us inhuman by hindering us from facing the promise and the claim of our own situation.

The image of Paul in research has been successively stamped by philosophy, psychology and the history of religion. With this varying approach the factual emphasis has changed as well. The career and message of the apostle released a till then unsuspected wealth of insights, but in the same degree they became increasingly complicated and mysterious. In the end, the historical problems choked theological interpretation to such an extent that only the fragments of a field of ruins could be detected. The people who roamed about helplessly in it were not greatly helped by the fact that a conservative system and a church which had grown up out of the revival clung to the old concepts, though these did not remain unscathed. They were rightly unable to accept solutions which by-passed the historical problems instead of overcoming them. Conscience must not be violated even in the name of the eternal verities, although the ecclesiastical establishment has taken little account of that at any period. It was thanks to outsiders rather than to the leading scholars of the day that the Reformed tradition was not entirely lost in the exegetical field. A counter-movement only began in Germany with Adolf Schlatter, Karl Barth and Rudolf Bultmann. But their interpretations of Paul, at any rate, barely penetrated beyond the German-speaking world and were not universally accepted even there.

We must be aware of this development if we are to understand why Paul's theology of the cross seems more of a provocation than a matter of course to contemporary Protestantism. We can only advocate it if we admit at once that it has remained largely uncomprehended even in our own history and that the Reformed attitude to it increasingly disappeared even in the Protestant churches. We must therefore be prepared from the outset to be thought dogmatically or denominationally prejudiced, and we cannot ignore the voices which remind us of the complex historical problems and the theological richness of Pauline theology. We are therefore maintaining a controversial thesis and we have to be able to justify it in discussion with people of other views and to relate it anew to the apostle's total message. This is a watershed of opinion, and has been since the church's history began;[1] and we can no longer be certain of understanding and agreement even within our own confessional tradition.

Of course, this does not mean that the importance of the death of Jesus for Paul's theology is called in question anywhere. No-one can seriously protest against a proper emphasis here or against the simultaneous assertion of the saving significance of Jesus' death for Paul. But the catchword 'theology of the cross' means more than this, and we must not turn it into something mildly edifying. For it belongs from the very outset to the controversial theology which Protestant fervour inaugurated through the *particula exclusiva* – the 'through Christ alone, through faith alone'. This means: *crux sola est nostra theologia.*[2] In his excellent essay, 'Das Kreuz: Grund und Mass für die Christologie', ('The Cross: the Basis and Test of Christology'), Martin Kähler interpreted this in precise terms:[3] 'Without the cross no Christology, and in Christology no single feature which cannot find its justification in the cross.' In a way, this statement introduces and anticipates the subject of demythologizing, which is of such concern today. Kahler therefore went on to say: 'At the same time, however, from this starting point and under this aspect, Christology is transferred from metaphysics, with its sterile logical necessity, into history and thus into the kingdom of our own reality.'[4]

It is worth pausing here for a moment. It is understandable that the discussion about demythologizing should have been kindled in our time over the question of the proper translation of the Christian message to the contemporary world. At the same time, we may well regret that it did not start from the theology of the cross, and may see here a considerable diminution of the theological perspective. Probably the battle would not have been waged any less passionately, but it might not have stuck fast in so many unclarified philosophical problems; perhaps, too, the controversy would not have been carried on in so sterile a manner or one so open to misunderstanding. In the light of a theology of the cross, demythologizing and an existentialist interpretation are inescapably demanded, and demanded more

[1] Cf. U. Wilckens, *Weisheit und Torheit*, 1959, pp. 214ff.
[2] M. Luther, *Werke, kritische Gesamtausgabe*, Weimar, 1883ff., 5, p. 176, 32f. on Ps. 5.12.
[3] BFCT 15, 1911, p. 13.
[4] *Ibid.*

radically than if we start from a modern world picture and modern self-understanding; for Jesus' cross is essentially directed against all religious illusion[5] and relegates man to man's humanity. Paul himself certainly permitted mythology an important place in his theology. But that is not a cogent counter-proof against the demythologizing programme. Beginners never see where their path is going to lead, and the truth can never be distilled with chemical purity on earth. A contemporary scholar carries the shell of an inherited tradition about with him just as much as a citizen of the ancient world. There is no language – and there has certainly never been a theological language – without unfamiliarity, misunderstanding and error. No methodology and therefore no hermeneutics can save people from surrendering to illusion, whether this meets them in the form of a mythology or in the ideology of a world which claims to have come of age. Theologically speaking, the ultimate decisions are not made in the sphere of language, where they are at most expressed; they are made at the point where we fall into arrogance or despair, or where we hear the call to obedience and true humanity – at the point, that is, where we make decisions of will. That is the case in confrontation with the one who was crucified and in the light of his cross; and that is why a theological hermeneutic – i.e., a doctrine about the understanding and right interpretation of the biblical message – can be established in the shadow of a theology of the cross. This must in fact be done if we are not merely to deal with a hermeneutical selection. We need not reject those analyses of structure which fall to our lot in the outer courts of philosophy, since open-mindedness towards every reality and human encounter is permitted us. But on the other hand, these analyses of structure must be viewed no less critically than mythology. For the cross of Jesus is for us the truly critical power both of the world and of every individual, because it determines existence as a whole – our wills as well as our thinking and our speaking.

This digression was designed to draw attention to the fact that the catchword about the 'theology of the cross' loses its original meaning if it is used non-polemically. It was always a critical attack on the dominating traditional interpretation of the Christian message, and it was not by chance that it characterized Protestant beginnings. It

---

[5] This is the beginning of both gloss and commentary in Luther's lectures on Romans 1515–1516 (ed. J. Ficker, 1925); and this is where Adolf Schlatter begins his essay on 'Das Kreuz Jesu unsere Versöhnung mit Gott' in *Gesunde Lehre*, 1929, pp. 7–14: 'Hence Jesus' calling and work begins with his destruction of our idols; and the weapon which he uses to annihilate our false gods is his cross.'

ought to drive us to self-reflection more clearly and more radically than our other current slogans. It demands of us whether the law we recognize is still valid or not, at least in the sphere of the Protestant churches. This would affect preaching and the piety of the church member, theology and ecumenical work alike. The needs and conflicts of our churches would take on a clearer outline and would be decisively helped. The different fronts would then, of course, separate out with extreme clarity where today general jungle warfare is the rule. Once more Paul proves to be of lasting and fateful significance for Protestantism, since his Christology brings us inevitably to a crossroads.

This explains why the Pauline and Deutero-Pauline letters especially talk about the cross and the one who was crucified instead of merely the death of Jesus or (in liturgical modification) about his blood. The heightening intention which guides Paul is shown very clearly in the supplementary phrase 'even death on a cross', which he probably added himself to the hymn to Christ in Phil. 2.6ff. If he here emphasizes the unusual degree of suffering and humiliation which was bound up with this death, Gal. 2.19, 21; 3.13 stresses another aspect. The Old Testament laid the man who died in this way under a curse, declaring him to be unclean and outside the divine covenant. This was evidently important for the apostle and had the deepest possible influence on his understanding of Jesus' death.[6] For Paul, that death incontestably contained the inherent conflict which is a central characteristic of his theology, with its irreconcilable opposition of law and gospel. The same fact is touched on in Heb. 13.12f., where the writer speaks of dying outside the camp of the people of the covenant. If we try to translate this statement into the world of our own ideas, the image of a criminal's death is joined by the other image of the man who dies in a state of godlessness. But the comparison is not an accurate one as long as we understand godlessness as being the description of a purely human attitude. In the ancient world temples were to be seen everywhere, visible abodes of the divine presence. People were consequently also aware of the place which was removed from God, a place where the religious man might not remain. Both Paul and the writer to the Hebrews preach that Jesus did not only die a criminal's death but that he died this death outside the limits of consecrated ground. We must here remember that the gospels tell us that even during his lifetime Jesus turned from his devout contemporaries to tax-collectors and sinners, thus thrust-

[6] Cf. G. Wiencke, *Paulus über Jesu Tod*, 1939, pp. 29ff.

ing forward in the very name of God into what was thought, religiously speaking, to be alien ground. The people surrounding Jesus found this scandalous. Today the cross is for us a religious symbol; but at that time, if it was set up in territory outside divine influence, the honouring of anyone who hung on that cross was from the outset a scandal of the most profound kind. This is what I Cor. 1.23 means by 'a stumbling block to the Jews and folly to the Gentiles'. These words have come to be embedded in so much pious cotton-wool that we are no longer conscious of their aggressiveness. In fact, elevating tendencies of this kind do more to hinder the gospel than the most radical demythologizing. For they free us from the brutal clutches of Christ's message and turn us into observers of a sacred pageant.[7]

Many Christians today are shocked by the slogan about the death of God, and the believer cannot be blamed for this. At the same time, we should be clear that we brought this slogan on ourselves. It is inevitable, if Christians fly from everyday reality (which ought to be the true place of their divine worship) behind church walls and into whatever is piously edifying. The man who surrenders reality in the slightest degree is treating the creator and Father of Jesus as dead, even if he unwearyingly goes through liturgical exercises, on Sunday or in the silence of his own heart. God dies at all times and in all places where his servants withdraw from the reality that he claims. This, too, can be learnt at the cross. But Paul goes a step further. For him hostility to the cross is the leading characteristic of the world – hence the statement in Gal. 6.14 that the Christian's existence is most deeply stamped by the fact that through Jesus' cross the world is crucified to him and he is crucified to the world. In the same way, this manifests itself physically in that (according to Gal. 2.20) we are no longer at our own disposal. Christ is our life and according to II Cor. 4.10 we only manifest Jesus' life if we carry his death about with us. For what the apostle says about himself here, applies to every messenger of the gospel; that is to say, it is true of every Christian. He is only a disciple as long as he stands in the shadow of the cross; and

---

[7] This danger would be even greater if we could trace the idea of the suffering and dying Messiah back to pre-Christian Judaism. The latest opponent of this view is W. Schrage in 'Das Verständnis des Todes Jesu Christi im Neuen Testament' (*Das Kreuz Jesu Christi als Grund des Heils*, ed. F. Viering, 1967), pp. 57f. There is obviously a connection between the proclamation and the death of Jesus, but the historian should not underpin this psychology by having recourse to Jesus' pre-knowledge of his passion, removing it from the sphere of historical contingency on the grounds of its logical necessity, cf. Schrage, p. 59.

according to the highly pregnant saying in II Cor. 13.4, Jesus shows himself to be a heavenly power of such a kind that his temptation is taken up by us on earth.

It is of the first importance not to wave aside sentences of this kind as if they were dialectical rhetoric. We fail to grasp the heart of Paul's teaching as long as we do not take his paradoxical praise of temptation seriously.[8] It is not only according to Gal. 6.17 that Paul views the stigmata of the one who was crucified (stigmata which even assumed physical form) as the sign of his belonging to Christ and as the mark of the true apostle and follower of Jesus. He was unable to separate faith from these stigmata. We have good reason to remember this fact, because faith which is lived and suffered is obscured in our theological thinking by what have become bloodless convictions, either vague or material. Dogmatic beliefs which do not realize themselves in suffering discipleship are turning the church's piety today into an illusion; and the world is not interested in a Christianity which has become an abstraction. It was not without profound truth that the heathen in the first centuries reproached the followers of the crucified Jesus with stripping the world of its gods; but the common use of the symbol of the cross on tombstones and in jewellery and art shows how the image of Jesus is everywhere overshadowed by Christian piety. This piety is itself often intolerant, but the world for its part tolerates it quite well; it is not normally disturbed by piety and may indeed value it, for one reason or another. What the world inevitably clashes with is whatever reflects the true image of Jesus in his cross. Here unrest and passionate disputes arise, even among Christians.

For it is important to see that although the Pauline message of the cross cites the behaviour of the Jews and Greeks as examples of enmity to the crucified Jesus, it is clearly the legalistic piety of Jewish-Christian circles and the enthusiasm of the Hellenistic church which is the real object of his attack.[9] Enmity to the cross does not end where the 'Christian' sphere begins. On the contrary: it shows itself there in its most dangerous form, distasteful though this statement may be felt to be. It is not by chance that the devoutest of men could be found at Golgotha together with Pilate's myrmidons. Thus Pauline theology (unlike countless sermons we have heard) significantly avoids directing its attack primarily against religious outsiders and the

---

[8] Cf. my essay 'Die Legitimität des Apostels', *ZNW* 41, 1942, pp. 53ff.
[9] For evidence, cf. Schrage, 'Verständnis', pp. 62ff.

morally unstable. Hate taught Nietzsche to see, not without a degree of truth, that the apostle almost exclusively attacks the strong and the devout. This is to shift the line of demarcation between the church and the world. We generally understand by the world the sphere in which the name of Christ is not acknowledged. Paul, on the other hand, is aware of a world which penetrates and gains ground within Christianity itself, dividing it into two camps. According to him there are actual enemies of Christ in the Christian communities in Galatia and Corinth, in Philippi and Rome; and they are not to be found so much among the waverers as among the keenest and most devout church members. The fact that Jesus is proclaimed and believed in as Lord is not the point. Everything depends on whether Christian devotion, in Kähler's words, finds its foundation and its criterion in the cross, right down to everyday life.

Paul often brought out what he found important through the use of already existing formulae, generally from liturgical contexts. Mention must be made above all of the frequently varied statement that Christ died for our sins, a statement already found in the oldest credal tradition, which is represented in I Cor. 15.3. This statement is undoubtedly taken from the proclamation of the suffering servant, and probably had its original place in the words used at the Lord's Supper. In its different variations, Jesus' death sometimes appears (as in Rom. 4.25; 8.32) as a divine sacrifice and the proof of God's love, sometimes (as in Gal. 1.4; 2.20; II Cor. 5.14f.) as the self-sacrificing love of Christ. Correspondingly, love in Paul always means the manifestation of existence for others, displayed in concrete form and with especial emphasis on the act of dying. The apostle introduces a personal and theologically important nuance into the formula when he talks about dying for the ungodly and sinners (Rom. 5.6ff.), or for the Christian brethren (Rom. 14.15), or for all men (II Cor. 5.14). The central theme is always the 'for us'. It covers the two meanings: 'for our advantage' and 'in our stead'; and the changing interpretations characterize Paul's intensity and range. What he is establishing is our incapacity to achieve salvation for ourselves. Salvation is always open to us without our doing anything for it – as a gift, according to Rom. 3.24, and, as Rom. 5.6ff. stresses with intense emotion, before we have fulfilled the will of God. It is only the love of our creator which saves. Otherwise God would not still, in his new creation, be the creator who, as II Cor. 3.5 tells us, makes the inadequate his instruments and is and remains (according to the definition of Rom. 4.17)

God only when he gives life to the dead and calls into existence the things that do not exist. It follows that the faith which receives salvation is simply an ever-new acceptance of the divine gift; and it must be understood in this sense. It includes the self-knowledge of enduring creatureliness, according to which we are entirely and continuously dependent on God's redeeming activity.

Let us pause here for a moment in order to make clear to ourselves that we have strayed imperceptibly from the formulae of the pre-Pauline tradition into the centre of Paul's own preaching. Of course, the traditional phrases that were handed down already stressed God's love and grace, Christ's representative act, our sins, which alienated our own activity from salvation. They, too, already understood Jesus' death as the great turning point, at which our affairs were no longer left in our own hands but were taken up by God. Thus far, Paul could take over views which had already been formed. But all this acquires a different depth and breadth in his thinking because it gives him a chance to consider who God really is, and who man. For him it is part of salvation that this should be recognized clearly and unforgettably in the light of Jesus' death. Indeed, it is only in this knowledge that we can fully understand salvation or enduringly possess it. The cross shows that the true God alone is the creator who works from nothing, who continually draws creation out of chaos and who has hence constantly manifested himself since the beginning of the world as the raiser of the dead. The cross also shows us that from the aspect of the question of salvation, true man is always the sinner who is fundamentally unable to help himself, who cannot by his own action bridge the endless distance to God, and who is hence a member of the lost, chaotic, futile world, which at best waits for the resurrection of the dead.[10] Morality and religion do not alter this at all; they only intensify the forlornness by arrogantly or despairingly permitting attempts at the impossible – attempts, that is to say, to achieve salvation and transcend the world. The cross always remains scandal and foolishness for Jew and Gentile, inasmuch as it exposes man's illusion that he can transcend himself and effect his own salvation, that he can all by himself maintain his own strength, his own wisdom, his own piety and his own self-praise even towards God.[11] In the light of the

[10] A. Schlatter, *Das Kreuz*, p. 12: 'Now God is really God and man is really man.'

[11] *Ibid.*, pp. 8f.: 'Why did he die? Because I make God into an idol to satisfy my hunger for life and blessedness. . . . Because I desire fellowship with God so that he can be my servant. . . . Because we all, theologians and laymen, churchmen

cross God shows all this, and ourselves as well, to be foolish, vain and godless. For everyone is foolish, vain and godless who wants to do, without God and contrary to God, what only God himself can do. Whether it is the devout man who makes the attempt or whether it is the criminal is in the last resort unimportant. Only the creator can be the creature's salvation, not his own works. Salvation always means resurrection from the dead, because that is what God effects in all his acts and gifts to us. Paul therefore basically defines God, on the model of a Jewish prayer, as the God who raises the dead and never does anything alien to that. To this degree, Christ's resurrection is the revelation of that to which all God's activity continually tends and of that which it has always achieved whenever it has achieved its goal. Its eschatological contingency merely shows that the true God, like true man, is completely concealed in the fallen world and only makes his appearance in the call of the gospel.

Paul sees the divinity of God revealed in the cross[12] because the cross is the disclosure and destruction of the illusion that man can transcend himself, either through his presumption or by his own piety; the cross leads us back from illusory heroism to the humanity of creatureliness. That is why Paul takes over what was evidently the traditional view and depicts the dying Jesus as the one who was obedient. Obedience here has nothing to do with mere humility, as the antithesis of Adam and Christ in Rom. 5.12ff. proves. The one who is obedient is the eschatological counterpart of the one who out of disobedience surrendered his creatureliness. He is hence the beginning of the new world, the manifestation of that freedom of the children of God for which earth cries out from its self-imprisonment – cries out without clearly understanding the meaning of its cry. Obedience is the sign of regained creatureliness; it is man's condition before the face of God in that it is simultaneously his condition when he ceases to reach out beyond himself. God rules over those who live and die under this insignia as creator and raiser of the dead; and in the Christian judgment it is only from his cross that the raising of the

---

and politicians, the converted and the fully converted, the saints and the criminals, want to rule – and to rule so that God will listen to us. . . . We pray to idols, the idols of power. That is why Jesus went to the cross. . . . Now the religion of claims and demands, our vainglorious devotionalism and pious behaviour, which we use to set ourselves up above God, comes to an end'.

[12] M. Kähler, *Das Kreuz*, p.45; 'The creed of the church adds to the cross's superscription the interpretation, "Behold your God".' Cf. also K. Barth, *Church Dogmatics*, IV, I, pp. 105ff., 109f.

dead is possible. For the raising of the dead does not mean mere revivification: it is *regnum dei* which raises us above rebellion and death. Cross and resurrection are here most deeply connected – distinguishable but not divisible. They are distinguishable even as 'true man' is distinguishable from 'true God', but they cannot be divided because true man only exists in the face of the true God, and the true God only exists over true man. For though God rules over the godless, this only becomes manifest where Adam's counterpart makes his appearance and joins himself to the godless, without godlessness but in reverence before the creator.

To sum up what we have said: Paul appropriated the tradition which was already in circulation about Jesus' cross in the sense of his doctrine of justification based on the cross; and this is, conversely, his interpretation of Jesus' death. For his teaching speaks of God only being 'for us' when he destroys our illusions and delineates the new obedience of the man who surrenders his autonomy in order to await his salvation from God alone. A man reverences the divinity of God when he remains an earthly creature instead of striving after heavenly translation. The dying Christ becomes creator of the new mankind by freeing us from the temptation to follow the way of the law on the one hand and from the rebel's despair on the other. He is the ground and sphere of reality of the justified.

This insight takes us a step further in many exegetical difficulties. The idea of the sacrificial death has often been unduly stressed.[13] It can, in fact, seem indicated when, in Rom. 3.25, we find Jesus' death described, according to the traditional interpretation,[14] as the instrument of atonement, if we go on to interpret the liturgical, pre-existing metaphor of 'the blood of Jesus' in that light, and if, finally, we think of the comparison of the eucharist with Jewish and pagan sacrificial meals in I. Cor. 10.18ff. Naturally, the 'for us' is then generally explained in corresponding terms. The radical denial of the idea of sacrifice which is occasionally forthcoming in Protestant circles[15] over-simplifies the problem to an inadmissible degree. Of course, Paul was familiar with the idea of sacrifice; he used it without scruple in Rom. 12.1; 15.16; Phil. 2.17 and the possibility, at least,

[13] Especially in J. Pascher, *Theologie des Kreuzes*, 1948; J. Jeremias, *The Central Message of the New Testament*, 1965, pp. 31–51.

[14] For another view see G. Fitzer, 'Der Ort der Versöhnung nach Paulus', *ThZ* 22, 1966, pp. 167ff.

[15] Cf. A. Seeberg, *Der Tod Christi in seiner Bedeutung für die Erlösung*, 1895, pp. 203ff.; Fitzer, *op. cit.*, pp. 173ff.

cannot be excluded that he even gave it Christological overtones. On the other hand, he never definitely called Jesus' death a sacrifice, particularly since it was in general accounted as God's action and God cannot very well sacrifice to himself. The cross's consequences for men dominate all Paul's statements to such an extent that the consequences for God simply do not enter his field of vision, and other concepts occupy the foreground so exclusively that for this reason alone no essential significance can be attributed to the theme of sacrifice. Only pre-Pauline formulae can be cited in support here, and a good deal of research into the history of religion is necessary before their cultic origin can be discovered. Thus, according to I. Cor. 5.7, Jesus is the Paschal lamb slain for us. But in the context the point is not the sacred rite but its result: for Christians, Easter has begun. Even if one does not want to surrender the atonement aspect entirely, the decisive point, at all events, is the ending of our separation from God. It is only the idea of vicariousness that has Christological importance.[16]

Here, too, we must define the point more precisely, however, because the old view of the vicarious punishment of Christ (a view resting on Gal. 3.13 and II Cor. 5.21) is still maintained even today.[17] The Pauline texts provide no basis for this. They do not speak of punishment but of the deep ignominy of the incarnation, which was the price of the salvation achieved without our aid, and of the divine condescension which abases itself to the level of our human sphere.[18] Even the associated group of statements which fall under the heading of reconciliation do not go beyond this. Again, Paul here finds himself in the realm of a traditional thematic which to begin with has nothing at all to do with the cult.[19] Throughout the New Testament, reconciliation means the end of enmity. Although originally this was talked about in relation to the whole world, Paul crystallizes the message, relating it more strictly to the church and the individual Christian, so to speak, as verifiable facts. Reconciliation is certainly offered to the whole world, and it is the service of the apostles to pro-

---

[16] Cf. Wiencke, pp. 63ff.; Schrage, 'Verständnis', p. 54; E. Schweizer, 'Dying and Rising with Christ', *NTS* 14, 1967, pp. 9f.; R. Bultmann, *Theology* I, pp. 295ff.

[17] Cf. Wiencke, pp. 83ff.; W. Pannenberg, *Jesus – God and Man*, 1968, pp. 258–82.

[18] K. Kertelge, *Rechtfertigung bei Paulus*, 1967, p. 211.

[19] Cf. my essay 'Erwägungen zum Stichwort Versöhnungslehre im Neuen Testament', *Zeit und Geschichte, Bultmann-Festschrift*, 1964, pp. 47–59. For a notably different view, cf. T. W. Manson, *On Paul and John*, 1963, pp. 50ff.

claim the offer everywhere. But it comes into effect only where people become disciples of Jesus, though even here faith has to accept what God does without our assistance. We cannot end the state of enmity with God by ourselves. Inasmuch as we look at ourselves instead of at Christ, who through his death leapt into the breach for us, we remain enemies of God and rebels against our Lord. That is why Rom. 5.10 takes up the message of reconciliation, intensifying what was earlier depicted in terms of justification: it describes the justification of the godless as the gift of the divine peace to those who would otherwise remain enemies and who now through the *pax Christi* are led back into obedience. Again, therefore, the pre-existing tradition is used to give a sharper profile to the apostle's own theology.[20] It is impossible to miss the fact that this tradition thereby takes on a new intention. For it spoke, as Rom. 3.25 does, of the forgiveness of previously committed offences in the reconciliation which II Cor. 5.19 tells us has been achieved through Jesus' death. It is striking that Paul hardly ever uses the expression 'forgiveness', although he must have been familiar with it from the context of the message of the Lord's Supper and probably also from baptism, and although he of course adhered to what was meant. But for Paul, salvation does not primarily mean the end of past disaster and the forgiving cancellation of former guilt. It is, according to Rom. 5.9f.; 8.2, freedom from the power of sin, death and the divine wrath; that is to say, it is the possibility of new life. He therefore gave a more radical turn to the tradition which he took over.

This leads us to the third variation of the message about the death of Jesus which was in existence before the apostle; it falls under the heading of redemption. An attempt was made to give clarity and colour to what was evidently, even in the earliest Christian period, a somewhat vague expression by linking it up with the buying free of a slave, a transaction which could be made in the name of a god. I Cor. 6.20; 7.23; Gal. 3.13; 4.5 show that Paul was familiar with this idea.[21] But it is never unequivocally ordered under the heading of redemption. On the contrary, Rom. 8.23 suggests that the chief meaning of redemption was liberation. For Paul himself, the law was the greatest of snares because it meant the perversion of the fundamental relationship between God and man; consequently Pauline anthropology contains in heightened form the idea which Gal. 1.4 terms, in

[20] Cf. Schrage, *op. cit.*, p. 74.
[21] Cf. Bultmann, *Theology* I, pp. 297f.

liturgical phraseology, 'delivering us from the present evil age'. The same notion is more extensively developed in Rom. 8.33ff.: since Christ died, the church has existed in that assailed but victorious liberty which grows from the love of God (i.e., from his existence and intervention on our behalf) and which reflects that love on earth. The condition of being once more the child of God is the fruit of Jesus' death and the expression of the kingdom of God, which he has newly set up on earth and which means the subjection of the cosmic powers. Through his death, the one who was obedient leads on eschatologically the people who have renounced Adam's arrogant claim to be a law to himself. The existence of this people is motivated by the fact that (like the apostle himself, and by virtue of the instruction he gives in II Cor. 12.9) it finds its sufficiency in the grace of its Lord and can now experience and manifest the power of heavenly freedom in the midst of its earthly trials.

To sum up: long before Paul, theological reflection and the liturgical creeds emphasize the death of Jesus as saving event. The apostle picks up the various variations of this proclamation without giving preference to any one in particular. The idea of the sacrificial death is, if anything, pushed into the background and can thus occasion a secular comparison in Rom. 5.7 which calls the uniqueness of Jesus in question by enrolling him among other heroes. But in taking over the tradition, Paul deepens it, sometimes corrects it – at all events gives it a new direction. We might even say that the tradition was not radical enough for him. It certainly gave the riddle of the cross a meaning, teaching people to see salvation in what was at first bound to appear a disaster. But it did this without that critical trenchancy which is the specific mark of Pauline theology; that is why it was suited to liturgical use. It is not by chance that the apostle, though by no means casting aside the doxology, puts it to anthropological use. In this way he brings it back into the field of earthly reality. For example, he talks in completely unelevating language about the gallows. His view of the saving significance of the cross, too, is shocking and paradoxical: God's love is given to the sinner, the ungodly, the enemy, thereby immovably determining the place where man belongs without grace. Despair ends on the cross of Jesus because pride ends there as well; the rebel's presumption as well as the arrogance of the devout, alienation from God together with the holy places, foolishness at the same time as the illusions of those who think themselves wise. Before the God who humbles himself,

self-transcending man comes to an end; even the mask of Christianity cannot save him.[22] The dying son of God does not give life without killing; he pardons, but as judge; he glorifies us by humbling us to the deepest degree; he illuminates by confronting us inexorably with the truth about ourselves; he heals by placing us among the poor in spirit. We imagine that we have come of age, but he calls us back to the relationship of being children, since that is the only possibility of true life. He de-demonizes the world by leading us back from the condition of potential heroes and gods into human reality and thus into the simplicity which breathes liberty in the midst of every entanglement. All this can be brought down to a common denominator: the justification of the ungodly is for Paul the fruit of Jesus' death, and nothing else. And this means *regnum dei* on earth.

When we have grasped this, we can understand why, according to I Cor. 1.23; 2.2, the apostle wants to preach and know only the one who was crucified, although Christian preachers and the Christian churches see this as an intolerable over-simplification and narrowing-down of the riches of Christ. In spite of an undoubtedly one-sided rhetorical and polemical emphasis, the centre of Pauline theology is fixed here. It cannot be anything but a theology of the cross, just as, and just because, it cannot be separated from the message of justification, and counters all enthusiasm with a critical and realistic anthropology. The protests against this which have been heard at every period and which can be heard again nearly everywhere today belong inevitably to Paul's way and work. Since the Corinthians first raised the objection, it has taken the form of a theology of the resurrection, and does so again throughout the Christian world today. Theologically speaking, Paul is a constant irritant to the ecumenicity which, as missionary to the Gentiles, he helped to build; it was not disrupted by him only at the Reformation. The ecumenical problem which is represented in the New Testament canon by Paul is still obscured by the reverential attitude of the churches and by traditional catchwords, none of which free Christianity from the difficulty involved. In Pauline interpretation the problem is still alive. Attempts to comprehend him mystically or sacramentally, or from the standpoint of the church, or from the angle of salvation history, all demonstrate this. The history of Pauline interpretation is the history of the apostle's

[22] Pascher (p. 40) takes a contrary view: 'The crucified humanity of the Lord is the fulfilled potentiality of humanity in general.' The *ad nihilum redigi* also receives too little weight if, like Delling (p. 86), one sees primarily love in the cross.

ecclesiastical domestication. The message of the cross as such is not disputed; what is in question is whether it is right to make this the real, or even the sole, theme of Pauline theology.

The protest appears to rest on irrefutable grounds. It is impossible to overlook the multiplicity of other themes in the apostle's letters. Even more tellingly, in Rom. 1.4; I Cor. 6.14; II Cor. 4.14; I Thess. 1.10 (to take only a few examples), the risen Christ appears as the ground of salvation as exclusively as does the crucified Jesus elsewhere. Although it is an established credal tradition about Jesus' resurrection which is passed on to us in Rom. 10.9, and although traditions of the kind undoubtedly influence the texts just mentioned, Paul for his part accepted the tradition without reservation, even in I Cor. 15.17 calling a belief which deviated from it 'futile'. It would be over-bold to conclude from this that confrontation with the cross alone is insufficient.[23] Yet the more challenging one's own defence of a theology of the cross, the more understandable one will find it that others should, with equal decision, describe the theology of the resurrection as the 'pivot of primitive Christian thought'[24] and the 'Archimedean point for theology as such',[25] and that they should maintain that this is true for Paul as well.[26] Do not passages such as Rom. 4.25 and I Cor. 15.3f. at least force us to recognize that the apostle's theology stresses Jesus' cross and his resurrection equally, and that it consequently has two focuses?[27] Admittedly, we will hardly find it satisfactory to apply the same dialectic as a corrective to every one-sided point of view. After all, the pre-existence of Christ, his incarnation, his exaltation to the right hand of God and his second coming are also, at least from time to time, stressed with no less emphasis. More – the salvation-historical antithesis of Christ and Adam and Moses, or the typological significance of Abraham are undoubtedly essential to Pauline Christology. Are we not therefore bound to conclude that even cross and resurrection are only links in a chain which includes, not least, the view of Christ as mediator in creation and to which only a theology of the facts of redemption (the

[23] See for example K. H. Rengstorf, *Die Auferstehung Jesu*, ⁴1960, p.63; W. Künneth, *The Theology of the Resurrection*, 1965, p.151: 'Without the Easter event, the cross of Jesus bears the stamp of a purely immanent happening.'

[24] Künneth, *op. cit.*, p.18.

[25] *Ibid.*, p.294.

[26] *Ibid.*, pp.150ff.

[27] Künneth is emphatically opposed to this view. But see Fitzer, *op. cit.*, p.175; K. H. Schelkle, *Die Passion Jesu in der Verkündigung des Neuen Testamentes*, 1949, p.247.

theology which enjoys such popularity today) can do justice?

We must raise this question bluntly because it is the hinge of the present Christological dispute and thus, inevitably, of the whole theological controversy. As long as no firm decision is made here, nothing is firm or decided at all; and unfortunately clarity has by no means been reached. The advocates of a theology of the resurrection and of the facts of redemption do not generally wish to set aside the theology of the cross; they want to give it a place in a wider context. But this is to overlook the fact that we are thereby levelling down the theology of the cross and giving it a merely relative importance; and this means, practically speaking, denying it altogether, if we take account of its original intention. For we cannot say *crux nostra theologia* unless we mean that this is the central and in a sense the only theme of Christian theology. The statement is rhetorical if the cross is only one, or even the most important, link in a chain. Whether we like it or not, the cross will then be overshadowed by the resurrection and the facts of redemption.[28] In this case, however, in spite of the apostle's most solemn declarations, I Cor. 1 and 2 are pure rhetoric, evidence of theological exaggeration and lack of control. According to this view, Pauline theology does not in reality go beyond a 'both . . . and'. In place of a clear answer to the question of the basis and criterion of Christian theology, we now have a complex theology of New Testament history. This is, in fact, our dilemma and it is here that the jungle warfare begins in which we are all involved today – theologians and church members, the churches individually and the churches in their conversations with one another: the Pauline texts as we see and understand them seem to contradict the theology of the cross held by the Reformers. Admittedly, few people have had the courage to say openly what simply cannot be concealed any longer: the theology of the resurrection and of the facts of redemption, which is making inroads on contemporary Protestantism everywhere, is no less polemical than once was the Reformation's theology of the cross, and it is therefore an attack on the Reformed basis of Protestantism, in so far as this has not in any case lost its validity. If we want to link up the one theology with the other, we are reverting to the pre-Reformation world. There the importance of the cross could be more

---

[28] Hence Künneth, *op. cit.*, p. 152: It is the 'presupposition' or 'key-signature', and this in 'the relationship of question and answer, riddle and interpretation'. 'The sense of the theology of the cross, accordingly, does not lie in itself.' For the opposing view see G. Bornkamm, *Paulus*, 1969, pp. 168f., 171.

impressively represented than we generally realize or would like to think, though it was admittedly only accounted the reverse side of a theology of the resurrection, the sacraments and the facts of redemption as these were represented by the church. It is not entirely by chance that contemporary Protestantism feels itself more at home with Orthodoxy and Roman Catholicism than with radical historical criticism and a demythologizing which I am convinced is the logical consequence and the admittedly rationalistic expression of a radical Reformed theology of the cross.

This diagnosis will hardly find general acceptance, but that does not greatly concern me. Taboos against which argument is of no avail are not only a reality and a power in primitive societies. The diagnosis can only be supported if we have a better understanding of the relationship of the cross to the resurrection than most Pauline interpretations display. And here we again start from an exegetical difficulty. Curious though it sounds, the apostle does not seem to have any precise knowledge about the concrete circumstances of the crucifixion. The statement in Gal. 3.1 that Jesus was publicly portrayed as crucified does not represent a detailed description, but an official proclamation made with the greatest possible emphasis.[29] In I Cor. 2.8 demonic powers, even, are made responsible for Jesus' death.[30] The hymn to Christ in Phil. 2.6ff. contains no direct historical reminiscence, but is a variation on the theme of the redeemer who descends from heaven and returns there. The scantiness of Paul's Jesus tradition is surprising in general, but his silence here, where he is so deeply engaged, is positively shocking. The theological interpretation drives out all historical information beyond the mere event of the crucifixion. Of course this is also true of the incarnation, which is linked up with Jesus' Davidic origin only in the fragment of tradition reproduced in Rom. 1.3. The same may be said of Paul's account of the resurrection, which only (in the tradition of I Cor. 15.3ff.) presents a list of witnesses no longer found in the gospels as proof of the factual nature of the event. And he proclaims the ascension as a pure article of faith, without any narrative accompaniment at all. On the other hand, this corresponds to the fact that I Cor. 1.8ff. knows no other approach to the cross than preaching and that

---

[29] Cf. G. Delling, 'Der Tod Jesu in der Verkündigung des Paulus', *Apophoreta, Festschrift E. Haenchen*, 1964, p. 93.

[30] For the contrary view see J. Schniewind, *Die Archonten dieses Äons. Nachgelassene Reden und Aufsätze*, 1952, pp. 104–9. Schniewind does, however, give a good account of the discussion.

the same is true of the resurrection and exaltation of Christ after the Easter appearances have come to an end. The sacramental mediation is not overlooked, but it does not exist without the essential co-operation of preaching.

This means that for Paul the 'facts of redemption' cannot be separated from the Word of Christian preaching; nor can they be played off against it. They are undoubtedly the basis of preaching, but without preaching we cannot have them at all. More – historical recollection is no longer able to say what really happened, and so nothing is said about this at all. When Rom. 10.14 tells us that all faith comes from preaching, this applies to faith in the facts of redemption as well. Of course Paul believes that one could have seen Jesus of Nazareth and the cross on Golgotha. But in this respect Jesus' life and crucifixion remain as ambiguous as the Easter events.[31] For the earthly facts do not merely create belief; they create disbelief as well. To say that salvation is to be encountered in these facts is a matter of revelation and faith. Assurance of salvation only comes through preaching. The person who wants to build on historical facts as such is bound to fall into uncertainty of salvation, and historical criticism confirms that this is the case. The inevitable conclusion is that the significance of the so-called facts of redemption for salvation can only be perceived and accepted on the basis of preaching. Thus far, preaching has saving significance for us and all salvation is for us bound up with it. Because there is no salvation without it, preaching brings about both life and death, according to II Cor. 2.15f. To isolate the facts of redemption from preaching, as one distils a chemical product, makes salvation intangible and inefficacious. The current talk about the facts of redmption which, we are told, can be objectively established, therefore conceals a deadly danger: for it is precisely talk like this which allows us to lose sight of the only place where we are not merely told about salvation but can find it. The cross helps no one who does not hear the word of the cross and ground his faith on that.[32]

---

[31] Consequently W. Künneth's statement in *Entscheidung heute. Jesu Auferstehung – Brennpunkt der theologischen Diskussion*, 1966, p. 38, is quite inadmissible: 'The facts alone have a fateful and destiny-determining quality.' The revealing 'alone' is simply anti-Protestant and betrays modern positivism. The Word appears as information about supernatural facts and faith is acceptance of those facts. Theology becomes a religious *Weltanschauung*.

[32] Cf. also Schrage, p. 76. For a characteristically different view, cf. Delling, p. 94: 'The event of the cross has validity *per se* . . ., not only at the moment when it is proclaimed to me.' It is frequently no longer realized that the 'objectivity' of the saving event is perceived, and only perceived, through the *verbum externum*.

The same is true of the resurrection, exaltation and incarnation of Christ; it is true even of the historical Jesus. Faith in them is only possible via the Word of proclamation, not on the grounds of their historical reality, which is as ambiguous as our own lives.

Whatever the reason for the talk about the facts of redemption, and whatever right the spiritualists may have on their side when they surrender the earth as a field of decision between belief and disbelief, this talk almost inevitably leads to the loss of a theology of the Word. We might also express it in religio-historical terms and say that this is to revert to a theology of manifestations and thus to a sphere in which Christianity and paganism can no longer be distinguished and divided – the sphere, that is to say, of general religiosity. The attempt to replace the theology of the Word by the theology of manifestations runs through the whole of church history. Apparently, in spite of the Reformation, we have still not learnt that faith derived from the Word and faith deriving from manifestations are two different things. That is why contemporary Protestantism is everywhere unsure of itself and has become questionable in general. The theology of the cross and the theology of the Word belong together and are won or thrown away together.[33] The person who sees has no need to hear, and the person who can no longer hear will inevitably want to see. According to Paul, whether one wants to hear or to see is what divides faith from superstition.

Let me explain this in more detail. The objection to the theology of the cross and the theology of the Word is not that they are completely wrong, but that they are an over-simplification. We are told that they only bring out part of the biblical message. That is the old reproach which the Roman Catholic and Orthodox churches levied against the Reformation's 'by faith *alone*'. The only thing that is new is that contemporary Protestantism has also, in polemical tones, taken up the cry about the riches of the bible. But how does this apply to the quarters where the importance of the facts of redemption is being preached today? It is clear that here individual isolable events are added together and connected through the system of ideas associated with the notion of a historical process. This raises two questions. In the first place, can, according to Protestant understanding, a historical process be an object of faith at all? Does this view not again reveal the idealist belief that history is the evolutionary process of the Godhead? The second question is no less important, namely: can the

[33] Cf. Bultmann, *Theology* I, pp. 301ff.

Protestant faith be appropriately described as the acceptance of individual events? For we are then compelled to make facts, which are essentially neutral, the object of faith; and it is extremely doubtful whether this is permissible, although we do it, usually without thinking about the matter. Personally I should answer 'no' to both questions. My generation at least (if we have profited at all from our own experience) should surely have lost its taste for the watchword of 'history as revelation', and as regards salvation history this watchword has always existed, even in secularized form. Anyone who has still not burnt his fingers enough can continue to pursue the subject. But after only thirty years it has apparently already been largely forgotten that it was at precisely this point that a choice had to be made in Germany between Yahweh and Baal, and that there is no way of wrapping up the basic nature of the choice. A discussion of this problem would extend so far, however, that I must content myself with a protest.

The second question is directed towards one aspect of the first and is hence easier to answer. The splitting up of faith into a number of different things which have to be believed runs parallel to the hypostatization of the object of faith itself. This would seem to be a crystallization, but in reality it means a process of abstraction. Pre-existence, incarnation, crucifixion, resurrection, exaltation and the second coming are not facts which follow one another like beads on a string and which indicate the saving and historical process inaugurated by Christ. It cannot be denied that this way of looking at things already begins in the New Testament and that Paul seems to encourage it when he describes the content of faith in relative and participial constructions. But then Christ must be made the initiator or first cause of an event which determines the path of a religion and its secular results and which makes the spread or decay of the church the object of salvation and its converse. Faith is here primarily the sum total of certain dogmatic convictions and a piety which puts particular ideals into practice or immerses itself in particular mysteries – in short a form of religiosity. It grows up basically in the environment of a general religious philosophy of life and can only be more precisely characterized as a type of the latter. In reality it exists at the cost of Christology, which then only forms the perspective of an evolutionary idea, that is to say it becomes a theory.[34] For Paul, faith

---

[34] Cf. B. Klappert (ed.), *Diskussion um Kreuz und Auferstehung*, 1967, and the comments by Bultmann (pp. 89, 93), Barth (p. 131), Moltmann (p. 251) and Iwand

means faith in one thing and one thing alone: Christ as Lord. All his paraphrases in relative and participial phraseology simply serve the purpose of substantiating and developing the lordship of Christ. Nothing earthly must take the place of this, and it can be resolved neither into a series of historical events nor into an institution for the transmission of salvation, nor into a specific piety. Christ as Lord will not be turned into an object, and faith which remains obedience and personal relationship[35] must be saved from being accounted a Christian ideology. But that is exactly the almost unavoidable danger of every theology which moves the 'facts of redemption' into the centre. The history of the churches illustrates this so cogently that one might suppose that no person of any discernment could overlook its warning. For Christianity has always made even Christ unbelievable, and has discouraged as many people as it has attracted. Today the church's bankruptcy in all its religious activities is so obvious that we can no longer afford to identify Jesus with Christianity. 'Facts of redemption' are offered on every religious and political market place, with the appropriate (and often convincing) historical interpretations thrown in. Many gods claim incarnation, resurrection and exaltation for themselves and find believers. This only draws us into the general competition and increasing scepticism, instead of freeing us from it.

We must learn again to spell out the question: who is Jesus? Everything else is a distraction. We must measure ourselves against Jesus, not measure him against our churches and dogmas and devout church members. Christianity is drowning, as the church in Corinth did in the past, in religious riches which are really a chaos. This does not mean that churches, dogmas or even the devout are irrelevant. But it is essential that they should not be defended for their own sakes, in order to preserve the *status quo* of any given tradition. Their value depends entirely on the extent to which they point away from themselves and call us to follow Jesus as Lord. They must also leave room

---

(p. 279). Elsewhere the church has integrated and practically domesticated its Lord; but a certain type of Protestantism (which oddly enough considers itself to be orthodox) has done the same for a particular history, which is *per se* supposed to be revelation.

[35] Although Künneth in *Entscheidung heute* (p. 150) also stresses the personal, not the factual, relationship, yet the *Christus praesens* mentioned on p. 212 is merely the code word for that reality which is described on p. 88 as 'the field of force of everlasting life' and 'transcendent existence' and which, according to p. 186, rests on the resurrection as 'universal elemental event'. Christ, the ancient god of the mysteries, turns up again in modern dress. Ultimately the Lord is the initiator and guarantor of a particular cosmology.

for varying dogmatics; Christianity has never owned a 'normal' theology and has always allowed different confessions their place, quite apart from the fact that from the very beginning it has a good deal to thank heresy for. After all, according to the gospels there were people who doubted the resurrection even among the first disciples, and I Cor. 15 tells us that there were even those who denied the future resurrection in the very first churches; and though these were admonished, they were by no means excommunicated. The decisive criterion of the church and of discipleship cannot possibly be the convictions we hold, especially since convictions change, even among Christians; we are never finished – we all have to go on growing. The decisive criterion for unity and division in our faith can only be how far we serve and follow Jesus as Lord and how far we deny his lordship, whether our denial takes the form of piety or impiety. Harsh though it may sound, it is obvious that Christ is denied today by Christians most of all, because his lordship over their organized religion and their dogmatic convictions has become illusory, theoretical and imaginary. But the token which distinguishes his lordship from the lordship of other religious founders is undoubtedly the cross and the cross alone. If theology is to make unique and unmistakable assertions about Jesus, everything it says must be related to the cross. In the same way, following Jesus means, uniquely and unmistakably, becoming a disciple of the one who was crucified. The cross is the ground and test of Christology.

Now of course we have not yet solved the difficulty that Paul proclaims Jesus' resurrection as exclusively as his cross. We must even call our theme in question by accepting the fact that Paul was only able to understand and preach the cross in the light of the manifestation of the risen Christ.[36] Just as, historically speaking, the crucifixion precedes the Easter appearances, so for the faith of the primitive church all knowledge of Jesus (in the sense of certainty of salvation) was only possible after Easter. This applies to the one who was incarnate and crucified as well as to the one who was pre-existent and exalted. Nor must we confine this observation to the experience of the primitive church. It is a basic truth and applies at all periods. If this were not so, a theology of the Word would be quite unjustifiable. For, according to the testimony of the whole of the New Testament, it is the one who is risen who acts through the Word of proclamation, even when the theme of that proclamation is the 'historical' Jesus.

[36] The view taken by Rengstorf (p. 69) and Künneth (*Theology*, p. 152).

We might even go a step further: anyone who analyses the New Testament texts will scarcely escape the insight that Jesus' cross was in fact first felt to be a dark riddle which found its solution in the light of the Easter events. It would otherwise be incomprehensible why the reaction of the first disciples to the cross was flight into Galilee, the shock felt by this community still finding its expression in the scriptural proofs which were to demonstrate the necessity of the cross. We therefore accept all the premises of the theology of the resurrection which is so effectively maintained today. But can we then escape the conclusions which follow from these premises? Must not the theology of the cross now turn into one chapter in the theology of the resurrection?

Before we can answer this question, two things must be made clear. Paul only spoke of the resurrection of Christ in connection with, and as the beginning of, the resurrection of the dead in general. It is not for him the individual event of the revivification of a dead person, as is generally assumed today. As the overcoming of death it is for him rather the beginning of the rule of the one with whom the kingdom of divine freedom begins, whose appearance means both calling and sending, who founds church and mission and who leads the new creature into a new world. As present Lord of the church, the risen Christ is for the apostle also the destined cosmocrator. This interpretation was facilitated by the fact that the pre-Pauline Christology preserved for us in the early Christian hymns has the heavenly exaltation of Jesus following directly on the cross.[37] This means that the raising of Jesus from the dead counted from the outset as an enthronement and the Easter appearances were conceived of as being manifestations of the one who was already exalted. This earliest view involved the danger that the cross could appear as a mere transit point on the way to the exaltation, and as a station which the exalted Christ left behind and which had therefore merely historical relevance. This was apparently exactly the way in which the Corinthians looked at it. Moreover, the Acts of the Apostles evidently reflects the same view, and this is the opinion repeatedly held by the churches. Enthusiasm and orthodoxy have always forged a curious alliance at this point. Here is the deepest root of that theology of the resurrection which is polemically played off against the theology of the cross and which enjoys the widest recognition today. 'Through cross to crown' is the

---

[37] Cf. G. Bertram, 'Die Himmelfahrt Jesu vom Kreuz aus und der Glaube an seine Auferstehung', *Festgabe für A. Deissmann*, 1927, pp. 187–217.

edifying vulgarization of this view, which moves Jesus' death into the shadow of his exaltation. It may do so in the framework of a theory of salvation history or may take the moralistic viewpoint, seeing this as model of the Christian path through which, not without divine initiative and co-operation, the transcending of our earthly being and the overcoming of nature by the supernatural can, after all, ultimately be proclaimed.

The Pauline letters are proof that the apostle passionately opposed this interpretation of the facts of redemption. They also give his reasons. He saw here an enthusiasm at work which was highly detrimental to Christology. Let me put the point more emphatically: although the Corinthians were already taking shelter behind the proclamation of a resurrection reality mediated through the sacraments (and were to this extent pursuing a theology of the facts of redemption), their Christology, according to Paul's understanding, suffered because it was overshadowed by a false anthropology and ecclesiology. And we shall have in all seriousness to face the question of how far a theology of the facts of redemption is not always pursued, consciously or unconsciously, in the interests of an enthusiastic anthropology and ecclesiology. The fact that its supporters believe that this is a defence against existentialism is no counter-argument. The opposing camps. could be much closer to one another in their approach and intention than their slogans would suggest. The criterion is not to be found in the alternatives of Christology or anthropology and ecclesiology, but in the alternative between a true and a false Christology which then projects itself into anthropology and ecclesiology. This latter alternative, however, is modified by whether the primacy of Christology is adhered to or jeopardized, either secretly or openly.

For Paul, too, the one who is risen is the one who enters into his kingdom. But the cross does not therefore become the way to that kingdom or its price.[38] It is rather the signature of the one who is risen. He would have no name by which he could be called were it not the name of the crucified. Moreover, otherwise he could not rule, because according to the apostle he bursts the bounds of personality as we understand it today and imbues the world with his body and through his members. He is unmistakable and identifiable with Jesus of Nazareth only as the man of the cross. No one has ever been able to talk about the one who is risen without meaning an ideogram

[38] Cf. Schrage, *op. cit.*, pp. 61, 65.

for the overcoming and transfiguration of the world (i.e., a cosmo-logical and anthropological ideology) unless the one who is risen remains the one who was crucified and is as such confessed as Lord.[39] Before Paul, the cross of Jesus formed the question which was answered by the message of the resurrection. The apostle decisively reversed this way of looking at things. In his controversy with the enthusiasts it was precisely the interpretation of the resurrection which turned out to be a problem, a problem which could only be answered in the light of the cross. This controversy shows for the first time in the history of the church that a theology of the resurrection which takes precedence over, and is isolated from, a theology of the cross leads to a Christian variation of a religious philosophy in which the imitation of Jesus and the lordship of Christ lose all concrete meaning. Paul, on the contrary, found it necessary to define sharply the sphere occupied by the reality of the resurrection in his eschat-ology and doctrine of the sacraments, as well as in his ecclesiology and anthropology: it is only the one who was crucified who is risen, and the lordship of the one who is risen marches with the present service of the one who was crucified. It reaches out into the world only in so far as it realizes itself in the community which is world-wide and universally confesses him as lord.

We cannot here enter in detail into the question of Christ's work for his own and for the cosmos, although our context really demands that we should. We must, however, make the distinctive facts of the case so clear that the Pauline perspective is visible and modern prejudices are excluded. Let me take as examples Paul's doctrine of the sacraments and his understanding of apostleship. The meaning of the sacraments for the apostle is obvious. The already-existing tradition unfolded a Christology which spoke of Jesus as the second Adam and a soteriology which allowed sacramental participation in the fate of this second Adam – participation both in his sufferings and in his glory.[40] His sufferings are mystically shared in baptism, but the fruit of baptism is a share in his glory. That is why groups in Corinth celebrate the Lord's Supper as the heavenly banquet, declaring the future resurrection to be unnecessary, understanding the Christian state as a foreshadowing of heavenly existence, with its freedom from

[39] Künneth (*Theology*, pp. 151ff.) significantly rejects the superiority of the *theologia crucis* over the theology of the resurrection, or its equal importance, but otherwise does not find it necessary to go into the question. It interests him in his context in a purely negative sense! Cf. also *Entscheidung heute*, pp. 16ff.

[40] Cf. Bultmann, *Theology* I, pp. 298f.

temptation, and behaving accordingly towards the brethren and the world. Here, too, Paul rectifies the tradition. He puts the main stress of the eucharist on the remembrance of, and participation in, Jesus' death and expressly denies that baptism, in which we die with Christ, also allows us to participate in his resurrection. It merely gives us the *expectation and hope* of the resurrection. That is why a paraenesis based on this enjoins the Christian with the greatest earnestness to mortify the flesh and allow the dying of the Lord Jesus to appear in his body. This makes it clear that Christianity carries the victory of Jesus into the whole world, but can only do so if and in so far as it takes up Jesus' cross after him. Its glory is hidden in being crucified with Jesus. Paul never tires of showing the same thing in his own case,[41] as the catalogue of his sufferings and his general exposition in II Cor. 10–13 show. At a time when the subject of the apostolic succession plays the greatest part in ecumenical discussions and in questions of church union, Paul's self-characterization is, however, passed over with staggering facility. And yet Paul is the only apostle whose writings have been preserved and passed down to us in the New Testament. To have seen the risen Lord and to have been sent forth by him: this is what Paul names as the precondition of apostleship. Yet he already knows of apostles whom he calls the enemies of the cross of Jesus. That is why he has to state the criterion of true apostleship in answer to the question forced upon him about the 'signs of an apostle'. The only infallible token he offers in his hard-fought controversy with the enthusiasts and his rebellious congregations is being crucified with Jesus and the service which is realized in this way. It is only where Paul is forgotten that the apostolic tradition (or what is considered to be the apostolic tradition) is assigned significance *per se* or on the grounds of its antiquity, so that it determines the nature of the creed, the canon or the church. Judas was an apostle, too, and the apostolic character is never completely unequivocal unless it bears the stamp of the cross. True apostleship may involve tasks which are different from the tasks of all other members of the church. But its absolutely decisive criterion does not divide the apostle from other Christians. It is the discipleship of the one who was crucified.

It follows from this that for Paul the cross was not a historically unique event, although it was certainly that as well.[42] It must not be

---

[41] Cf. E. Güttgemanns, *Der leidende Apostel und sein Herr*, 1966.

[42] J. Schneider, *Die Passionsmystik des Paulus*, 1929, p.24, rightly points to the characteristic aorists in which Paul talks about Jesus' death.

etherealized into an ideal of *humilitas* or something of the kind which can be made to cover the Christian life; for it cannot be detached from Golgotha. It is the foundation of the church and the salvation which has been prepared for us. On the other hand, Paul did not leave it in the historical dimension, because it would then have been outstripped and made a thing of the past by the later facts of redemption. It remains for him an eschatological event, to use our current phrase, because Jesus remains the one who was crucified; and it is only as the one who was crucified that he remains Jesus. Pauline theology therefore circles round in ever new attempts to bring out the saving significance of the cross. It is a theology of the Word because it is only through the word of the cross that Jesus' death remains present, remains grace, remains promise and covenant; and it is the work of the one who is risen to let this Word manifest itself in preaching, in the sacraments and in the Christian life. Does this mean that we must not speak of the glory of a Christian or of the church? The Pauline epistles everywhere contradict such an assumption. But everything depends on the way in which we speak of these things. The Corinthians already thought that Jesus bore the cross so that his own might partake of his exaltation. This idea came to be taken so far as to suggest that Christ was made man so that we might become divine. Paul contests this view passionately, in so far as it is supposed to be a description of earthly life in the present. He does so in the name of the truth of the crucified and the reality of Christian existence. For him, Jesus' glory consists in the fact that he makes his earthly disciples willing and able to take up the cross after him; and the glory of the church and of the Christian life is that they are thought worthy to praise the one who was crucified as the power and wisdom of God, to seek salvation in him alone and to turn their existence into the service of God under the token of Golgotha. Here the theology of the resurrection is a chapter in the theology of the cross, not the excelling of it. Since Paul, all theological controversy has radiated ultimately from one central point and can hence only be decided at that point: *crux sola nostra theologia.*

IIII

JUSTIFICATION AND SALVATION HISTORY IN THE EPISTLE TO THE ROMANS

Controversy is the breath of life to a German theologian, and mutual discussion is the duty of us all. For, in scholarship as in life, no one can possess truth except by constantly learning it afresh; and no one can learn it afresh without listening to the people who are his companions on the search for that truth. Community does not necessarily mean agreement. For this reason I should now like to join issue with the unusually provocative (and hence so important) article published by Krister Stendahl in the *Harvard Theological Review*, 1963,[1] under the title, 'The Apostle Paul and the Introspective Conscience of the West'. He thinks that the Pauline interpretation which he believes extends from Augustine and the Reformation to Bultmann's existentialist view is on the wrong road. According to Stendahl, the introspective attitude of the west has led to a false stress on Paul's struggle with the Judaistic interpretation of the law and hence to an equally wrong emphasis on the doctrine of justification which grew out of that struggle. The western churches' heightened idea of sin and conscience meant, he believes, an over-valuation of Paul's defence against Judaism, which was temporally conditioned and soon became obsolete. According to Stendahl, the main emphases have been confused in the process. The apostle's polemics assumed the dominating position. But, in fact, neither Paul the Pharisee nor Paul the convert possessed that pronounced awareness of guilt which his later interpreters imputed to him. His message rather centres on a concept of revelation based on salvation history. This can be seen

[1] *Op. cit.*, pp. 199–215.

most clearly in Rom. chs. 9–11.[2] In order not to go beyond the bounds of a lecture, I shall confine my reply to the Epistle to the Romans, tempting though it would be to analyse the whole Pauline *corpus* in the light of this question.

I. BASIC CONSIDERATIONS

First, I should like briefly to indicate the mental climate in which such a thesis could grow up. It is not only extremely surprising, when we remember that it is a former Swedish Lutheran who is supporting it. It also has the most momentous significance for the whole of Pauline interpretation, for our present theological discussions and for the situation of our churches. At bottom, Stendahl's conclusions are not new. William Wrede[3] and Albert Schweitzer[4] both already considered that the doctrine of justification was a mere tributary of Pauline theology (though they thought so for different reasons), and they were only expressing openly what was a widespread view in historical criticism. Long before, F. C. Baur saw Rom. 9–11 as the peak and thematic centre of the epistle, which he, too, pleaded should be understood primarily in the light of its own historical background.[5] The differences between the Pauline and the Lutheran doctrines of justification were brought out by P. Althaus.[6] Finally, J. Munck[7] and O. Cullmann[8] especially have recently proclaimed in unmistakable terms an interpretation not only of Paul but of the whole of the New Testament based on salvation history. Stendahl therefore belongs within the context of an established theological tradition. His essay is significant because he combines old questions and brings them up to date, thus becoming the spokesman of a line of approach which is beginning to find increasing acceptance in New Testament theology. Three general remarks may help to make clear what I mean.

What has been said indicates that today Pauline interpretation is just as controversial as, for example, the problem of the historical

---

[2] Cf. *ibid.*, pp. 204ff., 214.

[3] *Paulus*, 1904 (*Das Paulusbild in der neueren deutschen Forschung*, ed. by K. H. Rengstorf, 1964, pp. 1–97), p. 67.

[4] *The Mysticism of Paul the Apostle*, 1931, pp. 220f.

[5] 'Über Zweck und Veranlassung des Römerbriefs und die damit zusammenhängenden Verhältnisse der römischen Gemeinde', *Tübinger Zeitschrift für Theologie*, 1836, 3, pp. 59–178.

[6] *Paulus und Luther über den Menschen*, 1951.

[7] *Christus und Israel*, 1956; *Paul and the Salvation of Mankind*, 1959.

[8] *Salvation in History*, 1967.

Jesus or Lucan and Johannine theology. This means that at present the interpretation of the whole New Testament has become a highly uncertain matter, although the same historical-critical method is used everywhere, even if the ruthlessness with which the method is applied varies. Generally we do not give much thought to this. Scriptural theology has been pushed aside in many quarters by a theology which is guided by the needs of the church or its traditions. The intrinsic value of the bible is universally stressed, but its exposition is regulated and confined by considerations of edification or by the self-understanding which is prevailing at any given moment.

It follows from this that Protestantism is no longer generally in accord with the Reformation any more. The scriptures have ceased to be accounted the basis and tribunal of the church; they are now the documents of its tradition and spiritual devotion, as well as the instruments of its self-reflection and, occasionally, of any necessary self-correction. Practically speaking, the church takes precedence over the scriptures, even when this is not admitted in principle or is dialectically obscured. The Reformation, on the other hand, asserted, undialectically and inexorably, the pre-eminence of the scriptures over the church. In the process we have described, the interpretation of the bible as salvation history enjoys a particular function about which we are seldom clear. A glance at modern Catholicism may be helpful at this point. That the bible and its exegesis have taken on immense importance in the Roman Catholic church is one of the most remarkable features of present-day theology. Yet this process is mainly significant for the church as a whole because the rigidity which its dogmatics have acquired has been relaxed; they have by no means been subjected to fundamental criticism. Ultimately the interpretation of the scriptures based on salvation history actually strengthens the authority of the church, which has now become more elastic but has by no means been reduced to relative importance. Tradition and scripture continue to exist in a dialectical relationship which diminishes many of tradition's rigours, but not its still-prevailing dominance.[9] To put it bluntly: with salvation history one is always on the safe side. For it allows us to think in terms of a development which, in spite of many false starts and many needful corrections, leads to

---

[9] P. Benoit, *Exégèse et Théologie* I–II, Paris, 1961, is characteristic. But counter-tendencies, above all in Germany, must not be overlooked. A recent representative of these is K. Kertelge, *Rechtfertigung bei Paulus. Studien zur Struktur und zum Bedeutungsgehalt des paulinischen Rechtfertigungsbegriffs*, 1967.

growing understanding and ultimately to the goal which the church has before it, a goal whose outline is already to be traced in the church itself.

I have nothing against the phrase salvation history, although it is often used in what seem to me questionable ways; I would even say that it is impossible to understand the bible in general or Paul in particular without the perspective of salvation history. On the other hand, we should not isolate the phrase from the problems associated with it and, like all dangerous phrases, it should be defined as closely as possible. In no case should what we call the divine plan of salvation be absorbed by an immanent evolutionary process whose meaning can be grasped on earth, or which we can control and calculate. This would make the divine and the human interchangeable and would allow the church ultimately to triumph over its Lord, by organizing him instead of listening and obeying. The peace of God passes all understanding, and so does God's plan of salvation. The Stoic may imagine that he can look on at God. This is not open to faith. Thus the nerve of our discussion is exposed when we ask: is salvation history visible, and if so, in what way?

Before we answer this, we must consider the polemical direction which characterizes both Stendahl's thesis and the conceptions of salvation history held by Munck and Cullmann. All three of them attack Bultmann's theology. Interestingly enough, they do so primarily not because of its radical historical criticism but because of its systematic premises. Munck censures Bultmann's dependence on F. C. Baur's doctrines, and Cullmann complains of his exaggerated existentialism; but Stendahl ventures even further. He reproaches his opponent with a drastic 'prolongation' of the western misunderstanding of the Pauline doctrine of justification.[10] In Stendahl, consequently, the antithesis arises between salvation history as the apostle's fundamental position and his doctrine of justification as an early Christian defence against Judaism, conditioned by its time. Whether this view is tenable or not is for the moment unimportant. The remarkable thing is mainly the new position which is being built up here – a position which, if we look back, we can see has long since cast its shadow ahead of it.

Perhaps I may be allowed a personal reminiscence here. My theological youth was most strongly marked by the detachment of 'dialectical' theology from the nineteenth-century idealist view of

[10] *Op. cit.*, p. 207.

history, a movement which was supported by the historical criticism which goes under Bultmann's name. On the way to a theology of proclamation we rediscovered that Reformation doctrine of justification which had become largely incomprehensible to our fathers and grandfathers and which had therefore ceased for them to form the centre of the New Testament message. This discovery immunized us deeply against a conception of salvation history which broke in on us in secularized and political form with the Third Reich and its ideology. It will be understandable that as burnt children we are unwilling to add fuel to the fire which at the present day, for the third time in a century, is awakening such general enthusiasm. Our experience has made a theology of history suspect for us from the very outset, whatever the reasons may be which are urged in its support. It determined the liberalism whose faith in progress was finally shattered by the First World War. However erroneously and improperly, it was capable of serving as a shield for Nazi eschatology. We do not want to be called back to the place where our fathers and grandfathers stood a hundred years ago and where they came to grief fifty years later. But can this still be prevented?

If we view the matter dispassionately, we must see that for world-wide Protestantism in general the Reformation only produced the initial spark; apart from that, its influence has faded increasingly. In the English-speaking world, the key-words of law and justification are associated almost inevitably with a legalistic construction. The existentialist interpretation of faith rouses uneasiness because it seems to end in individualism. Finally, the ecumenical movement furthers the tendency to stress what binds rather than what divides, and looks for the same disposition in the New Testament. In this situation, the watchword of an attitude to the scriptures based on salvation history must seem to offer liberation, not only in modern Catholicism but also, and no less, in world-wide Protestantism: it offers the chance to be both progressive and conservative, to bring to the fore what is common ground, while tolerating what still separates us, and in a fallen world to see the church as the guarantor of divine salvation and as the pledge of a divine creation. It is in this mental environment that the alternative between justification and salvation history has taken form today – an alternative which may be of fateful significance for the whole of Christianity. To come to the point at issue itself, we must now ask how far this alternative can really be justified and whether it may be regarded as a clue to where we have to look for the real centre of Christian theology. Even if this cannot be decided on the basis of Paul's writings alone, he does at least give an answer which may serve as an example.

2. THE KEY-WORDS 'SALVATION HISTORY' IN THE EPISTLE TO THE ROMANS

As far as I am concerned, the dispute over the question whether Paul develops a concept of salvation history or not[11] is not a problem of Pauline theology; it is a specimen of the entanglement of all exegesis in systematic prejudices which we can diminish but never entirely rid ourselves of. Where existence and situation determine, and must determine, every theological statement, perspectives based on salvation history are bound to be passionately rejected. Yet this is to do violence to the texts. It cannot be denied that even the Pauline texts do not merely have an anthropology in view, and it is highly questionable whether anthropology even represents their central concern. One is thinking in terms of salvation history when one divides world history into the epochs of Adam, Abraham, Moses and Christ and sees creation tending towards judgment via fall and redemption. Theology cannot begin and end with the individual where world mission appears as the Christian task pure and simple, and where this task is seen against an apocalyptic background and is described in apocalyptic terms – i.e., when it is derived from the trial-situation presented by the conflict between the creator and his creatures. It is true that the category of the individual is unusually important with Jesus and even more so in Paul and John; and for us it is indispensable, because without this category theology, ideologically speaking, loses its concrete application. But it is both historically and factually quite wrong to make the individual the starting point of Pauline theology[12] even when we are considering Paul's concept of salvation history, which is certainly related to man.[13]

It has always been a characteristic of Pauline interpretation in Germany to fall from one extreme into another and often enough to postulate alternatives which destroy the apostle's dialectical treat-

[11] Unsatisfactorily illustrated from Rom. 4 by U. Wilckens, 'Die Rechtfertigung Abrahams nach Römer 4', *Studien zur Theologie der alttestamentlichen Überlieferungen*, 1961, pp. 111–27; G. Klein, 'Römer 4 und die Idee der Heilsgeschichte', *EvTh* 1963, pp. 424–47; U. Wilckens, 'Zu Römer 3, 21–4, 25', *EvTh* 1964, pp. 586–610.
[12] Contrary to Bultmann's view in *History and Eschatology*, 1957, p. 42.
[13] Bultmann, *Theology* I, p. 269.

ment of the facts. It is no comfort that in the English-speaking countries, for example, something similar came about under different omens. There the church is not infrequently played off against the individual, sacrament against faith, liturgy against *kerygma*, ethics against eschatology, the gospels against Paul and, in the same way, salvation history against the doctrine of justification. It is equally unhelpful to contrast the riches of the Bible with the Reformed stress on the *particula exclusiva*, that is to say, the *solus Christus* and, consequently, to set up *sola gratia*, *sola fide* against *sola scriptura*. Modern man is undoubtedly forgetting more and more how to converse with anyone else, in that he makes the world the object of his schemes and his neighbour the recipient of his proclamations. But the New Testament is the document and sphere of a conversation in which people, all starting from their different respective presuppositions, talk with and to one another. This dialogue must never be levelled down to the point where the differences and contrasts disappear. Still less is it a monologue in which only one voice is heard, or a report where the impressions of the hearer are of decisive importance. Every simpilfication which forces the primal variety into the already-existing ruts is a sin against the Holy Spirit.

It cannot be seriously disputed that salvation history forms the horizon of Pauline theology. But the significance of this horizon is anything but decided.[14] It could be a component part of a traditional early Christian *Weltanschaung* which Paul took over without reflection, and might then even be an inappropriate framework for his specific proclamation. On the other hand, it could be the key-note of his message or one of its most important aspects.[15] We must therefore inquire what meaning salvation history has for Paul and what function it serves in his theology as a whole. Because this question is also of paramount importance for Stendahl, he sets salvation history thematically over against the doctrine of justification.[16] This does in fact open up the absolutely decisive problem of Pauline interpretation. For all other questions can be fitted into this basic one. It is all

[14] Cullmann, *Salvation in History*, p. 248, asks directly whether salvation history constitutes the 'kernel' of Pauline theology.

[15] M. Barth's view in *Rechtfertigung*, 1969, p. 8; already anticipated by J. Jeremias, 'Justification by Faith', *The Central Message of the New Testament*, 1965, pp. 51–70: pp. 6of.

[16] *Op. cit.*, pp. 209, 211; he even describes Rom. 5.6ff. not only as 'the subsidiary conditional clause in an argument *e majore ad minore*' but as referring mainly to the past.

the more surprising that Stendahl does not make even an approach to an analysis of Paul's statements about salvation history, although it is above all the Epistle to the Romans which would suggest the necessity of such an analysis. Thus Rom. 5.12ff. makes it clear that the apostle does not understand history as a continuous evolutionary process but as the contrast of the two realms of Adam and Christ. Pauline theology unfolds this contrast extensively as the struggle between death and life, sin and salvation, law and gospel. The basis is the apocalyptic scheme of the two successive aeons which is transferred to the present.[17] Apparently Paul viewed his own time as the hour of the Messiah's birth-pangs, in which the new creation emerges from the old world through the Christian proclamation. Spirits, powers and dominions part eschatologically at the crossroads of the gospel. We thus arrive at the dialectic of 'once' and 'now', which is absorbed into anthropology in the form of 'already saved' and 'still tempted'. In the antithesis of spirit and flesh this dialectic determines the cosmos until the parousia of Christ. Christians are drawn into this conflict all their lives. Every day they have through obedience to authenticate their baptismal origin anew. The churches, too, are exposed in the same way to the attacks of nomism and enthusiasm, which threaten the lordship of Christ. The church lives under the sign of the cross, that is to say, given over to death inwardly and outwardly, waiting longingly with the whole of creation for the liberty of the children of God and manifesting the imitation of Jesus through the bearing of his cross.

This means that Paul's view of salvation history does not differ from Augustine's. Salvation history is the battle field of the *civitas dei* and the *civitas terrena*. No conception which disregards this reality and does not, from this starting point, assume a constitutively dialectical form can invoke the authority of the apostle. In Cullmann's words,[18] he thought that Victory Day was just ahead and proclaimed the gospel's triumphant progress throughout the world-wide church. At the same time he urged the Corinthians, and with them the whole of Christendom, not to celebrate this victory with the banquet of the blessed, as if they were members of a mystery religion, but to enter with Christ into the shadow of the cross. For Paul, as for the writer of Revelation, the only people who overcome are the dying, the temp-

---

[17] On this point see P. Stuhlmacher, 'Erwägungen zum ontologischen Charakter der καινὴ κτίσις bei Paulus', *EvTh*, 1967, pp. 1–35.

[18] *Christ and Time*, rev. ed., 1962, p. 141.

ted, the mocked, the weak – in short, believers. The person who does not share in the carrying of the cross, leaving the things that lie behind, has no part in the church; nor has the man who does not stand in the no-man's land before the gates of this world's permanent camp, repeating Israel's Exodus. He is in truth not a Christian at all, but a member of the old world, whose characteristic is enmity to the cross. No one can take on the likeness of Christ in the birth-pangs of the Messiah without having become a disciple of the one who was crucified. Although the enthusiasts raise their cry of victory, according to Rom. 8.36 believers are regarded as sheep to be slaughtered. Measured by human criteria, salvation is fundamentally rooted in disaster. That means that the Pauline proclamation of the reality of salvation history is deeply paradoxical.[19]

This paradox is retained when, in Rom. 4.12ff.; 9.6ff., the apostle discusses the problem of the continuity of salvation history as exemplified by Abraham. Paul really does talk about continuity in time and space and does not yet understand the sonship of Abraham in the metaphorical sense which was adopted later. Apparently he finds it important to preserve the fulfilment of the promise to Israel in its character as historical power as well. Thus in Paul the historical and eschatological dimensions do not yawn apart in the sense that they are essentially and *ab initio* different. The eschatological breaks in upon earth in a very real sense, taking root not only in the sacraments, the church and the Christian life, but even in history. Hence its manifestations can be pin-pointed in, for example, baptism, conversion or the birth of the church. The eschatological is neither suprahistory nor the inner aspect of a historicity; it is power which changes the old world into a new one and which becomes incarnate in the earthly sphere. For it is corporeality which is the sphere of revelation – inevitably so, since this is the nature of the world and everyday life. Only a complete misunderstanding can make a spiritualist out of Paul, though strangely enough such attempts have repeatedly been made. For him, salvation history has a spatial and temporal dimension, frontiers dividing off the cosmic spheres of power and a cohesion which leads from creation to Christ and the parousia by way of the choosing of Israel and the promise.

But when all this is conceded, so that the idea of incarnation receives its due, dialectic and paradox must not be overlooked. Rom. 4.17ff. depicts Abraham's faith as a relation to that God who reveals

[19] G. Bornkamm, *Paulus*, 1969, p. 157.

himself in history, gives offspring and hence sets faith in the continuity of promise and fulfilment, present and future. We misunderstand the tenor of the whole passage if we lose sight of the fact that faith goes beyond individual existence and situation. It has its concrete place and its particular time, and cannot be detached from the fact that in faith a particular man calls God Lord and Father. At the same time, however, it has a horizon which reaches from creation to parousia, which spans, that is to say, the whole of history. Yet faith must remain separate from a religious philosophy of life or a Christian speculation about history. For its horizons do not give faith its content. They can, on the contrary, be falsely placed and in fact generally are. Abraham does not know the country to which his exodus is to take him. He hears the promise of heirs without understanding how that promise can be fulfilled. What he sees speaks against it. From a human and earthly point of view, Sarah's laughter is completely justified and the expression of a realism which the church ignores at its peril. Sarah's laughter is faith's constant companion. It is not merely heard at the beginning of salvation history; it remains audible even when we look back at its different pages and chapters. For each of these pages and chapters contains, like the bible, the tragi-comedy of broken hopes and realized stupidities, disagreeable developments and vain service, broken existences and triumphant worldliness. Ishmael and Esau belong to it, just as much as Isaac and Jacob. For there is no Christ without Antichrist; there are no apostles without Judas, no prophets without the enthusiasts, no fields ripening to harvest without weeds; and the letters of the Apocalypse have to tell the churches at all times what their Lord has against them.

It is only from a great distance that we can read salvation history without being aware of its catastrophes. But faith must not fall a victim to docetism, must not separate itself from what is human, must not miss the cry of the dying, the despairing, the people at the end of their tether, the erring, the waiting, the complaints of the Psalms and Job's rebellion. Seen at close quarters and from the standpoint of the actors, salvation history generally looks different from what the books which are written about it would like to think. It is the story of Adam and the prodigal son, of the crucified Christ, the sheep without a shepherd, the warring confessions; a story in which faith and superstition cross and recross each other without pause. The man who places himself in its ranks does so hoping against hope, believing that God is constantly calling into being the things that are not, that he

raises the dead, lifts up the fallen, forgives sinners and makes the ungodly the instruments of his grace. The dimension of faith is framed
by creation and parousia. Our everyday life, however, is seldom
aware of this; it merely hears the context in which it stands preached
to it. For Paul, salvation history is therefore exodus under the sign
of the Word and in the face of Sarah's justifiable laughter. Its continuity is paradoxical because it can only endure when God's Word,
contrary to the earthly realities, creates for itself children and communities of the pure in spirit.[20]

3. OBSERVATIONS ON PAUL'S DOCTRINE OF JUSTIFICATION

It has rightly been repeatedly noticed that the apostle's message of
justification is a fighting doctrine, directed against Judaism. But to go
on to say that, since this is so, it holds a subordinate place in Paul's
theology, is an assertion which divides modern Protestantism inevitably and finally from the Reformers' interpretation of Paul and
hence from the Reformation itself. A breach of this kind may perhaps
be unavoidable. But at the same time we ought to realize clearly
what is afoot. It is not without irony that it is left to radical historical
criticism, as represented by the Bultmann school, to defend the
Reformed heritage. It does so in the face of a theology of history
which has lost its past revolutionary fire and is now planting con-
servatively laid-out gardens on the petrified lava. The curious ex-
change of fronts which is familiar to us from the dispute over the historical Jesus is no less prominent here. The iconoclasts of a former day
are becoming orthodox again,[21] and the custodians of ecclesiastical
tradition are turning liberal. The theology of the Word and the theology of history are still in conflict. But the two have exchanged teams.
We ought to consider on what side we want to be found in the future.
Otherwise we could one day make the discovery that in trying to make
the earth turn we were simply being whirled round on a roundabout
ourselves. It was looking back that turned Lot's wife into a pillar of salt.

Two questions must be asked and answered if the unique character
of the Pauline doctrine of justification is to be clearly recognized.

[20] Cullmann, *Salvation in History*, sees the problem clearly, as his chapter on constant and contingency shows, pp. 122ff., as well as his rejection of the scheme of promise and fulfilment, p. 159. But his notion of development does not permit him to
bring out the paradox I have stressed above with equal sharpness.
[21] For an example see E. Jüngel, M. Geiger, *Zwei Reden zum 450. Gedenktag der
Reformation*, ThSt 93, 1968.

First, is it, as a fighting doctrine, so conditioned by its time that we must call it obsolete today? Secondly, does it, as Protestants generally suppose, primarily take its bearings from the individual, so that it has to be supplemented or even replaced by a standpoint based on salvation history? Stendahl answers 'yes' to both questions, and I would agree with him that it is impossible to overstress the polemical character of Paul's doctrine of justification. It does not retain its true character if its antitheses are softened or abolished – a process which is already at work in the Pastoral Epistles. It is paralysed if its attacking spear-head is blunted, and for that reason it is only seldom that it has been able to determine theology and the church. For Jews and Greeks alike, Paul was a lone wolf and an alien; and in contemporary Protestantism he is increasingly overshadowed by Peter, because his polemics are at most understood in their historical bearing. This tendency is increased because at the moment both tolerance and neo-positivism consider polemic to be the expression of subjective feelings, and hold up to it the duty of objectivity.

Transferred to the theological sphere, this of course means that the portrait of the benevolent God has more or less pushed out the picture of the judge, and the function of the Holy Spirit is now only viewed as edification, although the New Testament ceaselessly shows him as a polemicist. But can the imitation of Jesus ever cease to be a scandal, even when it is silent? Are not all the revolutionary slogans harmless compared with the message about the raising of the dead? Does the preaching of the forgiveness of sins no longer shock modern man when it touches him personally? Will the crucified Christ which Grünewald painted ever lose its frightfulness? Strangely enough, Christianity has contrived to draw so many pious veils over all this that it has quite ceased to give offence. For Christianity has long told a story of salvation which justifies the institution of the church as the community of 'good' people. The muted colours of our church windows transform the story of the Nazarene into a saint's legend in which the cross is merely an episode, being the transition to the ascension – as if we were dealing with a variation of the Hercules myth. If we want to understand the polemics of the Pauline doctrine of justification, we must remember this development. The doctrine undoubtedly grew up in the course of the anti-Jewish struggle and stands or falls with this antithesis. But the exegete must not make things easy for himself by simply, as historian, noting this incontrovertible fact. If he does, he could equally well call Jesus a pious Jew who had a memorable fate and left behind him a series of impressive sayings. Our task is to ask: what does the Jewish nomism against which Paul fought really represent? And our answer must be: it represents the community of 'good' people which turns God's promises into their own privileges and God's commandments into the instruments of self-sanctification.[22]

The New Testament scholar must not fall a victim to the view of Gentile Christians from the end of the first century onwards; their interest in the Jewish law was purely ethical[23] – apart from that, they allegorized it. The reaction to a law viewed in this light inevitably expresses itself in psychological terms, i.e., in the consciousness of guilt and sin. Since a consciousness of this kind does not in fact play the same part in Paul that it does in the later western world, it would seem necessary to deny the Pauline teaching about the law anthropological depth and to push it into the historical distance. The doctrine of justification is of course affected simultaneously, because the doctrine of the law is its radical spear-head. Such self-contained and logical argumentation merely fails to realize that the apostle did not for a single moment detach the ritual from the ethical law – nor, as Jew, could he possibly do so. The *nomos* is for him, precisely because he was unable to confine it to the moral sphere, power which was part of salvation history and had even cosmic force – a power like sin and death.[24] This power leads man astray into the paths of demonstrable piety. It creates the sphere within which man tries to sunder himself from immorality and godlessness, views the history of his fathers' redemption as the guarantee of his own election and claims God's grace as his personal privilege. But Paul calls this attitude to God sin, because these pious claims and works are an attempt to bring God into dependence on us. It is the gospel which, for the first time, lays bare this sin and the true part played by the law which produces it. For the gospel does not begin with subjective feelings of guilt but with the objective fallenness of man, who is his own victim, the victim of the forces of his own world, a state which displays itself in its most sinister form in his reliance on his own goodness.

Now we must consider whether the struggle is really superseded

[22] This problem is nicely brought out when T. W. Manson, in *On Paul and John*, 1963, p. 58ff., states that the justification of the ungodly does not apply to 'every sinful Tom, Dick and Harry', because it is the work of Christ to alter man's moral attitude also.

[23] Cf. U. Luz, *Das Geschichtsverständnis des Paulus*, 1968, p. 142.

[24] Bultmann, *Theology* I, pp. 259f.

at this point and whether it is a merely anti-Jewish affair. If it were, then Christianity must already have become the company of the poor in spirit which, with the whole of creation, waits for the day of redemption. But then it would no longer be permissible for it to erect the fences of a sacred enclosure round itself. For, unlike the Pharisees, the Zealots and the Qumran community, its Lord did not want to make the pious man more pious still. He set out to go to the tax-collectors and sinners, that is to say, into the world of the ungodly. The pious were, generally speaking, against him and finally crucified him, if what the evangelists tell us is true. Is the story of this Jesus not our story and our reality? On which side does Christianity really stand when it is confronted with Jesus? The fact that we confess him by no means proves that we are his disciples.

We can now draw some preliminary conclusions from what has been said: Paul's doctrine of justification, with the doctrine of the law that belongs to it, is ultimately his interpretation of Christology.[25] It proclaims the 'true God and true man' in its way by expressing the fact that the true God joins himself to the ungodly and brings them salvation, as he did through Jesus – the ungodly, but not the Pharisees, the Zealots or the men of Qumran. It proclaims true man by depicting the one who is intolerable to the good people of his time, the one who breaks through their taboos and can only die for them. The Pauline doctrine of justification is entirely and solely Christology, a Christology, indeed, won from Jesus' cross and hence an offensive Christology. Its point is the *ecce homo* presented so that we, confronted with the Nazarene, learn how little our illusions about ourselves and the world can stand up to his reality. But it is this which is the breakthrough to the new creation.

The Gentile Christianity of which Paul was one of the founders saw the apostle's struggle with the Jewish law as obsolete; but it soon became itself the sphere of the *nova lex* and then no longer knew what to do with the Pauline doctrine of justification. Its Christ became the God of the mystery plays, the conqueror through suffering, who makes his believers like himself. He becomes man so that we can become as gods. Protestantism would do well to remember this development. It might then learn that the Pauline doctrine of justification is a protection not only against nomism but also against enthusiasm and mysticism. It calls the church, no less than the synagogue, in the name of Jesus, out of its pious dreams back to earth and to the humanity of

[25] G. Bornkamm, *Paulus*, pp. 128f.

the creature. The justification of the sinner is the only path on which God's creature remains before and under God and at the same time part of mankind, so that while he is in this world of ours he is also beneath the open heavens.

But what, then, of salvation history, if the justification of the sinner is the centre, not only of the Pauline message but of the whole Christian proclamation? With that we come to the second question which we raised at the beginning of this part of our essay. If the doctrine of justification holds fast to the Christology which does not turn its gaze away from the one who was crucified, it neither can nor may continue to be interpreted in exclusively individual terms. Protestant theology always circles round the question: how can I find a gracious God? This question retains its abiding rightness. We ought not to throw out the baby with the bath water by pushing this question out of the centre of our concern, for the sake of proclaiming Victory Day. The Jews also expected the final victory down to the very last moment when they defended the temple against the Romans; and they buried their eschatological hopes in its ruins. When we cease to ask, 'How can I find a gracious God?', we find ourselves in that curiously diffused world history which Kierkegaard unmasked with such acid irony. The message of God's victory is only credible, and can only be taken seriously, as long as there are people who take the *absolvo te* seriously and risk living by it. The church can take the burden of faith from no one; each must hazard for himself. Nor does the church save; and to believe out of *fides implicita* is not open to Protestants, although a Protestantism which has lost its proper instincts is everywhere being taken in by this slogan today.

Yet Stendahl and his friends are right in protesting against the individualist curtailment of the Christian message. Here the twentieth century must dissociate itself from the nineteenth. The Pauline doctrine of justification never took its bearings from the individual, although hardly anyone now realizes this. It does not merely talk about the gift of God to the individual. If that were so, the cosmic horizons of Rom. 1.18 – 3.20; 5.12ff.; 8.18ff. and especially chs. 9–11, would be incomprehensible. We should then also have to shut our eyes to the fact that Paul can depict God's righteousness as a power which reaches out towards our lives in order to make them obedient. Salvation never consists in our being given something, however wonderful. Salvation, always, is simply God himself in his presence for us. To be justified means that the creator remains faithful to the creature, as the father remained faithful to the prodigal son, in spite of guilt, error and ungodliness; it means that he changes the fallen and apostate into new creatures, that in the midst of the world of sin and death he once more raises up and fulfils the promises we have misused. All his separate gifts are pointers towards these self-manifestations of his in a world which has turned away from him. But where he appears, he also meets us as our lord and judge; we experience his gifts, but also the power which lays claim to us, the sovereign rights of the creator to his whole creation.

This means that in justification it is simply the kingdom of God proclaimed by Jesus which is at stake. His right to us is our salvation, if he does not let it drop. It will be our misfortune if we resist him. Paul's doctrine of justification is about God's *basileia*. The apostle generally expresses it in anthropological terms because he is concerned that it should determine our everyday lives. God's *basileia* seizes territory wherever we are and will be entirely human. Otherwise it would be illusion. The Christology inherent in the doctrine of justification corresponds to the existence led in the everyday life of the world. Justification is the stigmatization of our worldly existence through the crucified Christ. Through us and in us he simultaneously reaches out towards the world to which we belong. Paul's doctrine of justification means that under the sign of Christ, God becomes Cosmocrator, not merely the Lord of the believing individual or the god of a cult; it is not by chance that the doctrine has its roots in apocalyptic.

That is why Rom. 9–11 can describe God as also reaching out towards unbelieving Israel. He does so in accord with the eschatological law of the revaluation of earthly values, a law revealed in Christ, according to which the first is last and the last first. Israel, too, falls under the justification of the ungodly, not, as the Jews (including Qumran) suppose, the justification of the godly. The doctrine of justification dominates Rom. 9–11 no less than the rest of the epistle.[26] It is the key to salvation history, just as, conversely, salvation history forms the historical depth and cosmic breadth of the event of justification. Since creation, God has acted no differently with Jews and Gentiles. His being is the justification of the ungodly and hence the raising of the dead and creation out of nothing. For he acts under the token of the crucified Christ, whom Israel, too, cannot escape. Because this is so, salvation history is not the consummation of, let

[26] G. Bornkamm, *Paulus*, p. 160.

alone the substitute for, justification, but its historical depth, i.e., one of its aspects. Neither the scriptures nor the world can be adequately grasped except through belief in the justification of the ungodly. It is impossible to play off justification and salvation history against one another. To do so would be to fall a victim to individualism or ideology; and in either case God would cease to remain for us the creator of the world. Justification and salvation history belong together. But everything depends on the right co-ordination of the two. Just as the church must not take precedence over Christ, but must be Christ-determined without itself determining Christ, so salvation history must not take precedence over justification. It is its sphere. But justification remains the centre, the beginning and the end of salvation history. Otherwise the cross of Jesus would also inevitably lose its central position and then everything would be distorted – anthropology and ecclesiology as well as Christology and soteriology. For our God would then be once more the God of the 'good' and would cease to be, as the Father of Jesus Christ, the God of the ungodly.[27]

[27] I have purposely left my account in its original form, as a lecture for a general audience. We must not merely talk esoterically, especially at the very centre of theology. Moreover, because I adhered strictly to the antithesis of the theme, I was unable to enter in detail into the present German debate about the Pauline doctrine of justification, especially among Bultmann's adherents. The tendency of the essay and its conclusions ought to be enough to show that I still participate in our common heritage. On the other hand, the debate shows that I apparently stand between two fronts in refusing either to subordinate the apostle's doctrine of justification to a pattern of salvation history or to allow it to turn into a mere vehicle for the self-understanding of the believer. I would recognize both as necessary. What I would dispute are the respective emphases which are associated with these aspects. Perhaps it is best to consider the complicated historical and philological problems involved (in which I continue, broadly speaking, to agree with P. Stuhlmacher's book, *Die Gerechtigkeit Gottes bei Paulus*, [2]1966) from the aspect of the basic decisions which have to be made.

These questions are forced inexorably upon us through Hans Conzelmann's essay, 'Die Rechtfertigungslehre des Paulus. Theologie oder Anthropologie?', *EvTh* 28, 1968, pp. 389–404. Even if the alternatives formulated here were already suggested earlier, as Conzelmann says on p. 390, they are still accepted on p. 393 and are identified in sharpened form with the antithesis between mysticism and justification. The apparent presupposition – and it is characteristic of our present situation – is that metaphysics and mysticism can only be avoided through an anthropological approach. My objection to this alternative is that it by-passes the problem and the relevance of Christology. My partners in debate force me to move into the centre with increasing deliberation and decision what was once, if only hesitatingly, touched on in relation to the earthly Jesus. Paul's doctrine of justification is more than a logical conclusion; it is the specific Pauline interpretation of Christology in its relation to man and the world: that is the theme of this essay – in a nutshell, but maintained in all seriousness. His teaching about justification gives a clear definition of what the apostle understands by the lordship of

Christ. I understand all the arguments of his theology from this starting point, and therefore feel bound to judge present-day Pauline interpretation by the degree to which it is able to bring this out. Difficult though it may otherwise be to distinguish those allied in the spirit from those related in the flesh, under this aspect everything becomes clear. Here everyone shows whose child he is.

Friends and opponents must be tested against the question whether they only feel able to talk about the lordship of Christ as a mythological, mystical or metaphysical figure of speech. Precisely that is the kernel of the dispute about whether God's righteousness means in Paul solely and exclusively the gift conferred on us, or whether it also means the power of salvation which reaches out towards us – a meaning which is demonstrable even philologically. I have set up no alternative here, nor can I find any. I have never maintained that the righteousness of God means exclusively or primarily a subjective genitive (unlike Conzelmann, *op. cit.*, p. 398; N. Gäumann, *Taufe und Ethik*, 1967, p. 156). On the contrary, I have called, the *genitivus auctoris*, i.e., the soteriological sense of the phrase, the dominating one. I have never denied that the righteousness of God establishes a relation (contrary to G. Klein, 'Gottes Gerechtigkeit als Thema der neuesten Paulus-Forschung', *VF* 2, 1967, pp. 5f.). It is for that very reason that I so vigorously deny an attributive interpretation (contrary to Gäumann, *op. cit.*, pp. 146, 153). One cannot simply build up a false position in this way, and sound and fury is not enough to solve a genuine problem.

The only real point is whether it is philologically and theologically justifiable to confine the Pauline statements to the gift of salvation and with Conzelmann (*Outline of the Theology of the New Testament*, 1968, p. 220) to call the divine righteousness the presupposition but not the goal of our movement. It is this and this alone which I reject. According to my understanding of the apostle, every gift has the character of power. It seems unjust, particularly since I combine the two aspects, to reproach me with stressing the 'power-aspect in isolation' (Conzelmann, 'Rechtfertigungslehre', p. 399), or even to talk about a label 'which can be adopted here or there at will' (*Outline*, p. 219). In his exposition of Paul, Bultmann used the idea of power frankly and unswervingly, and I understand divine righteousness, where it does not merely mean the gift, as being at least the power to achieve salvation. Schlatter finds that the genitive in the phrase 'the righteousness of God' sometimes has the same meaning as, and always a similar bearing to, the genitive in the gospel, the power or the wrath of God. I do not consider this to be a 'philological error' (Conzelmann, *Outline*, p. 215), but rather a philological achievement, and one which can also be justified exegetically. Philological acrimony should not allow us to forget that God here is always seen and proclaimed as active revealer, not merely as the origin or owner of certain properties. Why does no one mention that the phrases about the spirit, the grace, the love and the peace of God also belong to this series and that in them the dialectic of gift and power is indisputable, a dialectic which recurs in the apostle's doctrine of the sacraments and ultimately permits God to remain both his gift to us and our Lord and judge? That I turn God's Word into 'a formal proclamation of power', 'faith into formal submission', 'abandoned by the Word at the decisive moment' and that God becomes *numinōsum* (Conzelmann, 'Rechtfertigungslehre', p. 400), or that I have perverted obedience into the attitude of *humilitas* in a *devotio moderna* (Gäumann, *op. cit.*, p. 151), no longer reflects my interpretation but nightmares for which I have neither an explanation nor an answer.

But misunderstandings of this kind do arise when one starts from the alternative between theology and anthropology, reduces faith to self-understanding and ends up in a liberal-Protestant variant of Christ as the cultic deity who brings the true gnosis to his people. Here faith is still threatened by unbelief, but it is no longer seriously endangered by superstition, and New Testament theology shrinks to a doctrine of faith. There the decisive category is inevitably 'individualization' (Conzelmann, 'Rechtfertigungslehre', pp. 401ff.; G. Klein, *op. cit.*, p. 11). I, too, have maintained that God's righteousness and grace are verified in the individual. If this destroys 'the objectivity of salvation history' (Conzelmann, 'Rechtfertigungslehre', p. 402), that may have its uses polemically speaking, if we are once again forced into the alternative of contrasting universal history and the individual. That God's grace and righteousness relate to the world and intend a new creation, not merely a number of believing individuals, seems to me an irrelinquishable truth if the Christian proclamation is to be the foundation of anything more than merely private piety. I must therefore once more replace the alternatives by a dialectic. The justification of the ungodly certainly in the first place affects, in concrete terms, myself. But the phrase is robbed of its full significance if it does not mean salvation for everyman and for the whole world. For even the ungodly only exist, in a remarkably transsubjective way, in the entanglement of all earthly things in sin and death. Adam takes on concrete form in the individual life. But every individual life, with all its possible differentiations, is, conversely, the representation of Adam and of the individual's world. In the struggle with superstition, faith experiences that righteousness of God which was part of the design before faith arrived at its self-understanding and which does not stop there, because it forces faith to go out in service to the world. Salvation reaches out beyond our experience, which is always incomplete and often enough deceptive. Salvation lies in the fact that Christ becomes our lord; and Christ becomes a god of the mysteries when this lordship is restricted to the individual sphere. I did not talk about the gift in isolation for the sake of using abstract terminology or making a perverse distinction (contrary to G. Klein, *op. cit.*, p. 11). I was deeply aware that in the whole of theological history down to the present day the gift has always been isolated from its giver; and that in the gift the Lord who gives himself to us and who reaches out towards us in that gift is pushed into the background. If that is the effect of the Pauline doctrine of justification – and it was already so with the Corinthians and remains so wherever ecclesiology or anthropology move into the centre of theology and obscure the primacy of Christology – then this doctrine is, according to my understanding of it, being deeply misunderstood, both theologically and in its philological and historical sense. For the doctrine is concerned with the one who sets up his kingdom on earth, thereby becoming salvation for all who receive him in faith.[28] It is the theological summing-up of a Christological interpretation: Christ rules over his enemies throughout the world and, as the one who was crucified, gives his grace to the ungodly.

[28] This is why I do not understand G. Bornkamm's criticism, (*Paulus*, p. 156) that the co-ordinate relation of God's righteousness and faith recedes curiously into the background in my writings. The following essay will, I hope, refute this judgment.

IV

THE FAITH OF ABRAHAM IN ROMANS 4

Romans 4 holds a key place in the epistle. Here the scriptural evidence is marshalled for the theme of the righteousness of faith which has been expounded in 3.21–31.[1] This only has a point if the faith of Abraham in some respects anticipates Christian faith and was, ultimately speaking, even identical with it.[2] This has now to be proved. The question then inevitably arises how far Paul could establish the existence of Christian faith in the pre-Christian era, and how he was able to get over the apparent contradictions involved.[3] Everything which is irrelevant to this point will be left on one side, since it is not our intention to offer a detailed exegesis of the chapter.

Philo also already depicted Abraham as the prototype of faith, thus taking over the Jewish tradition which calls the patriarch 'our father'. Paul's argument, therefore, belongs within a firm traditional context. At the same time, it moves out of that context when it makes Abraham the prototype of Christian faith. By so doing, Paul does not merely demonstrate a different understanding of faith. The polemic which runs through the whole chapter shows that we are dealing here not with an extension or modification of the Jewish view but with its contrast. But this means that in fact the ground is cut away from under

[1] For another view see, for example, A. Schlatter, *Gottes Gerechtigkeit*, 1935, pp. 158f.; T. Hoppe, *Die Idee der Heilsgeschichte*, 1926, p.65. But this involves the structural division which links ch. 4 with chs. 5–8.

[2] For another view see V. Taylor, *Forgiveness and Reconciliation*, 1948, pp.47f. Taylor does not think that the centre of Paul's teaching is touched on here, and he distinguishes the content of Abraham's faith from the justifying faith of the Christian because it is related to the promise, not to redemption.

[3] For the same question cf. P. Vielhauer, 'Paulus und das Alte Testament' (*Studien zur Geschichte und Theologie der Reformation, Festschrift für E. Bizer*, 1969, pp. 33–62), pp.43f.

the feet of the Jewish tradition and the Jewish interpretation of the scriptures, and that the patriarch himself is removed from its context. With unbelievable boldness, the apostle always attacked his opponents at the point where they themselves felt most unassailable. Nowhere does this come out more strongly than when he unfolds and defends his doctrine of justification. The point at issue here is the centre of his theology. That is why he shrinks from none of its consequences, however radical. In harsh antitheses he confirms the sovereign freedom of the Christian out of which, in I Cor. 3.21, he cries to his people, 'all things are yours'. The same applies to the patriarch, the tradition based on him and the interpretation of the Old Testament from which Judaism derived its exclusive claim. We must remember that with this a controversy flared up about the true interpretation of scripture, and that for the first time the problem of a Christian hermeneutic became a theological theme.

But it must also be remembered that although Paul occasionally mentions other models of Christian faith out of the Old Testament as well, he sets Abraham apart from them all as prototype. It is only Abraham who is talked about in this way throughout the whole of our chapter. For Paul's remarks about David in v.6 also have provocative force: together with the patriarch, Israel is also deprived of the crown witness of the Messianic king – the second dominating figure of Jewish history as regards its expectations of the future. With the saying from the Psalms ascribed to David, Paul underpins the Christian interpretation of Gen. 15.6 according to the rabbinic rule which demanded two witnesses for every dispute. With this David's function is exhausted, for it is not equal to Abraham's. Finally, it must be noted that no comparison is made between the patriarch and Christ. Liturgical fragments, which Paul puts to paraenetic use, show that the apostle was familiar[4] with the view of Christ as prototype, a view which finds expression in Heb. 12.2, where Christ is described as the 'pioneer and perfecter of our faith'. But the notion that this view had a decisive Christological relevance for Paul must be disputed. Whereas through Jesus the lost divine image is manifest once more and is conferred on Christians as their share in the Son, so Christ appears as the second Adam, who ushers in the eschatological creation and thereby remains, as the 'first born', incomparable with his brethren. He is not, like Abraham, the prototype of faith; he is the

[4] E. Larsson's book, *Christus als Vorbild*, 1962, calls for a thorough critical examination.

Lord of his church and the predestined cosmocrator. It is only through this differentiation that the patriarch acquires his proper place in salvation history. He belongs to the old covenant, but unlike Moses he does not mark the antithesis to the proclamation of the gospel, but rather the point at which the old covenant points beyond itself to the new; that is to say, he represents the promise.

After these preliminary remarks let us consider what each of the sections 1–8, 9–12, 13–22, 23–25 have to say about Abraham's faith. If my opening thesis is correct, the nature of the Christian faith according to Paul's understanding of it must here also be summed up in its essentials. According to Rom. 3.21–31 this centre is belief in justification. But Paul was not content to derive this assertion from the scriptures as a necessary conclusion, important though the appeal to divine documentation was for him. The unusually careful and detailed argument has evidently a particular trend which leads from belief in justification to belief in the resurrection, its point lying in the fact that the two are identical. The thesis of 3.21ff. takes on a sharper emphasis and a clearer significance from the context of scriptural proof. Our analysis must show whether this last assumption holds water – whether, that is, we are confronted with a self-contained argument without significant deviations. First, admittedly, Paul's dominating concern is to give 3.21ff. scriptural support as a firm legal basis, which would also be binding on his Jewish opponents, and to screen it against possible objections.

As in Gal. 3.6, Paul draws on Gen. 15.6 for support. From I Macc. 2.52 onwards, rabbinic reflections on this passage[5] (which are still reflected in James 2.23) allowed faith as trust in the divine promise (and especially the monotheistic confession as the sum of faith) to be itself a work; and the divine acceptance was hence considered as a juridical ratification of an existing piety. Philo was thus able to talk about the specific work of righteousness.[6] The apostle does not avoid the arena prescribed by his opponents, but he enters it under the presuppositions of his own theology. For Paul, faith does not mean, as it does for Philo, that a devout disposition of the soul builds character in the storms of life and proves itself in faithfulness. Like Palestinian Judaism, the aspect of faith he stressed was action; that is why he talked about the obedience of faith. This was admittedly somewhat dangerous because of the possible misunderstanding that what is

---

[5] Cf. Billerbeck on the passage; Heidland, *TWNT* IV, p. 292.
[6] *Quis rer.div.her.*, 95.

aimed at here is a life lived in increasing holiness. This would be to give increased countenance to the notion of 'works', which Paul wants fundamentally to exclude. The lack of clarity was increased by the long and bitter dispute about whether the apostle preached a forensic-imputative or an effective righteousness. The alternative is a false one, because it is directed against two opposing modern misinterpretations. Of course, the apostle did not interpret the divine promise in the sense that it sets us under an 'as if' as recipients of a righteousness which has no earthly equivalent. Nor, on the other hand, did he permit righteousness to be considered as a gift which could be detached from the giver and transferred to our possession. God's Word is for him, as it is for the Old Testament and for Judaism, creative power; but for that very reason it is incalculable; it is not at our disposal or demonstrable to human controls. We remain constantly dependent on it afresh, and we possess it only so long as it possesses us. It sets us in the kingdom of Christ and deprives us of our autonomy. Thus the obedience of faith means essentially the existence and the abiding under the promise which we have heard, and which must prove itself in the Christian life. The missionary situation, in which faith was in the first place acceptance of the Christian message, has kept alive this understanding.[7] Old Testament passages such as Gen. 15.6, which stress the aspect of trust in the divine promise, see to it that the 'forensic' relation of the declaration of righteousness as being a free pardon (a relation which also dominates the verb 'to justify') cannot be forgotten.

Faith therefore does not take on independent existence as a religious attitude or Christian virtue. It is not *fides historica* or *fides implicita*, i.e., the acceptance as true of certain facts of sacred history or an assent to an acknowledged ecclesiastical dogmatic. In so far as he accepts both, the believer does so in order to characterize his Lord, not in order to establish a certain *Weltanschauung* or theological system. Otherwise he would simply be ceasing to remain in the obedience of constant listening, which also makes him critical towards any existing historical or dogmatic tradition which takes on an independent existence. The Lord who speaks to him cannot be replaced by institutions, theologies and convictions, even when these interpret themselves as being the documentations of that Lord. Of course we must now be equally vigilant towards the opposite danger: faith must be rescued from the dimension of recurrent religious experience.

[7] Bultmann, *TWNT* VI, p. 209.

Demons also produce overpowering events; so ecstasies, visions, miracles and experiences determined by these things can by no means count as a specifically Christian characteristic.[8] According to Paul's view, faith is not yet in a position to see directly; it is bound to preaching's power of revelation, which we cannot perceive once and for all. The Lord remains the one who acts towards us in his Word, and he remains this only when the message about him reveals the unmistakable features of the Nazarene and moulds us accordingly.

To talk about the 'object' and 'content' of faith is completely inadequate and highly confusing, because the Lord who acts is here forced into a neutral category and thus into the dimension of what is at our disposal and can be replaced by something else. This is not avoided even when, as in recent times, faith is made 'primarily God's decision'.[9] It is true that Gal. 3.23ff. talks about the manifestation of faith in personified form, which would seem to lend support to this way of looking at things. But this is a description of the earthly effect – almost the objectification – of the gospel which replaces the power and human representation of the law; and that fits into the wider context of those passages in which a pale version of faith in faded form is identified with Christianity or, as *fides quae creditur*, means the crystallization of the gospel in the creed. These definitions are designed to bring out the fact that faith must not be turned into a hypostasis which can be separated from the believing person.

In view of certain tendencies which are again common today, we must put this point more precisely: as the acceptance of the divine address, faith in Paul remains primarily a decision of the individual person, and its importance must not therefore be shifted away from anthropology to ecclesiology.[10] It is true that a man never believes in isolation; but he is none the less irreplaceable in himself, and the Christian community is the company of those who have personally turned away from superstition and cannot be dispensed from this by anything or anybody. In so far as the renunciation of the superstition which is a constant threat and temptation even to Christians is a

[8] That is why it is so open to misunderstanding and so problematical when O. Cullmann, *Salvation in History*, 1967, p. 323, says that salvation history overwhelms us and that we are included in it in such a way that faith involves both the facts communicated and the interpretative revelation about these facts.

[9] F. Neugebauer, *In Christus*, 1961, p. 165ff.

[10] *Ibid.*, pp. 167ff.; E. Jüngel, 'Theologische Wissenschaft und Glaube im Blick auf die Armut Jesu', *EvTh* 24, 1964, p. 430; P. Stuhlmacher, *Gerechtigkeit Gottes bei Paulus*, [2]1966, p. 81.

characteristic of faith, it can be described as a movement between 'no longer' and 'not yet'.[11] On the other hand, this pattern characterizes the whole of life and hence is not sufficient for a precise definition. The real point is the constantly new hearing of, and holding fast to, the divine Word, which drives us to constant exodus and always strains forward to what lies ahead, that is to say to God's future. The essential thing is still that we do not set ourselves in motion, but that we are called out of ourselves through God's Word and miracle. We cannot therefore interpret our faith as our own work, but only as grace, which is conferred on us, in the face of the world, without our deserts and in the midst of unavoidable temptation. Faith is brought about by the creator by means of his mighty Word.

These are the theological premises which lie behind Paul's reading and interpretation of Gen. 15.6. Abraham submitted without reservation to the divine promise and was therefore 'righteous'. Righteousness before God and righteousness received from God cannot be acheived in any other way. The apostle draws a conclusion from this which shocked both friend and foe during his own lifetime and has remained a stumbling block to the devout ever since. He proclaims the justification of the ungodly and thereby gives his theology its sharpest spear-head. Admittedly this is only explicitly stated in this one passage. But that does not mean that we are at liberty to brush aside the statement as a rhetorical exaggeration. Statistics cause just as much confusion and have just as many unfortunate results in theology as they do elsewhere. It is important to see that it is only the formulation used here which makes the whole of the rest of the chapter's argument possible, and that it yields up the indispensable key to Paul's doctrine of justification. We are not taking it seriously if we explain it psychologically in terms of the apostle's strong ethical self-criticism, in which the distinction between the 'righteous' and sinners becomes first relative and then irrelevant.[12] It is equally inadmissible to use the formula which is apparently based on the divine predicates of the liturgy (and which is consequently a fundamental characterization of the divine action) in order to deduce a process of development from it: before justification man was certainly ungodly – Israel and all the 'godly' would bitterly oppose this! – but he ceased to be so when once he was set upon the

[11] R. Bultmann, *Theology* I, p. 322.
[12] The view taken, for example, by T. Zahn, *Der Brief des Paulus an die Römer*, ³1925, p. 223; E. Kühl, *Der Brief des Paulus an die Römer*, 1913, p. 135.

path of sanctification.[13] Finally, it shows a complete misunderstanding of the statement if we translate it into moral terms and talk about the justification of the wicked.[14]

Because he lays claim to no religious achievements and merits, and precisely because he is *not* to be viewed as 'an example of an outstanding religious personality',[15] Abraham is ungodly, in so far as he cannot be called 'good', measured against the standards of the Jewish[16] and Greek worlds. He does not deal in works. For that very reason he is, on the other hand, the prototype of faith,[17] which always has to be viewed in antithesis to a piety of works. Thus he receives the blessing spoken to David in vv.7f.: forgiveness inevitably only falls to the lot of the man who is not 'good' in the usual sense of performing good works, i.e., the man who is ungodly. On the other hand, God shows his divinity in that he acts forgivingly, i.e., turns towards the ungodly. The present tense in v.5 shows clearly that he always behaves in this way, just as according to v.17 he is always the God who gives life to the dead and calls into existence the things that do not exist. The centre of our passage is to be found in Paul's separation between faith and what is generally called goodness; and he can only bring this out, as he does in 3.29f., when he gives a challengingly new definition, contrary to the prevailing view, of what the nature and work of the true God really is.

Verses 9–12 assume that the blessing which we have quoted applied to Israel. It must then be asked whether the righteousness of faith does not also remain confined to the sphere of the circumcision. The apostle, following the official view of the synagogue, argues that Gen. 15.6 precedes the demand for circumcision in Gen. 17.10f. by twenty-nine years.[18] Accordingly, circumcision cannot have been the presupposition; it must have been the 'seal' (i.e., the documentation and legitimation) of Abraham's justification. Since the meaning of circumcision is discussed in this way, the problem of the righteousness of faith enters the sphere of salvation history, and we make things too easy for ourselves if we brush that aside out of our historical knowledge as being the abstruse reasoning of Jewish scriptural exegesis and

---

[13] Taylor, *Forgiveness*, pp. 57f.
[14] H. Lietzmann, *An die Römer*, ⁴1933, p. 52.
[15] C. H. Dodd, *The Epistle of Paul to the Romans*, ⁸1941, p. 64.
[16] Cf. Stuhlmacher, *op. cit.*, p. 226.
[17] G. Bornkamm, *Paulus*, 1969, p. 152,: 'man's prototype'.
[18] P. Billerbeck, *Kommentar zum Neuen Testament aus Talmud und Midrasch* III, 1926, p. 203.

as having no importance for ourselves. Even if we no longer accept Paul's argument, we have by no means finished factually with the link between justification and salvation history. Behind it lurks the problem of the relationship between faith and the world, which the Christian simply dare not avoid. Moreover, not to take it into account is to miss the path of access into the third section of the chapter, as we shall see.

For Judaism, Abraham counted as the father of all proselytes.[19] The apostle does not dispute this view in principle. But it would be too little if we see what he says simply as an expansion of the notion. For, practically speaking, he reverses its intention. The proselyte receives a share in the divine covenant and its righteousness. But Abraham received this share before his circumcision, and is hence the father of all believers who are not proselytes. Verse 12 seems to limit this statement. A permanent relationship between the patriarch and the circumcision is in fact preserved, in order not to rob Israel of its right of succession, in salvation history, to the promise.[20] On the other hand, to concede the text merely a co-ordinating 'both . . . and' sense is to miss its tendency. For the Jews it was already unendurable that the circumcision should only be mentioned second. And Paul goes even further when, as in 2.25ff., the circumcision of the heart is made the decisive thing. The promise to Abraham then really only applies to the group of the circumcised who have become Christians.

These insights make it necessary to take up a double front in the present discussion about Pauline salvation history. The choice of the patriarch as example and prototype would be absurd if we were meant to confine the possibility of experiencing the divine righteousness to the period *post Christum crucifixum*.[21] Moreover, the appeal to the Old Testament so characteristic of Paul would then lose all positive theological significance, so that, following Marcion's footsteps, we should also have to draw the necessary conclusions as regards the canon. The slogan 'no theological differentiation of Jews and Gentiles'[22] does not commend itself as the bearing either of this passage or of 3.29f., because it formalizes the idea of the *justificatio impii* and at most describes its highly problematical effect in Gentile

[19] *Ibid.*, p. 211.
[20] U. Wilckens, 'Zu Römer 3, 21–4, 25', *EvTh* 24, 1964, pp. 599ff.
[21] G. Klein, 'Römer 4 und die Idee der Heilsgeschichte' (now in the collection of essays, *Rekonstruktion und Interpretation*, 1969, pp. 145–79), p. 148.
[22] *Ibid.*, p. 151.

Christendom, a point which Paul himself considers in Rom. 11.15ff. The view that the history of Israel is 'radically profaned and paganized'[23] demonstrates precisely the arrogance against which we are warned in 11.20. No one can be forbidden to go beyond the apostle if his own theology forces him to do so. But to do this in the name of the apostle and of our chapter is simply unjustifiable, because that is to do violence to both. On the other hand, it is completely true that here not only is a particular understanding of salvation history being expounded – another one is being simultaneously destroyed;[24] and 'that the category of a salvation history running its course in chronological continuity is inappropriate as a hermeneutical principle for the illumination of Paul's picture of Abraham'.[25] It is not by chance that the idea of the holy remnant (which was so important to Jewish Christianity, providing a verifiable transition from Israel according to the flesh to Christianity) plays no part in Paul's writings except for Rom. 9.27ff.; 11.4f., 13ff. But there it is offered as a highly paradoxical indication, contrary to all appearances, of a divine mystery and a miracle which is only credible in the light of the divine promise. What Paul is *not* doing is guarding a perceptible and in the earthly sense unbroken continuity between Abraham and Christ, which could fit into the theological formula of promise and fulfilment. After all, it is a pure postulate that Abraham was bound to believe in the eschatological ratification of the promise.[26] In reality he would then, stripped of his historicity, be nothing more than a mysterious cypher in a plan of salvation reconstructed by the Gnostics.

In the face of both viewpoints we must cling to the fact that the apostle did not detach faith from world history. Nevertheless, it shows a gross misunderstanding when on the one hand the decisions of faith are belittled and the problem of Israel, with which Paul wrestled so hard, is got out of the way by means of a theological amputation; or when, on the other hand,[27] faith is defined as being fundamentally faith in history and history as being faith's primary foundation. Whereas in the first case the divine Word becomes a promise to curiously isolated individuals, in the second it becomes an interpretation of history which merely satisfies speculation. In vv. 9–12 the privileges claimed by Israel are demolished. God's righteous-

[23] *Ibid.*, p. 158 and passim.
[24] *Ibid.*, p. 164.   [25] *Ibid.*, p. 169.
[26] U. Wilckens, 'Die Rechtfertigung Abrahams nach Römer 4', *Studien zur Theologie der alttestamentlichen Überlieferungen*, pp. 111–27; p. 125.
[27] *Ibid.*, pp. 123, 127.

ness cannot be limited to the realm of the circumcision, which even Abraham entered as one already justified and which is not able to guarantee true faith. Abraham is not to be interpreted through Moses or determined by him. For then, according to 3.29, God would become the private idol of the Jews instead of the creator. On the other hand, there is the Abraham who believed, and who was justified by his faith, and there are his successors in the form of those Jewish Christians who have undergone the circumcision of the heart. Salvation does not belong merely to the Gentiles who have believed. There is an Israel under the promise which can only be denied if, like Marcion, we replace creation by Christology. For the abolition of the privileges claimed by the Jews does not mean the abolition of the *protevangelium* in the promise, which was bound to Israel. Justification does not set aside salvation history, but it removes its barriers by tearing down the fence of the law and refusing to leave salvation in a private reserve. It shows that God deals with the world, not merely with the godly. Israel can only follow Abraham's footsteps through faith, i.e., it is saved not through its piety and its tradition, but through the *justificatio impii*. Salvation history is the history of the divine Word, which finds out faith and makes superstition possible; it is, therefore, not marked by a visible earthly continuity but by interruptions and paradoxes; again and again its path leads over the grave out of which it brings the dead to life. We must not deny salvation history, however, because God's Word in its activity permeates the world in its breadth and depth.

This is the only key to the theme of the third section of the chapter, which is determined by the catchword of Abraham as 'heir of all things' and weaves unwearying variations on this theme in unmistakably polemical tones. That is why Paul talks in v. 16 about 'all his descendants' and 'the father of us all', and this is taken up in v. 17f. in the biblical predicate, 'the father of many (Gentile) nations'. The promise of Israel's occupation of the promised land was extended as in Eccles. 44.21: 'He promised him . . . to cause them to inherit from sea to sea, and from the River (Euphrates) to the ends of the earth.' Matt. 5.5 and I Cor. 6.2 show that the promise could be transposed into the eschatological sphere. Applied to the bearers of the promise, it is summed up in the technical formula, 'heir of all things', which in Heb. 1.2, in accordance with the apocalyptic tradition, also characterizes the Messiah. The Pauline polemic which is associated with these statements brings out the point that the universalism of such assertions of salvation cannot be attained via the law.[28] This universalism expresses itself most sharply in the fact that the apostle undoubtedly understands by the nations mentioned in Gen. 17.5 the Gentiles who have become Christian. Again the promise to Israel, which is valid and has been fulfilled through the Jewish Christians, is not abrogated. But the stress lies unmistakably on the point that the promise bursts apart this circle of receivers. To be the child of Abraham is no longer the privilege of Judaism; it is not even the mark of Jewish Christians alone. The patriarch is the heir of all things in that the Gentiles, too, are his children, in the form of those of them who are Christians; they are his 'seed', and not merely if they are proselytes. Abraham, who was himself justified before his circumcision simply on the basis of his faith, not his works, is the prototype of the justification of the ungodly and, as the Gentile Christians prove, is thus also the father of the justified ungodly. The theological formula found in v.5 has therefore now been historically illustrated and interpreted, and the thesis of 3.21ff. is thereby confirmed at the same time.

Meanwhile, however, the horizon of these statements has broadened out to universal dimensions. The faith which accepts God's promise, and is thereby justifying faith, lays claim to that participation in the universal kingdom of its Lord which was already promised to the prototype of this faith. The hearing of the promise does not end with the listener, but sends him out to be tested in the world and in history. If we are separated from the world and history by the cross, then what belongs to the world cannot become the content and foundation of our faith, even in the form of salvation history. But the world remains faith's battleground and the horizon of the divine grace which reaches out to the world and history in the divine Word. Faith only lives from hearing, not from seeing miraculous events. But it does not remain mere hearing to the extent that it does not have to prove itself, or as if hearing were the final goal of the promise. In order to prevent a common misunderstanding, it must, on the other hand, be stressed that faith is not identical with love. Hearing has a primacy which cannot be replaced by anything else. Faith is not *fides caritate* but *verbo formata*, so arriving, nevertheless, at the universality of being open for everything and everyone and of breaking out of an isolable and abstract *punctum mathematicum* into the sphere of love which stands the test.

[28] J. Moltmann, *Theology of Hope*, 1967, p. 146.

At this point, in order to make the boldness of the following statements comprehensible, we must briefly consider the relationship of promise and gospel. Here it is all important to avoid that formalization of the concepts used which the idea of development, and especially the scheme of promise and fulfilment, suggests. The point in Paul is that the promise, according to Gal. 3.8 for example, is to be understood as the anticipation or complement[29] of the gospel, is substantially identical with it, and is termed only another aspect of the revelation in the Word.[30] It is the gospel pre-given in salvation history, its historical concealment, whereas the gospel itself is the promise eschatologically revealed and open to the day. The gospel replaces the law but not the promise; indeed it has itself the character of promise in that it does not free us from temptation and gives us, with the gift of the spirit, expectation of final redemption. The co-ordination of promise and gospel brings out the fact that eschatological happening breaks into real history, thus designating the latter as the sphere in which the divine creativity and providence have always ruled. The distinction makes it clear that history and eschatology do not coincide, but are united merely through the Word of the divine self-promise. The promise entered history by concealing itself in the scriptures. The gospel, with its universal proclamation and revelation of the depths of history, liberated the promise from this concealment.[31]

It is essential to recognize this substantial identity of promise and gospel if we are to understand why, in a difficult transition, the faith of Abraham is depicted from 4.17b onwards as faith in God's power of resurrection. As in II Cor. 1.9, Paul here picks up the divine predicate out of the second of the Eighteen Benedictions of the Jewish liturgy: 'Yahweh, who givest life to the dead'.[32] That explains his unusual use of the verb 'give life to' instead of 'raise'. Another common Jewish formula is linked with it and (at least here) is also adapted to the liturgical style. This proclaims that God's sovereign creativity takes the form of the Word, that the call of the creator constantly issues forth and that the raising of the dead must be shifted into this context. For the point of the resurrection is not survival beyond the grave but an eschatological *creatio ex nihilo*, since it has

[29] J. Schniewind, *TWNT* II, p.575.
[30] Moltmann, *op. cit.*, p.147.
[31] As against this, H. Ulonska's remarks in *Paulus und das Alte Testament*, diss. Münster 1964, pp.207f., 216, seems grotesque.
[32] Billerbeck III, p.212.

been from the beginning of the world the work of the creator who acts through his Word.

The theologoumenon of the *creatio ex nihilo* has been disputed as regards Jewish tradition.[33] This is correct, in that it is not, as in a certain Greek philosophy,[34] thought of as a principle or in the abstract. 'Formless matter' is the presupposition for creation in Wisdom 11.17, for example, and II Macc. 7.28 states polemically and contrary to Greek speculation that God 'did not make them out of the things that existed'. Interest is directed, not towards the origin of matter, but towards the almighty power of the creator, whose Word breaks through all resistance. But this is the starting point for liturgical addresses such as that in the Syriac Apocalypse of Baruch (II Baruch) 21.4: 'O Thou . . . that hast called from the beginning of the world that which did not yet exist.' 48.8 is especially impressive: 'With a word Thou quickenest that which was not.' Philo is also familiar with this tradition (whether Greek material also influenced him need not concern us here). In *De specialibus legibus* IV, 187, he writes: 'He called the things that are not into being', and in *De opificio mundi*, 81: 'He brought the things that were not into being.' We need not follow up other parallels and their survival, for example in Hermas, *Mandates* I; II Clement 1.8; *Apostolic Constitutions* VIII, 12.7. But it is important that in 1QH 3.11ff.; 11.10ff., entry into the community is viewed as a new creation.[35] Finally, we cannot dispense with *Joseph and Asenath* 8.9: 'Thou who givest life to the universe and callest it out of darkness into light and out of terror into truth and out of death into life.' For here, as in the two strophes of Col. 1.15ff., we find a link between the creation of the world and redemption, interpreted as the resurrection of the dead; and this also explains the connection of the liturgical formulae in Rom. 4.17b. According to *Barnabas* VI. 13, the primal period and the end-time correspond, so that the resurrection of the dead appears as the eschatological new creation. But that must be termed *creatio ex nihilo*. If it were not so, the whole association of ideas would lose its point: the resurrection of the dead is, as is nothing else, creation out of nothing. But if it points back to the first creation, that means that God's action in history is always brought to bear, from the beginning to the end, on what is in

[33] A. Ehrhardt, 'Creatio ex nihilo', *The Framework of the New Testament Stories*, 1964, pp. 200–34: pp. 210ff.

[34] W. Bauer, *Wörterbuch zum Neuen Testament*, ⁵1958, col. 442.

[35] E. Sjöberg, 'Neuschöpfung in den Toten-Meer-Rollen', *St. Th.* 9, 1955, pp. 131ff.

itself nothing; this is what the apostle expressly states in II Cor. 3.5f. in reference to service in the proclamation of the gospel as well. II Cor. 4.7ff.; 12.9; 13.4 are variations on this idea, which is constitutive for Pauline theology, while I Cor. 1.26ff. formulates it with an eye to the make-up of the church. It is not a theology of revolution which finds its expression here, but a radicalized doctrine of God and creation, acquired in the light of the cross of Christ. Unlike the idols, the Father of Jesus works with poor, fundamentally perishable material, and always most profoundly for and with the dead.

The point of such statements lies in the fact that justification is part of this context. It is the *creatio ex nihilo* which takes place in the eschatological era; it is an anticipation of the resurrection of the dead in the midst of still-existing earthly temptation. As such it must necessarily be, and is bound to remain, *justificatio impii*. It does not base salvation on what we are capable of and what we do; consequently it shatters every human (and more especially every religious) self-sufficiency and self-security. We remain at the point where the justification of the ungodly is valid, in the condition of those who are incapable of self-praise and who have to live from faith alone. To this extent the reverse side of true faith is always the *redigi ad nihilum*, as is made plain from the example of Abraham in vv. 19–21. It is grotesque if the theme of these verses is clouded by the assumption that the patriarch's generative powers were miraculously preserved.[36] But it is not doing justice to the text, either, to follow the *koine* reading in v. 19, according to which Abraham 'paid no regard' to the death of his own powers and Sarah's. This destroys the paradox that (as is expressly stated in verse 18) the believing man hopes at the very point where there is, in the earthly sense, nothing more to hope for. He does not by-pass realities, but is aware of them and holds his ground notwithstanding. He does not escape into illusion, not even in the name of piety and edification. He sees himself confronted with death and nothingness on earth, both in himself and in what he sees in the world surrounding him. Thus far it is not the *credo quia absurdum* that describes man but, in the judgment of human reason, the *credo absurdum*. He dares to trust the divine promise, contrary to every earthly reality, and to rely on him who raises the dead.[37] For this he

---

[36] O. Kuss, *Der Römerbrief*, 1957, p. 192. For the opposing view, cf. Bornkamm, *Paulus*, p. 153.

[37] Conzelmann, *Outline*, p. 171: the object of faith is not the man who is delivered, but the delivering Word of God. O. Cullmann's opposing view in *Salvation in History*, pp. 70f., 120, is problematical, and probably not merely in its formulation.

has no pledge except the promise; and he has experienced no miracle; no redemptive history taking place before him, on his behalf or after him, frees him from the necessity of living every day anew, simply from the promise of the God who has given that promise to him. That is what the justification of the ungodly means: where it is a question of salvation or disaster the believer does not look to any verifiable, already existing facts – either to facts of world history, or the facts of his own moral and religious existence, or to pious traditions. He stands fast at the point where *creatio ex nihilo* has to take place and man's becoming man has always to begin anew, i.e., at the point where God in his sole efficacy and grace remain the first Word and the last. Even the sanctification of the Christian life does not change this. It does not remove us from the place where God's Word has to create us afresh every day, has to call us anew from nothingness into being, has to bring us out of death into life. It is constantly *reditus ad baptismum*, a lived hearing of the Word of creation which proves itself in the response of our acting. Without this Word we are and remain ungodly, even in our 'goodness'. That God has spoken to us, and does not cease to speak to us, is our only salvation; that we allow this Word to be spoken to us and dare to live by it is our sanctification and justification. No achievement of our own annuls our ungodliness, which can always only be ended through the divine promise given to us, hence only in faith as the state of being *coram deo*. We do not transcend ourselves. God comes to us in his promise and makes us righteous – righteous in that we, as the receivers, allow him to come to us.

Verses 23–25 do not add any new argument to the scriptural proof but appeal to the reader from the liturgical tradition: *tua res agitur.* The relation of the scriptures to the present is brought out, as vv. 23f. expressly stress. This does not mean that the historical events, as Paul was capable of seeing them, lost their independent significance, as would have been the case if they had been pure illustrations and more or less arbitrarily chosen examples.[38] Admission into the scriptures undoubtedly gave the apostle access to the historical dimension and the course of history, although he did not, of course, share our modern way of thinking. The antithesis between historical

He talks about the 'aligning' of oneself in the sequence of events presented by salvation history.

[38] Against Conzelmann, *Outline*, pp. 169f.

and eschatological was once a great help in critical research. As a principle it can hardly be maintained anywhere at all in the New Testament. The two are joined together through a singular dialectic in which the eschatological view first encroaches on mere history and what it understands as such, and turns the past into eschatology's dimension in depth; whereas later (in a change which introduces a new theological phase) eschatology is increasingly historicized, i.e., is incorporated into a process of development. Paul did not yet use the Old Testament as a book of images and a collection of examples, like I Clement. For he was not yet interested in an ecclesiastical morality and in the divine *paideia* as education in Christian character. As is clear from our text as well as from Rom. 15.4; I Cor. 9.10; 10.11, he related all history, in so far as it was preserved in the scriptures, to the end-time, finding in it the harbinger of what was to come and the criterion for a proper understanding of the present. He holds fast to the identity of the God who reveals himself in history, because not to do so would be to lose the creator, as was the case with Marcion. Historical interpretation as a whole is alien to Paul. He refuses to surrender the documentation of the divine will towards salvation throughout all history. It is deposited in the scriptures, but is also concealed in them, because these scriptures were only available to Israel. It was only the inspiration which came about with the proclamation of the gospel that brought out of its historical conceal-ment this documentation of the divine will towards salvation and its eschatological relationship, revealing it to the whole world as the now open secret of the eternal faithfulness of God.

This eternally faithful God had always brought about and had always intended the justification of the ungodly. Verse 24 describes this as the insight of the man who believes in Jesus as the Lord who has been raised from the dead. It stands in the clarity and openness which was denied to Abraham. Abraham's faith as paradoxical trust in the mere divine promise which contradicted every human expectation was not an act of perversity and despair which for some incompre-hensible reason had a happy ending. In the light of Christ its right-ness and its necessity is proved. This is what always happens when faith encounters the true God and surrenders to him. Abraham is the prototype of Christian faith which reads the justification of the ungodly, unmistakably and scandalously, in the message of the cross. Christ was put to death for our trespasses. But, as always in Paul, the cross and the resurrection count as a single event. The two are coordinated in v. 25, to begin with rhetorically and liturgically. But as in v. 17b, the justification is obviously and markedly aligned to the proclamation of the resurrection. What was once and for all substantiated through the death of Jesus happens afresh wherever faith in the one who is risen is present. The reign of the risen Christ is the sphere of revealed righteousness. This statement offers the transition to chs. 5–8, which have to deal with justification as the reality of new life under the sign of our own coming resurrection.

Belief in God's power of resurrection is identical with belief in justification, in so far as the justification of the ungodly must not only be experienced once and for all, but must be clung to as constitutive of the whole Christian life and the constant action of the creator. Here we are not only dealing with a beginning, but with the central theme of salvation history in general and hence also with the central theme of our own future. Since it is the activity of the creator directed towards nothingness, the resurrection of the dead is the presupposition for the justification of the ungodly; and, as our hope, it is the ultimately unassailable ratification of justification. Abraham reached out for it merely on the strength of God's promise. Anyone who reads the scriptures in the light of the eschatological event understands that in so doing he was reaching out towards the reality of Christ, which was still hidden from him.

We have now, finally, to make clear to ourselves what intellectual premises allowed Paul to depict the patriarch as the prototype of Christian faith, thus bridging the temporal gap with unusual boldness. This question inevitably brings us to the problem of typology, which is factually and conceptually hotly disputed but is still ultimately unresolved. It has even been denied that typology is present at all in Rom. 4, because the apostle's scriptural proof does not draw on the aspect of repetition.[39] This view is undoubtedly mistaken. We have been ceaselessly concerned to show that Abraham prefigures Christian faith; and v. 24 presents him expressly as what Neugebauer calls, with epigrammatic terseness, 'the type of the new people of God' and 'pre-existent member of the *ekklesia*'.[40] Yet the dispute remains hopeless as long as people continue to discuss the general nature and structure of typology or its individual characteristics

[39] R. Bultmann, 'Ursprung und Sinn der Typologie als hermeneutischer Methode' (now in *Exegetica*, 1967, pp. 369–80), p. 377; H. Conzelmann, *Outline*, p. 170; K. Kertelge, *Rechtfertigung bei Paulus*, 1967, pp. 185, 193; U. Luz, *Das Geschichtsverständnis des Paulus*, 1968, p. 179ff.; Vielhauer, *op. cit.*, p. 41.

[40] *In Christus*, p. 168.

instead of first confining the problem to Paul and working out the basic nature of typology from there.

It is superficial to talk about a unique form of comparison[41] or analogy,[42] because the borders between typology and imagery, symbol or allegory then become fluid.[43] It is still only a short step from this, if we set Pauline typology in the framework of the difference between the provisional and the final,[44] or, more concretely, in the framework of salvation history, so far as this is determined by analogy and climax, repetition and consummation.[45] Whatever may be correct about this, an exact clarification is not to be achieved along these lines. On the other hand, this desired precision is not achieved either if typology is traced back in religio-historical terms to the context of a cyclical thinking, and is ordered under the heading of repetition.[46] If that is correct, it certainly does not take us any further in Paul. For him, history is directed towards a fixed goal, and the background is no longer a cyclic view of history but the doctrine of the two aeons. From the starting point of this presupposition, the existence of typology in its original sense in Paul must be denied, or it must be seen as being the remains of an earlier view which was no longer of decisive importance for him. In either case it must be subordinated to his prophetic argument. From the perspective of radical historical criticism, however, the opposite attempt is also somewhat improbable, if not impossible: this traces back New Testament typology essentially to Jesus and calls its Pauline variation the spiritual interpretation of Scripture, which it considers the constitutive interpretation for Paul.[47] For though it cannot be denied that this use of the Old Testament has its importance, it is parallel to the argument from prophecy, to allegory and to paraenetic application, and is by no means paramount.[48]

If we try to distinguish Pauline typology from other kinds of interpretation, we must first be clear that, like the rest, the Pauline method is bound to the scriptures and therefore does not apply to non-biblical events and figures. That at least already distinguishes it from

[41] K. Galley, *Altes und neues Heilsgeschehen bei Paulus*, 1965, pp. 161ff.
[42] H. Müller, *Die Auslegung alttestamentlichen Geschichtsstoffes bei Paulus*, Dissertation, Halle, 1960, pp. 93ff.
[43] Cullmann, *Salvation in History*, pp. 133f.
[44] W. Huber, *Passa und Ostern*, 1969, p. 90.
[45] Cullmann, *op. cit.*, pp. 132f., 146.
[46] The view taken by Bultmann in the essay mentioned above.
[47] L. Goppelt's view in *Typos*, 1939.
[48] Contrary to Goppelt, *Typos*, p. 154.

cyclical thinking in general. It differs from prophecy and allegory in that, though it certainly implies a biblical text, it views it as the tradition of an event;[49] the exegesis of details is only of secondary importance. Prophecy and allegory basically maintain the fulfilment of a particular text and the relevance of its details. Moreover, prophecy appears as applying directly to the future event of its eschatological fulfilment. It has an exclusively forward-pointing significance. For typology and allegory, this application to the future is at least not direct or exclusive; it at most arises out of the subsequent comparison of a present situation with a historically veiled past. Here correspondences or antitheses are brought out. Moreover, in allegory the historical event counts as the shroud for a veiled allusion to the future, which is the sole point. In typology, however, the historical has its own reality and importance. Its relation to the future belongs to a deep-lying stratum which has first to be laid bare – laid bare not as the hidden meaning of a text, but as the correlation of events which either correspond or stand in defiant contrast to one another.

In the light of all this, current categories associated with typology lose much of their value. That is true, for example, of the catchword 'prefiguration',[50] because in Rom. 5.12ff., for example, type and antitype are seen antithetically and in counter-movement. The same passage shows that no decisive weight, at least, is assigned to the aspects of climax or repetition. We must firmly lay aside the perspectives of promise and fulfilment. The relation of the bearers of curse and blessing is based on the fact that both are bearers of the world's destiny. If the blessing proves itself mightier than the curse, that is not substantiated in the typology as such.

For Pauline typology, the correspondence of primeval history (to which, in the Jewish view, the Exodus tradition also belongs) with the end-time is constitutive; here repetition and climax may play their part. It is the events which are important, not the individual words. The development from type to antitype is normal because the end-time will be more glorious than the primeval period. But it can be omitted for the sake of contrast. The repetition, as we find it in exemplary fashion in Rom. 4, is now no longer to be explained on the basis of a cyclical course of events; it represents the unique correspondence of the primeval era and the end-time. Consequently

---

[49] L. Goppelt, 'Apokalyptik und Typologie bei Paulus', *TLZ* 89, 1964, cols. 329f.

[50] cf. Goppelt and also E. Fuchs, *Hermeneutik*, 1954, p. 192.

typology is in fact well suited to minister to the outlook based on salvation history. At the same time, it is not the continuity of a development which it brings out but, through the correspondence or antithesis of beginning and end, the pivot of history. Here attention is not directed towards the individual as example but towards whatever is pregnant with destiny, which spreads over into individual existence. Typology has a cosmic dimension and to that degree belongs to the sphere of Pauline apocalyptic.[51] Because this is so, it modifies the pattern of the two aeons, which either follow one another in time or, as the heavenly and the earthly, are contrasted with one another in space. Typology can take up both variations, i.e., the prefigurations and antitheses of the eschatalogical event in the primeval period, as well as the reflections and contrasts of the heavenly in the earthly. The New Testament's merging of the temporal sequence and the spatial gradation is shown more especially in the Epistle to the Hebrews, but also in Gal. 4.25f.

Let us now revert to our theme. In Rom. 4 the scriptural evidence is marshalled in different ways. Reflection on particular passages of scripture (Gen. 15.6; 17.11) serves a methodical argument from prophecy: God's will is unambiguous and finally laid down in the Old Testament. It demands the righteousness of faith which was revealed in Christ. This argument, however, is fitted into the wider framework of the whole story of Abraham, which typologically anticipates the story of Christ. That comes out clearly in vv. 17ff. The text used there is interpreted as a pointer to the Christian belief in the resurrection. With this the patriarch no longer counts merely as an example of the believing person; he has the Jewish meaning of being the bearer of the promise *per se*, who is replaceable by no other figure. The whole chapter has previously worked towards this theme, in that Abraham is removed from the sphere of the circumcision, unless circumcision follows on the faith that was his. He has not merely representative significance but, since he is the ancestor of the believing Gentiles as well, universal significance also. Like Moses in Rom. 5.12ff., he is the bearer of destiny, though not in antithesis to eschatological reality but in anticipation of it. Typology made possible the Pauline statement about the identity between the faith of Abraham and that of Christianity, faith which interprets the justification of the ungodly as a

[51] A partial approach to this view, at least, may be found in H. J. Schoeps, *Paulus*, 1959, p. 246; K. Kertelge, *Rechtfertigung bei Paulus*, 1967, p. 140; U. Luz, *Geschichtsverständnis*, pp. 56, 60.

creatio ex nihilo and an anticipation of the raising of the dead. For typology allows the primeval period and end-time to correspond and the promise hidden in the scriptures to be revealed by the gospel.

This analysis has tried to show how the apostle arrived at his train of thought and the ideas inherent in it. The question remains, in what way can we listen to his message, not only grasping its content but continuing to think systematically along the same lines. We can only indicate the direction in which an answer lies. Still, we are in a position to say that the problem of Pauline typology and the problem of the meaning of the equally controversial formula 'in Christ' touch nearly upon one another. Here, too, the faith of the individual becomes part of an all-embracing context. Scholars have expended much energy on making this context comprehensible. For a long time, interpretation was dominated by the mystical view, which attempted to understand the formula in the light of devotional experience,[52] or of the sacramentally founded, eschatological community of Christ.[53] The preposition was here mainly understood in the sense of locality. It was entirely logical that a generation for which the catchword 'mysticism' had become, for various reasons, suspect, should interpret the formula in an ecclesiological sense, in so far as it thought itself forced to hold fast to this 'local' meaning for the preposition, at least largely speaking: a person is in Christ when that person is in his body, that is to say, the church.[54] We are indebted to Neugebauer[55] for raising the question anew. He understands the preposition almost exclusively as instrumental, which is not only linguistically possible but is undoubtedly justifiable in many cases. But it is unfortunate that a consistent historical interpretation, based on salvation history, is not only sweeping away mysticism but also, ultimately, the eschatological point of view. What Christ once did has continuing efficacy and gives us a part in him, so that 'in Christ' means belonging to the historical extension of the saving event which once took place in the past and the sphere which is indicated by that event.[56] Eschatology is talked about here in order to bring out the

[52] Fundamentally in A. Deissmann, *Die neutestamentliche Formel 'in Christo Jesu'*, 1892.
[53] Cf. A. Schweitzer, *The Mysticism of Paul the Apostle*, 1931.
[54] E.g. my dissertation, *Leib und Leib Christi*, 1933, p. 183; Bultmann, *Theology* I, p. 31. The view is a common one among Roman Catholic and English-speaking writers.
[55] *In Christus*, 1961, with an extensive account of the research up to date on pp. 18–33.
[56] Cf. pp. 84f.

salvation-historical character of the redeeming event in past and present. This means, practically speaking, that what was begun through Christ is continued in the church.

We shall not enter into detailed exegesis in order to show that the 'local' sense of the preposition simply cannot be argued away in many places.[57] We must, however, be aware of the theological implications of this historicizing interpretation. Jesus becomes in this way again the author of our faith. He appears as Lord largely in that his demands retain their validity for us.[58] The gospel inevitably changes into the communication of ecclesiastical tradition. The presence of salvation resides in the remembrance of what has happened and in appropriate conduct. The sacraments then serve the same purpose. The fact is completely overlooked that the so-called saving events have determined not only believers but also the enemies of Christ, and have kindled not only faith but superstition as well as dubious piety and theology. The sphere of influence of a historical event comprehends many potentialities; and the history of the church proves that Christianity and its traditions are not capable of providing and guaranteeing clarity about the meaning of the saving event. With this in mind, the rights and wrongs of the interpretation presented above should at least be examined once more.

At the same time, Neugebauer's outline is important. He does not only do much to correct a questionable exegesis. He attacks in his own way the same problem which also faces us in Pauline typology. Here the individual person is similarly moved into a context which is wider, spatially and temporally, than himself and which makes him the member of a world-wide event and the successor and exponent of one who has gone before him. Not even the believer lives in isolation, or in an association of many individuals. 'In Christ', as under Adam, Moses and Abraham, we stand in an already-existing world and history, which we ratify in faith or superstition. Our essence does not lie in free decision but in our affirmation or denial of an event which confronts us from outside ourselves. What was called Pauline mysticism points most sharply to the fact which the Reformed *extra se* was designed to characterize. Man never belongs to himself; he always has a lord whose power is manifested through him. We might

---

[57] Cf. the recent criticism made by E. Brandenburger, *Fleisch und Geist*, 1968, pp. 20, 26ff., 54.

[58] Neugebauer, *op. cit.*, pp. 61, 137ff., 148f. See also E. Lohse's criticism in *TLZ* 87, 1962, cols. 843f.

also put it as follows: we live in and from spheres of power. If one interprets the 'in Christ' simply in the light of the 'through Christ', one certainly arrives at a supra-individual event, but still only at the context of a tradition. To attach the name salvation history suggests that another causality than the causality of, for example, the history of ideas is intended and that the ultimate salvation or disaster of man is seen as being already inherent in it. Basically, however, our relationship to Christ remains thereby that of a historical development stamped by ecclesiastical tradition, a development whose initiator was Jesus. Here Christ himself becomes the cypher for a movement which he started: *Christus prolongatus* can be preached even by Protestants and even in the sense of salvation history.

As against this, Rom. 4 reminds us that Christology and the doctrine of justification mutually interpret one another. It tells us that Christ is always drawing us afresh even out of our inner-ecclesiastical traditional associations and that his sphere of power is that of the gospel of the justification of the ungodly. We do not simply enter into this. We must be called to it afresh every day. 'In Christ' is really not primarily an ecclesiological formula at all. To see it as such is to endanger and obscure the primacy of Christology over ecclesiology. 'In Christ' is the state of those who through the gospel are called out of the old world and who only belong to the new creation in so far as they continue to be confronted with the Lord who justifies the ungodly. His sphere of power has, however, for the sake of the gospel, a universal breadth and also, as the promise to Abraham shows, the depths of salvation history. For both in the primeval period and in the end-time the point at issue is more than individual salvation or disaster; what is at stake is the destiny of the world.

V

THE THEOLOGICAL PROBLEM PRESENTED
BY THE MOTIF OF THE BODY OF CHRIST

In all probability, the nature and task of the church has seldom been
the subject of more intensive consideration in the Protestant churches
than during the last forty years. In Germany the reaction against
liberal individualism, the struggle against national socialism, and the
ecumenical movement, have all played their contributing parts here.
In this way the theme of the body of Christ has also taken on a significance for my generation which would have been unthinkable
earlier; and it has frequently been of determining importance. At the
same time, the debate over the question among New Testament
scholars has here as elsewhere been marked more by the conflict of
the interpretations offered than by an increasing clarity. It is almost
the hall-mark of our scholarship today that the decisive questions
have everywhere turned into problems again and that hermeneutical
premises, historical judgments and theological interpretations differ,
sometimes to an extreme degree. Although our knowledge increases
and our horizon is constantly being extended, our common viewpoint is diminishing. Probably the very increase in our knowledge
intensifies the confusion instead of reducing it. In these circumstances you must not expect more of me than a number of observations on
a subject which I myself consider to be of paramount importance. I
should like to strike out a path through the wilderness of individual
questions in order to fix the focal points and to arrive at a bird's eye
view of the whole. The trend of the present outline is determined by
the work already done on the subject, together with the problems
which have thereby emerged, and my view of the most likely solutions.

    1. The unavoidable starting point seems to me the necessity of

breaking away from the view once current (at least among Protestants), that in describing the church as the body of Christ, Paul, who inclined to bold statements, was using a beautiful metaphor.[1] We do not need totally to exclude the pictorial aspect of this theologoumenon, any more than we have to with the descriptions of Christendom as the people of God, the *familia dei*, the heavenly city or the sacred temple.[2] This pictorial aspect can also be stressed to a greater or lesser degree according to one's respective judgment about the derivation of our motif in the history of religion. I shall go into this question as little as possible, because it is extremely intricate and would extend beyond the bounds of a lecture on my particular theme. Generally speaking, it is possible to shed light on Paul's meaning even without detailed investigation into the history of religion. At the same time, in tracing the scope of the concept of the body of Christ, it cannot be overlooked that three perspectives are under discussion. The influence of the Stoic notion of organism, which (as in Menenius Agrippa's famous fable) permits a community to be described as a body, will hardly be denied by anyone, especially since I Cor. 12.14ff. is clearly a reflection of it. But this is hardly enough, in view of the statement in I Cor. 12.12, with its sacramental substantiation in the following verse. For Paul does not simply establish the fact that the church is a body; the argument is a Christological one, as in Rom. 12.4: it is with Christ himself (to take the most cautious interpretation) as it is with the body; 'in Christ' the church is a body. In order to give full force to this nuance, scholars have drawn on the Jewish idea of 'corporate personality'[3] as well as on the Anthropos myth.[4] There is no reason why all three elements should not combine syncretistically, even if decisive importance is assigned to the last named.

[1] This is still the view emphatically taken by P. S. Minear, *Images of the Church in the New Testament*, 1961, pp. 173ff.

[2] Contrary to E. Schweizer, *TWNT* VII, p. 1069, I would not include the symbol of the vine in this context, nor can I see that this is exactly the same as what is meant by 'body' in Paul. If even an analogy were present, this would at most shed definite light on the apostle's horizon, not on his own view.

[3] Cf. H. Wheeler Robinson, 'The Hebrew Conception of Corporate Personality', *BZAW* 66, 1936, pp. 49–62; a theory supported by E. Percy, *Der Leib Christi in den paulinischen Homologumena und Antilegomena*, 1942, p. 41; E. Best, *One Body in Christ*, pp. 20ff.; J. J. Meuzelaar, *Der Leib des Messias*, 1961, pp. 11ff., 124ff.; J. de Fraine, *Adam et son Lignage*, 1959.

[4] Cf. H. Schlier, 'Corpus Christi', *RAC* III, 1957, cols. 437–53; A. Wikenhauser, *Die Kirche als der mystische Leib Christi nach dem Apostel Paulus*, 1937, p. 239; A. Nygren, *Corpus Christi (Ein Buch von der Kirche)*, 1950, p. 19ff.

In any case, neither Judaism's 'corporate personality' nor the middle Stoa's cosmic organism was a mere image which could be set over against reality in the modern manner. In both cases the ancients believed that they were dealing with an actually existing reality.[5] The position is no different when Paul talks about the body of Christ. It is true that what he says in Rom. 12.4f. and I Cor. 12.12ff. is introduced by a comparative particle, and that a comparison determines the progression of his argument. But the first passage says, 'We are one body in Christ', and that is explained in the second: 'For by one Spirit we were all baptized into one body.' This is not a metaphorical figure of speech.[6] To deny that these are assertions of identity affects the whole of Pauline theology. For the apostle (as Gal. 3.27f. shows particularly clearly), the sacrament effects a metamorphosis in which the old man dies and a new creature comes to life. It is not meant metaphorically when Paul says that baptism and the eucharist involve us in Jesus' death, incorporate us 'in Christ' and allow us to participate in the divine Spirit.[7] Disinclination to talk about Paul's mysticism is understandable in view of the many excesses in this direction. But we do not therefore have to go to the opposite extreme. The apostle uses the expression 'the body of Christ' because he really means to point out the structural characteristics of a body; that is why he makes a detailed comparison in I Cor. 12.14ff. But this way of speaking does not indicate that what is being described is any different. On the contrary, the comparison brings out the reality which is intended through the concrete application of the statement of identity to the life of the Christian community.[8] The exalted Christ really has an earthly body, and believers with their whole being are actually incorporated into it and have therefore to behave accordingly. From the point of view of the history of religion, the idea of organism which Paul takes up in the comparison presupposes a mythological conception which he presses into service in his paraenesis.[9]

It follows that the Pauline idea of the body of Christ is by no means equally obvious or immediately accessible at all periods. Like every

[5] N. A. Dahl, *Das Volk Gottes*, [2]1963, p. 225.

[6] Contrary to Meuzelaar, p. 172ff. and passim.

[7] H. Conzelmann, *Outline*, p. 261.

[8] E. Käsemann, *Leib und Leib Christi*, 1933, p. 161f., 170f.

[9] I am unable to accept Conzelmann's alternative (p. 261) between a mythological and a realistic conception of the body, because I believe that what seems to us mythological was viewed by Paul quite realistically.

concept, it has its historical situation, its '*Sitz im Leben*', and can only be properly understood in this light. We must not separate it from its situation and its time in order to turn it into an indispensable component part of what we consider to be a timeless metaphysic. The Roman doctrine of the *corpus Christi mysticum* rightly protects the Pauline theologumenon from being understood in a purely pictorial sense and from being degraded to the level of one metaphor among many. But it does so by metaphysically excluding the concept's historical ties. It thereby incurs the danger of treating the text as evidence of a dogma and of interpreting the dogma (according to the needs of the moment) but not the apostle's intention. Here as elsewhere, only a historical interpretation makes it possible for us to arrive at a correct understanding of the biblical facts.

2. Talk about the body of Christ is the ecclesiological formula through which Hellenistic Christianity armed itself for world-wide mission. In spite of a wide consensus of opinion among scholars,[10] the view that Paul invented this formula himself must be called highly problematical. He used it relatively seldom, and even then without any painstaking development of its underlying mythological conception, merely touching on it.[11] He made use of the concept primarily in paraenesis[12] and hence modified it in the direction of popular philosophical tradition, which described a political or cosmic entity as a body. All this is more understandable, at least, if he already found the mythological view to hand and if he was able to presuppose that it was familiar to his readers. In a Christianity which organized itself in analogy to the Hellenistic mystery religions, which understood the sacraments as participation in the fate of the Lord of the cult and viewed that Lord as the second Adam on a cosmic scale, this is completely conceivable.

We are unfortunately dependent to a great degree on conjecture here, and must not deceive ourselves into the belief that we have achieved any certainty. On the other hand, the apostle's originality ought not to be exaggerated. It is clearly evident in his doctrine of the

[10] E.g. Wikenhauser, p.1; W. Goossens, *L'Église corps du Christ d'après S. Paul*, 1949, p.80; Best, *op. cit.*, p.94; R. Schnackenburg, *The Church in the New Testament*, 1965, p.77; E. Schweizer, *TLZ* 86, 1961, p.172; Conzelmann, *op. cit.*, p.263.

[11] Conzelmann, *op. cit.*, p.263.

[12] Meuzelaar, *op. cit.*, p.172; E. Schweizer, *TWNT* VII, pp.1067ff.; *TLZ* 86, 1961, cols. 288, 291; P. Bonnard, 'L'Église corps de Christ dans le Paulinisme', *Revue de Théol. et de Phil.* VIII, 1958, pp.281f.; Conzelmann, *op. cit.*, p.261; H. Küng, *The Church*, 1967, pp.227f.

justification of the ungodly and his teaching about the charismata; it can very probably be found in the Christological associations of the spirit, which (in close connection with the ideas mentioned above) set firm limits to enthusiasm; and it may be seen generally in the clarity and depth with which he is able theologically to subordinate all these things to his chief concerns, determining the Christian way of life also from that self-same centre. On the other hand, he generally derives his individual motifs from Jewish, pagan or Christian tradition, though, unlike later writers, he does not pick up fragments of these and force them into a new framework, but penetrates and varies them in sovereign manner. Because we have only fragmentary knowledge of his Christian environment (pre-Pauline Syria in particular is practically unknown to us), we incline to ascribe to the apostle everything which we meet for the first time in his writings. This attitude still conceals the idealist superstition about the great personality, who has to be original at every point, whereas in theology the important things are, after all, concentration on the essentials and a combination of consistency and flexibility in their application.

It therefore seems to me idle to consider whether the notion of existence 'in Christ' precedes the idea of the body of Christ.[13] The two belong together in that they mutually interpret one another; and perhaps this very parallelism is best explained by a common underlying tradition. It can hardly be by chance, at least, that we encounter the motif of the body of Christ for the first time in Paul, and that it fits with such smoothness into his theology.[14] Although he did not initiate the world-wide mission, he advanced it programmatically like no one before him and even saw mission as his specific task. No other concept of the church represents his work and his message more adequately, because no other concept characterizes the world in the same way as the kingdom claimed by Christ.[15]

Similar importance is at most to be ascribed to the idea of the church as the eschatological people of God. This, being the constitutive idea of Pauline ecclesiology, really does link up with the idea of

[13] Contrary to E. Brandenburger, *Fleisch und Geist*, 1968, p. 49.

[14] Conzelmann, *Outline*, pp. 262ff., holds a different view.

[15] Conzelmann formalizes my precise definition when he talks about a 'mythical conception concerned with space and collectivity' and he distorts it when he warns us against the 'vision of the world-embracing Christ' as 'our possibility of ascent'. He too speaks about the 'sphere of Christ's rule' (p. 264), though as the 'sphere of faith' and not the universal kingdom claimed by Christ.

the body of Christ, either taking precedence over the latter[16] or sup-plementing it.[17] It must freely be admitted that the theme of the people of God, which has its roots in the earliest Christian tradition, is far more frequently touched on in all its different variations and associated theological complexes by Paul as well, and would there-fore seem to have the greater weight. But the question can hardly be decided merely statistically, even if, as in this case, statistics give a completely clear result. The fact that in the Deutero-Pauline epistles the picture changes just as clearly, so that the general trend is towards the body of Christ motif, should warn us to be careful. We must also remember that the apostle already found the idea of the eschatological people of God to hand in the traditions of Jewish Christianity. Why was this not enough for him? Finally, we must not overlook the fact that contemporary Catholicism is most strongly con-cerned to relax the fixed dogmatic system which, perhaps starting from the idea of the body of Christ, stresses the hierarchical structure of the church[18] and allows the notion of the priesthood of all believers to recede into the background. The salvation-historical approach, which is inevitably associated with the theme of the people of God, is undoubtedly calculated to counteract this tendency and there is no need to expound at length the many Protestant trends which are also determined by this view. In the face of these facts we are bound to enquire into the respective functions of the two ecclesiological images in the apostle's theology.

If the texts are examined under this aspect, it immediately becomes evident that Paul talks about the people of God exclusively in con-nection with Old Testament quotations, typologically in paraenetic admonition, or in direct controversy with Judaism.[19] He is therefore guided here by a polemical intention. That manifests itself in the harsh antithesis between Moses and Christ, the old and the new covenant, the heavenly and the earthly Jerusalem, in the retreat of the theologumenon about the holy remnant, and in the absence of the theme of Israel's restoration. In the antinomian dispute, the theme of the people of God is picked up in order to prove that the church is the

[16] A. Oepke, *Das neue Gottesvolk*, 1950; 'Leib Christi oder Volk Gottes bei Paulus', *TLZ* 79, 1954, cols. 363–68; F. Neugebauer, *op. cit.*, pp. 94ff., whereby on p. 98 the body of Christ becomes 'glorified Israel'; H. Küng, *The Church*, pp. 224f.

[17] E. Schweizer, *TWNT* VII, p. 1072; N. A. Dahl, *op. cit.*, pp. 255f., 228.

[18] T. Soiron, *Die Kirche als der Leib Christi*, 1951, pp. 188, 213, is characteristic.

[19] G. Delling, 'Merkmale der Kirche nach dem Neuen Testament', *NTS* 13, 1967, p. 302.

true Israel, in which the Old Testament promises are fulfilled and in which, apocalyptically, Israel according to the flesh must also incorporate itself, under the token of the justification of the ungodly. Since Paul is constantly involved in controversy, it is entirely understandable that there is a preponderance of texts in which Judaism's claim to be the true people of God is wrested from it and in which the enthusiasts have held up to them, in typological paraenesis, the warning of the past as attested by the Old Testament. Nor did the apostle fail to hold fast to the ecclesiology already offered to him by Jewish Christianity, because he was unwilling to surrender, not only the scriptures and the scriptural bearers of the promise, but also the God of his fathers and the heritage of the election of the people of the old covenant. Salvation history keeps its significance for Paul and lends his ecclesiology the dimension of depth. The promise is not obsolete, like the Mosaic law.[20] To this degree the church remains the people of God of the eschatological era.

Yet that is only one side of Paul's attitude. It points to the connection with the sacred past, but paradoxically. The idea of the people of God is closely connected with the establishment of the covenant on Sinai and can be applied to Gentile Christians who have not become proselytes merely in a transferred sense. Where the old and the new covenants diverge in eschatological contrast, it is no longer a question of development and continuity in the historical sense, no longer a matter of the correlation of the two covenants, but of their antithesis. The centre of ecclesiology is now the contrast of the aeons of Adam and Christ, of fallen and redeemed creation. This dualistic aspect cannot be adequately grasped through the concept of the people of God. The body of Christ is more than the category of a people is capable of expressing; it is a new world or, better, a new creation in universal dimension.[21] It is not enough simply to establish the fact that the spatial category replaces the more temporal one of the people of God,[22] or that universality takes the place of particularism.[23] The question of universal rule certainly arises here. But it

[20] The alignment with salvation history is stressed by E. Schweizer, *TWNT* VII, p. 1072; Minear, *op. cit.*, pp. 233ff.

[21] When Conzelmann (pp. 263f.) instead considers that the essential point is the 'temporal priority', the contrast of our interpretations is brought out sharply. The theology of existence is no longer in a position to talk seriously about the universal rule of Christ, and in addition ultimately sacrifices the primacy of Christology to a particular ecclesiology.

[22] E. Schweizer, *TWNT* VII, p. 1072.

[23] Minear, *op. cit.*, p. 229.

is answered in the light of Christology, which also could not directly be the case from the starting point of the idea of the people of God. Again, it is not enough to stress the stronger Christological alignment,[24] because the point at issue is an exclusively Christological consideration. Finally, it is evident that the Pauline conception must not be interpreted primarily from the Jewish view of the father of the race, who includes in himself the succeeding generations. Jewish Christians would have liked to find access to the body of Christ motif from this angle; but it only offered a general horizon under which the motif could find a place; its essential stress remained unrecognized. The universal sovereignty claimed by Christ and already manifesting itself in his body is not ultimately comparable with the sphere of activity of a father of the race. All this leads to the conclusion that the facts do not permit the starting point to be the theme of the people of God,[25] whose specifically Christian character is to be brought out through the motif of the body of Christ;[26] on the contrary, here completely independent conceptions supplement one another. The interests of salvation history and his own polemical intentions make the apostle cling to the pattern of Jewish-Christian ecclesiology, although it no longer corresponds at the deepest level to his theology and his work. Why, on the other hand, he gives so little space to the motif of the body of Christ, which does actually express his understanding of the church, must be discussed later.

However, it is worth while pausing for a moment at this point and remembering that the letter to the Ephesians, which is otherwise completely dominated by the specifically Pauline theologumenon, seems to reverse this development in 2.11ff. There the conversion of the Gentile Christians is depicted as incorporation in the Jewish-Christian people of God, and the body of Christ is correspondingly interpreted as a union of Christians, both Jews and Gentiles, i.e., a union of two nations. The text presents complicated problems.[27] We shall pick out only one of these: the fact, namely, that here the two theologumena we are considering compete with one another. This is a highly remarkable fact in the case of a writer who was undoubtedly a disciple of Paul's, and we must ask the reason. I can find only one satisfactory explanation: at the time when the letter was written,

<hr>

[24] *Ibid.*, pp. 229f.
[25] Contrary to Oepke, *TLZ* 79, 1954, cols. 363f. as well as Schnackenburg, *op. cit.*, pp. 142, 150f.
[26] Contrary to Dahl's view, *op. cit.*, p. 228.
[27] Cf. my meditation in *Exegetische Versuche und Besinnungen* I, 1960, pp. 280–3.

what Paul considered in Rom. 11.17ff. as a threatening possibility
had already happened. The Gentile Christians were pushing the
Jewish Christians aside. The writer therefore reminds them (as the
apostle himself had already done from time to time) of the Jewish
Christians' priority in salvation history. Consequently the continuity
with Israel as the people of God is energetically stressed. This is a
further confirmation of the fact that every definition of the church
relates to a concrete situation and must be interpreted in that light.
But every definition also contains its own particular danger if it is
transferred into absolute terms, i.e., if it is removed from its historical
situation and used in a timeless sense. The way in which the motif of
the body of Christ is used in Ephesians discloses the danger of this
particular ecclesiological aspect. The mythological world of ideas
from which it derives tempts one to forget the concrete history of the
church and to replace it by metaphysics. Consequently here the Christian community does not merely extend throughout the world but,
with its members, simultaneously rises into the heavenly places of
which the opening of the letter already speaks. The shift from the
Pauline conception, which allowed the Lord alone to be exalted and
made the Spirit the medium of his presence in the church, must be
critically noted; it is the first sign of a misinterpretation which has
endured to the present day.

3. Ecclesiological metaphysics are read even into the Pauline
statements in a highly dangerous way. Thus the church as the body of
Christ is associated with the crucified body of Jesus;[28] and by declaring that the latter is the prolepsis of the body of Christ in the
church,[29] the two are made to coincide;[30] or the crucified body may
even 'in its continuing efficacy' be identified with the body of the
exalted Christ and called the 'sphere of the church'.[31] I must admit
that I am unable even to associate any clear concept with specula-
tions of this kind, if they are intended to be more than highly over-
charged metaphors. They are apparently occasioned by what the
apostle has to say about the sacraments, especially in I Cor. 10.16f.
Just as baptism makes the believer a member of Christ, so, according
to this latter passage, the eucharistic element allows us to participate

[28] E. Percy, *op. cit.*, pp. 28ff., 44.
[29] H. Schlier, 'Die Einheit der Kirche' (*Die Zeit der Kirche*, 1958, pp. 287–99),
p. 288ff.
[30] L. Cerfaux, *The Church in the Theology of St Paul*, 1959, pp. 236f. and passim.
[31] E. Schweizer, *TWNT* VII, pp. 1066, 1070; see E. Güttgemanns' criticism in
Der leidende Apostel und sein Herr, 1966, pp. 252ff.

in the body of the crucified Christ in such a way that we manifest and lay hold of our membership of Christ's body in the church afresh. It is not infrequent for the whole conception of the church as the body of Christ to be deduced from these comments on the sacraments.[32] In this way the concept can be explained as a genuinely Christian creation, detachable from the religio-historical context of the heavenly, world-embracing *anthropos*.[33]

Within the framework of a lecture it is impossible to enter into an exegetical examination of the details which are marshalled in support here.[34] I must confine myself to setting up counter-theses and to drawing attention to the systematic consequences of the position I have just indicated. First, it may be emphatically maintained that I Cor. 10.16f. above all demands a differentiation based on a critical analysis of the tradition. The description of the eucharistic element as the body of Christ was apparently already in existence liturgically before Paul. It is highly unlikely that it originally had anything to do with the body of Christ as an ecclesiological formula. It rather corresponds to the other expression, about partaking in the blood of Jesus, and merely presupposes the mystery-like notion that the two sacraments incorporate the believer in Jesus' death. The connection of this view with the ecclesiological one about the church as the body of Christ is created by the apostle, by means of a comparison. He is concerned with the unity of the Christian community. Those who eat of the same bread become physically united. Now comes the decisive leap: this physical union through the common bread and participation in the eucharistic element (traditionally called the body of Christ) brings about a renewed and confirmed incorporation in the church in its character as the body of Christ. This is a leap not merely from one formula to another, but at the same time from the 'mystery' concept that the believer is incorporated in Jesus' death to the other idea that he is incorporated in the body of the exalted Lord. The difference lies in the fact that the church as the body of Christ is the earthly body of the risen and exalted Lord – i.e., it is not the crucified

---

[32] Wikenhauser, *op. cit.*, pp. 112ff. J. A. T. Robinson, *The Body*, 1952, pp. 47f.; Conzelmann, *op. cit.*, pp. 261f.; Schnackenburg, *op. cit.*, p. 170, calls the church an extension of the crucified body.

[33] A. E. J. Rawlinson, 'Corpus Christi', in Bell/Deissmann, *Mysterium Christi*, 1931, pp. 275–96; J. A. T. Robinson, *op. cit.*, pp. 56f.; J. Reuss, 'Die Kirche als "Leib Christi" und die Herkunft dieser Vorstellung bei dem Apostel Paulus', *BZ*, NF 1958, pp. 103–27, especially pp. 108, 118.

[34] Cf. my article, 'The Pauline Doctrine of the Lord's Supper', in *Essays on New Testament Themes*, 1960, pp. 108–35.

body, which was Jesus' alone and in which no one can be incorporated. If this distinction is overlooked and if everything is transferred to the same level, one arrives at an abstruse result from which only a mystical devotion to the Passion would fail to shrink. It is forgotten here that according to Paul the church as the body of Christ is created and held together by the spirit of Christ; i.e., it has only been in existence since Easter and Whitsun.

But the anthropos myth cannot and ought not to be passed by either. According to both the apostle and his followers, the statement about being in Christ runs parallel to the other statement about incorporation in his body. The two themes are united when in Gal. 3.27f., for example, the writer talks about putting on Christ and the solidarity to be won in that way. The sacramental context does not exclude the anthropos myth but pre-supposes it. The motif of the church as the body of Christ cannot be isolated from the characteristic Pauline Christology of the second Adam. Otherwise the idea of the people of God takes on an ascendancy which it does not deserve and which allows room only for the idea of the father of the race and a community incorporated in him. But this is to truncate the universality of the church in favour of the view of an ecclesiological group or eschatological nation; and it also overshadows the decisive and permanent primacy of Christology over ecclesiology. A father of the race is in the first place necessarily the initiator of the generations which follow him; and his efficacy will lie primarily in his historical influence, i.e., it will be caught up in the ecclesiological tradition. This then expresses itself – not without logical consistency – in the tendency to interpret Jesus' crucified body docetically, as being no longer truly earthly and perishable but the prefiguration of the body of Christ in the church; secondly, the spirit no longer constitutes the church but only sustains, fosters and nourishes it; and thirdly, the church is inevitably involved in the fundamental saving event, whether as the bride of Christ, the mother of the faithful, or whatever it may be.[35] Christology and ecclesiology merge into one another: the church becomes the prolongation[36] and representative of her Lord, in whom she integrates herself, though as her author and head.[37]

---

[35] Cf. Schlier on this point, *Einheit*, pp. 288ff. (on Eph. 2.11ff. and then transferred to Paul).

[36] J. A. T. Robinson, *op. cit.*, p. 49ff.; T. W. Manson, *On Paul and John*, 1963, p. 67.

[37] Credit is due to Bonnard (in the article cited on p. 105, n. 12) for his opposition to this view. Conzelmann (p. 263) has the same concern.

Contrary to this view, it must be emphatically stated that according to Paul it is the risen Lord alone who creates for himself his earthly body, just as it is he and he alone who confers the spirit, grants the sacraments and, through spirit and sacraments, incorporates believers in his body. The church is the place of his presence only in so far as the spirit remains the medium of that presence. This idea is so important for the apostle that, unlike the Deutero-Pauline writers, he does not call Christ the head of the body. He had good reason to avoid doing so, since the letters to the Colossians and Ephesians divide Christ from his body, even in space. It is in this way that they thus characterize him as the enthroned Lord, to whom the rule of the world is due, thus bringing out the Pauline concern, i.e., the rule of Christ over his church as well. That rule is present only where there is dependence on him and obedience to him. The church is in no way independent. That is exactly the point Paul wants to make when he clings to the assertion that the spirit is the founder of the body and holds it together. If the crucified body already proleptically depicts the body of the church, then the latter exists, *idealiter* or *realiter*, before the spirit and the enthronement of Christ. That inevitably alters the whole of the apostle's ecclesiology and gives the church an importance in his theology which is not its due, as is already indicated by the sparseness of the evidence in his epistles for the motif of the body of Christ.

It is only when once this is clear that we may and must ask whether the body of Christ in the form of the church then has nothing to do with Jesus' crucified body. That this cannot be what Paul means is clear from his comments on the sacraments. Christians, above all, are drawn into Jesus' death – through the eucharistic gift according to I Cor. 10.16f.; through baptism according to Rom. 6.3ff; through their missionary activity according to II Cor. 4.10f. The church is not proleptically prefigured in the crucified body; it is subsequently made a partaker in the event of the cross[38] by the one who is risen (whose earthly body it represents after his exaltation) in such a way that, moulded into the likeness of the one who was crucified, like him it manifests life *sub contrario* as God's work in the act of dying physically. At the same time the church's difference from its Lord is also preserved in this way: his death has not led the church to exaltation and a transcending of itself. Christ's exaltation rather makes the church the means whereby his earthly fate cannot be forgotten. Pauline

[38] I hope that I am in agreement with Güttgemanns (pp. 259f.) here.

ecclesiology is part of the apostle's theology of the cross and to that degree can only be understood in the light of his Christology.

4. We must now go on to consider whether and how far the theme of the body of Christ takes its bearings from Paul's anthropological concept of the body. Since the apostle uses the same expression on both occasions (Rom. 12.4f.; I Cor. 12.14ff.), comparing the body of Christ with the human body and finally, with the greatest emphasis, describing the bodies of Christians as 'members' of Christ, a correlation is unmistakably implied.[39] In that case, the question of what Paul understood anthropologically by body and corporeality is bound to be of some importance for our theme.[40] It is generally assumed as a matter of course that 'body' is primarily a term describing the human 'self' as person. I would urge against this that what is meant is man as a non-isolable existence, i.e., in his need and real capacity for communication as friend or foe – man as a being who finds himself in and is aware of an already existing world, and is conscious of his dependency on certain forces and powers. Thus far, this earthly existence of ours is always characterized by membership and participation. That forms the existential presupposition for the fact that we as believers can be incorporated into the kingdom of Christ, and that not only for ourselves, let alone merely as soul or in our inner lives, but with all our potential and actual relationships to our world. Where that happens, Christ on the other hand reveals himself in this very process as the one who is destined as future cosmocrator and today already secretly exerts this function everywhere through his earthly body. He fills the world with his promise and his claim, under the sign of the cross and in the power of his resurrection. He takes possession of the world by calling men to his service, in their creatureliness and involvement with that world, with all their capacities, without distinction of sex, party, nation, race, religious tradition, education or talent. He, the exalted one, can only come to everyone on earth if our bodies become members of his kingdom. For he has these members everywhere, since he creates believers in every station of life and every camp. What he wants is the world, and that is only

[39] Cf., for example, Robinson, *op. cit.*, pp. 47f.; E. Schweizer, *TWNT* VII, p. 1071; Neugebauer, *op. cit.*, pp. 97f. On the other hand, for Güttgemanns, *op. cit.*, p. 276, 'body' is a 'purely anthropological structural concept', which according to p. 261 must not be transferred to the Christological level.

[40] The question has surely never been put more forcibly than by A. Schweitzer, *The Mysticism of Paul the Apostle*, 1931, p. 116, where he speaks of a riddle unparalleled in the whole of mystical literature.

possible if he wants our bodies. We are denying him the world whenever we think that we have to give him less or more than our bodies.[41]
Our bodies are the part of the world which he claims, the only part
which we are capable of giving and with which according to I Cor.
6.20 we have to glorify God.

But that is only one side of the facts we are considering. By
incorporating our earthly bodies in his kingdom, Christ at the same
time shows that the sphere of his earthly kingdom is a body. Christ
communicates with his people – and beyond them with the world as
well – through sacrament, Word and faith. As the sphere of this
communication the church is the earthly body of the risen Lord. Paul
was not particularly fortunate in his attempts to organize the
communities he had gathered, which detracted from his work considerably. Consequently it was not without reason that the Pastoral
Epistles saw in this their most important task. The body of Christ
which the apostle had before his eyes included the individual and
filled the world. But a firm internal order could not be guaranteed.
Paul strove for this all his life, and his letters were apparently in part
also preserved because people found directions for a congregational
order in them. He had as little enduring success here as he had with
his characteristic theology. But we must not therefore conclude that
he did not think that the demonstrable nature of the church was of
much consequence. We still have to consider why he deals with the
theme of the church relatively seldom in the letters which have come
down to us. He concerned himself all the more frequently, however,
with the criteria of the Christian condition and the right proclamation. He undoubtedly did this not only – and probably not even
primarily – in order that faith might arrive at consciousness of itself.
He wanted to see the earthly incarnation of Christ emerging in the
world itself and appealed to every individual Christian to make this
possible. Wherever Christians prove themselves as such, they are for
Paul manifesting the body of Christ, which is accordingly represented
by every individual congregation.[42] Thus the slogan about the un-
worldliness of the believer is highly dangerous, although it certainly
has its particular meaning. It is the apostle's constant concern that
faith should not remain unworldly, because Christ wants his rule to
be documented in the world. According to Paul it is precisely in
physical things that spiritual reality must show itself, just as true

[41] Cf. Güttgemanns, *op. cit.*, p. 231.
[42] E.g. Wikenhauser, *op. cit.*, p. 8.

worship today finds its expression in a Christian's everyday life, and the heavenly sacrifice consists of the earthly surrender of our bodies to Christ's service.

5. Up to now we have only considered certain individual aspects, as a preparation for a consideration of our theme as a whole. We must now pass to this overall view, first of all with a critical observation. It is noticeable that, unlike many of his interpreters, the apostle did not talk about the body of the church. Otherwise it would be clear that here he was using a purely metaphorical figure of speech, i.e., that the basis is a mere comparison of statements about the body of Christ. It is the religio-historical, historical and theological problem of our motif that it is not talking about the body of a collective (i.e., the body of the messianic community) but the body of an individual, namely Christ.[43] The starting point is not a plurality from which the eye is directed towards the unity which holds it together, Christ therefore being understood as the inner unity of his members.[44] What is stated is the exact opposite: the heavenly Christ has a body which fills and embraces the earth. This body is then identified with the church, after which finally, in a last step, the relationship of the members of this body is described (in a comparison stemming from the idea of an organism) as mutual and general solidarity.[45]

We make things too easy for ourselves if we fail to notice that here, as in other of the apostle's genitive constructions, the stress lies on the genitive itself. We must hold fast to the fact, even if it sounds exaggerated, that we, since we have a part in Christ, become members of the church and not the reverse: we do not partake in Christ because we are members of the church. Here the irreversibility of the order is of vital importance. Christ is there before the church and he is not absorbed into that church.[46] As creator and judge, he remains the

[43] Contrary to Meuzelaar's basic thesis; but cf. also Neugebauer, *op. cit.*, p.98 and, it would seem, T. W. Manson, *On Paul and John*, 1963, p.69. J. A. T. Robinson brings out the problem sharply, *op. cit.*, pp.58ff.

[44] This danger is still not avoided when Robinson (p.51) talks about 'not . . . a supra-personal collective, but . . . a specific personal organism'. Cerfaux (*op. cit.*, p.228) can say unreservedly: '. . . the life of Christ, as the spring from which the Christian life and the churches flow, leads to the unity of the Christian world.'

[45] R. Bultmann, *Theology* I, p.310; E. Schweizer, *TLZ* 86, 1961, cols. 173f., seems inclined to reverse the order.

[46] It is therefore impossible to accept either Nygren's statement (p.22): 'The church is Christ as he is present among us after his resurrection'; or H. Schlier's: 'Christ's body is the body of those who believe in him. The body of those who believe in him is the body of Christ' ('Zu den Namen der Kirche in den Paulinischen Briefen', *Besinnung auf das Neue Testament*, 1964, p.303).

counterpart of his members. The ideas of organism or corporate personality are incapable of expressing this; it was necessary for the motif of the body of Christ to be linked up with the theme of the eschatological Adam. There is wide agreement today[47] that Pauline ecclesiology is basically Christology. But this statement can be interpreted in different ways. The prevailing ecumenical trend undoubtedly means that the statement is used as evidence for the glory of the church: it participates in the being of its exalted Lord and is his earthly projection, being the prolongation of the act of incarnation. As against this, it is impossible to stress too strongly that the tendency of Paul's argument lies in the reverse direction: the body is destined for service and only participates in the glory of the exalted Lord in so far as it remains his instrument in earthly lowliness. For it is this which gives the church its unique character and eschatological significance. The mystery religions also promise participation in the glory of the cultic God. The whole context of Rom. 12.3ff. and I Cor. 12.12ff. is clearly directed against an enthusiastic *theologia gloriae*. Nor can those who already participate in heavenly glory pervade the world; they can only separate themselves from it. The world-wide church about which Paul talks can only be achieved when it remains part of the world's everyday life and does not fly from the lowliness which was the mark of its Lord before his resurrection.

To put it somewhat too epigrammatically, the apostle is not interested in the church *per se* and as a religious group. He is only interested in it in so far as it is the means whereby Christ reveals himself on earth and becomes incarnate in the world through his Spirit. The human body is the necessity and reality of existential communication; in the same way, the church appears as the possibility and reality of communication between the risen Christ and our world, and hence is called his body. It is the sphere in which and through which Christ proves himself *Kyrios* on earth after his exaltation. It is the body of Christ as his present sphere of sovereignty,[48] in which he deals with the world through Word, sacrament and the sending forth of Christians, and in which he finds obedience even before his parousia.

6. That is the reason why the motif of the body of Christ in Paul

[47] Wikenhauser, *op. cit.*, p.89; Percy, *op. cit.*, p.45; Best, *op. cit.*, p.191ff.; Minear, *op. cit.*, p.208.

[48] G. Bornkamm, *Paulus*, 1969, p.201; in contrast Manson, *op. cit.*, p.80: 'The church is just the society wherein the love of Christ is the law.'

only crops up in paraenetic contexts. If we look at the letters to the Colossians and Ephesians, this can no longer appear either a matter of course or a matter of chance. There the doxological way of speaking about the body of Christ is dominant, a mode of expression which ought, in fact, to precede the paraenetical one, both factually and logically. Here lies a decisive difference between the genuinely Pauline and the Deutero-Pauline letters. It may be objected that the paraenetic argument necessarily presupposes that Paul developed our theme theologically and dogmatically in his preaching. The objection is incontrovertible. But it is not, of course, open to proof. It certainly cannot be called firmly established. For in the extant letters the subjects of the spirit and faith, justification and law, discipleship and suffering, worship and proclamation, and many more, are, after all, thematically dealt with. It is difficult to see why the *topos* of the church particularly should get such short shrift. Of course Paul is always presupposing congregations such as the ones he so unwearyingly founded himself and addresses in his letters. But he left it to his successors and our contemporary interpreters to write a theology of the church. This noticeable fact is generally overlooked. It becomes understandable when one realizes that the body of Christ has a functional meaning for the apostle. Everything that is important in his ecclesiology then expresses itself in the relation of Christology to the spirit, word, service, faith and sacrament and to the concrete state of affairs in the churches. Thus paraenesis remains the proper place for an explicit discussion on the theme of the church. Unlike the writers to the Colossians and Ephesians, and determined by paraenetic considerations, Paul pursues his argument largely through an immediate acceptance of the idea of organism and in the form of a comparison. The important thing is that existence in the body of Christ is lived and realized. That can be made clear from the anthropological aspect if the solidarity of the members is the most important concern of this paraenesis.

Why is this solidarity so strongly stressed? When he talks about the body of Christ, Paul is dealing with the problems presented by largely enthusiastic congregations. Unlike today, the point is not to rouse 'the laity' to activity. Rather, the multiplicity of gifts, possibilities and demonstrations is threatening to break up the unity of the church. The task of the paraenesis is hence to give the theological reason for the unity in the midst of multiplicity, to put that unity into practical effect and then to preserve it. The watchword is solidarity, not uniformity. Paul finds it important for the church to remain polyform. Only in this way can it pervade the world, since the world's everyday reality is not to be conformistic. It is impossible to cope with the everyday life of the world if one is out for uniformity. Uniformity is petrified solidarity. People who are the same have nothing to say to one another and cannot help one another. They remain introverts and cannot do justice to the constantly differing situations of life, a changing environment or people in their varying individualities. The necessity and blessing of Christian liberty as the state of being in the presence of Christ is not to give everyone the same thing but to give and allow everyone what is his. This is in accordance with the demand for everyone to be in his own place a member and reflection of his Lord, where what is at issue is the world-wide sovereignty of Jesus. Consequently the ecclesiology which is stamped by the motif of the body of Christ must radically maintain and effect the priesthood of all believers. The fact that for a long time people were only capable of deducing purely hierarchical structures from this ecclesiology is grotesque, but characteristic of the misunderstanding of Pauline theology in general. It is only the priesthood of all believers which manifests the reality of the body of Christ as his sovereignty with its universal claim.

But does not a view of this kind inevitably lead to the chaos of religious anarchy? The apostle's letters show how legitimate a question this is. For Paul had in fact to fight against religious anarchy all his life. From what angle did he try to meet this danger? Of course everything with which he combated disorder must be taken into account. But this does not bring us to the centre of his teaching and activity. That centre lies in the Christological aspect of his ecclesiology, which is the starting point for the link between promise and demand. In a sentence – every Christian in his own place, in his particular situation, with his specific capacities and weaknesses, may and must be a 'place holder' for Christ until death. This does not mean being a substitute, because no one can be a substitute for Christ or even represent him. But the place where we stand is to be kept open for him, and this is the case wherever the spirit makes us obedient and prepared for the waiting of hope, the service of love, the joy of faith. If everyone does this in his own particular place, solidarity is born, i.e., the unity of those who are different which through their belonging to the same Lord, allows the strains otherwise existing between them to be endured and made fruitful for the whole and the world around them. Thus is expressed in the midst of the world the rule of him who creates a new world, the one body out of many members.

7. A glance forward may end our account. In the letter to the Ephesians we find a variation of our motif, which shows a changed perspective. The idea of the people of God supplements the concept of the body of Christ, giving it historical depth. Instead of the spirit which rules the body, talk is here of the head which holds the body together. The mythological language is intensified, whereas the anthropological comparison retreats into the background. Paraenesis is now embedded in doxology. The theme of the church moves into the centre and takes on independent life (as 5.25ff. shows particularly clearly) even as against Christology, although the motif of the body of Christ still remains dominant.

This shift resulted from a different historical situation in the church. World-wide mission had assumed proportions which made a total ecclesiastical consciousness necessary. The beginnings now belonged to the more distant past and thus the problem of continuity with those beginnings made itself felt more strongly than before. The unity of a church made up of Jewish and Gentile Christians lost its balance in favour of the latter. The attacks of enthusiasm were a threat as well. Unity was shielded by the setting up of the *notae ecclesiae*. The voice of prophecy largely gave way to the voice of Christian tradition, so that even ethics had to take fresh bearings. The dimensions and solution of all these problems was sought for in the question of the nature of the true church. The faithfulness of his followers preserved the Pauline *Leitmotif* of the body of Christ. But we can perceive clearly that it is impossible to bathe in the same river twice, even if one enters it at the same point. There is no such thing as an unchangeable ecclesiology.

To put it as a thesis: contrary to the general view,[49] it must be contended that the thematic treatment of the concept of the church cannot be called Pauline. Wherever ecclesiology moves into the foreground, however justifiable the reasons may be, Christology will lose its decisive importance, even if it does so by becoming integrated, in some form or other, in the doctrine of the church, instead of remain-

---

[49] Cf., for example, T. W. Manson, *op. cit.*, p. 78; Robinson, *op. cit.*, pp. 65f.; above all V. Warnach, 'Kirche und Kosmos' (*Eukainia, Ges. Arbeiten zum 800 jährigen Weihegedächtnis der Abteikirche Maria Laach*, ed. by H. Edmonds, 1956), pp. 17 f.–205.

ing the church's indispensable touchstone. That very thing has already happened in the letter to the Ephesians. Here, as the opening hymn already brings out, the church has become the central eschatological event. What Paul preached in Christological terms has now been turned into the function of ecclesiology – namely, the unity of the world in the *pax Christi*. The function of Christology in the letter to the Ephesians consists in caring for the orderly growth of the church. The problem of church and world does not replace the question of the relation of Christ to the world, but it embraces it. We ought to be concerned as to the necessity and justifiability of this theological shift. Even if the change was inevitable historically, we cannot avoid the decision whether it was a change which we must ratify or one which we have to reverse.

VI

THE CRY FOR LIBERTY IN THE
WORSHIP OF THE CHURCH

The boldness of the train of thought in Romans 8 is constantly surprising, even to the person who expects this of Paul from the outset. The question under discussion is what the Holy Spirit means for the church and the Christian life; the pre-Pauline view is taken up, but modified by new aspects and relations. Although I only propose to interpret two verses, 26 and 27, it may be useful for us to remind ourselves of their context.

I. THE CHARACTER OF PAULINE PNEUMATOLOGY

Experience of the spirit is the real hall-mark of post-Easter Christianity. It was also the moving force which allowed Jewish Christianity to turn to the Gentiles and at the same time the strongest incentive for those Gentiles who attached themselves to the Christian community. It made possible the formation of purely, or predominantly, Gentile-Christian congregations, which were nevertheless able to view themselves as being in continuity with Jewish Christianity. All this was possible because the spirit represented the eschatological gift *per se*, and post-Easter Christianity constituted itself the community of the end-time. This is classically formulated in Acts 2.17 in the already interpreted words of Joel 3: 'In the last days it shall be, God declares, that I will pour out my spirit upon all flesh.' Since Gunkel made his famous debut in 1888 with a study on the operations of the Holy Spirit, we know that the whole of primitive Christianity viewed *pneuma* as the power of ecstasy and miracle. According to Gunkel, Paul then gave this view ethical depth. Although Gunkel

was not entirely wrong in certain respects, we are bound to characterize these facts differently and differentiate them more sharply today.
We have a better overall view of the development of early Christian
pneumatology and now understand that it was the very eschatological
understanding of the spirit which first allowed earthly manifestations
of supernatural power and wisdom to be stressed. In the same way,
alterations in eschatology also determine the further development of
the doctrine of the spirit, which is particularly concerned to associate
the *pneuma* more closely with the context of soteriology. Ecstatic
practices tend to split a community rather than to further it. This
danger is only prevented if such ecstatic practices can be included
under a wider and governing viewpoint without, of course, the
manifestations of the heavenly world (which were so important to
primitive Christianity) being allowed to be pushed aside or robbed
of their character. The theological and practical conquest of enthusiasm was the first test to which the young church was exposed, and
nothing less than its whole existence and future depended on its
mastery of this problem.

Admittedly this task could not be taken up everywhere simultaneously and in the same way; the organization of the different
congregations was not sufficiently developed for that, and practical
differences were bound to be a serious hindrance. It is therefore not
by chance that the path chosen is marked by tentative attempts,
varying models and severe set-backs. We shall view it with admira-
tion notwithstanding, because both insight into what was necessary on
any given occasion and subsequent improvisation (it might be
through recourse to traditions preserved elsewhere or through the
trying out of new conceptions) was both called for and practised.
Certain approaches which were capable of development became
evident early on. Ecstatic and miraculous powers counted as being a
gift to the whole congregation. That baptism conferred the spirit on
everyone who was received into the church was never in dispute.
Finally, people saw the spirit revealed in the worship of the congregation in all sorts of forms of proclamation, eucharist and liturgy. The
orientation of the spirit towards the congregation was the most
immediate way of confining the dangers of ecstatic manifestations,
even in the sphere of enthusiastic Christianity. The church appears as
the earthly manifestation of the transcendent world and hence, also,
as the sole sphere of the spirit's operations. In this view Paul and Luke,
for example, are entirely at one, since it determines Hellenistic

Christianity as a whole. At the same time, the stress is different in the two writers. For Paul, the ecclesiastical alignment, which for Luke ultimately makes the spirit the moving force of salvation history, does not supply the dominant. In Paul, the ruling factor is the Christological qualification of the spirit, which on the other hand noticeably recedes in Luke – that Christological qualification which is the essential legitimation of the ecclesiological tie. Thus it is not by chance that Paul, unlike Luke, does not yet develop in institutional form the approach which suggests that the holders of the charismata are in a special sense the bearers of the spirit in the church, so that spirit and office are more closely linked. The spirit holds sway in the church and the Christian life because, and in so far as, it constitutes, as the spirit of Christ, the body of Christ and its members. In this way Paul also preserved the older Jewish-Christian view, which allowed prophets to speak in the name of the exalted Christ and as his mouthpiece, therefore relating the spirit and the word of Christ to one another, a view which is later found only in the Fourth Gospel. The ecclesiastical domestication of the spirit is more strongly resisted by these means because the confrontation of Christ with the church and his precedence over it can be brought out more sharply. On the other hand, the Pauline concept of the spirit is more open to the danger of charismaticism. Although miracles and ecstatic manifestations take up the greatest space in his writings, Luke is very much less exposed to the threat of enthusiasm, just because the ecclesiological connection of the spirit cannot be constantly paralysed by its Christological qualification.

Paul was not blind to the danger which inevitably set in with the parallelism and practical identity of 'in the spirit' and 'in Christ'; he was therefore forced to incorporate further safeguards against it. There are, if I am right, three of these safeguards: (1) He so interpreted the spirit as the power of the risen Christ that it had to be proved daily in the individual Christian's life as the power of the *nova oboedientia*. (2) Starting from the identity of the risen and the crucified Christ, he allowed the spirit to be the power of standing fast in temptation and suffering. (3) Like the Jewish Christians, he understood the spirit as an 'earnest' and hence placed pneumatology as well as Christology and anthropology under the eschatological proviso.

2. ON THE CONTEXT OF ROMANS 8.26–27

It is only against this background that we can understand the way in which our passage fits into its context. All the criteria of a true experience of the spirit which have been mentioned above turn up here. The revelation of the spirit cannot be separated from the reality of the sufferings of Christ. Its goal is that eschatological sonship which unites the characteristics of liberty and obedience and thus leads man back to the lost *imago dei*. The two are united in a splendid apocalyptic vista: the present counts as the era of the eschatological birth-pangs, in which the liberty of the children of God takes form and emerges, at first assailed, ultimately in perfection. In this way Paul offers his own variation on the first beatitude. For him, therefore, what appears to the Hellenistic enthusiasts as irreconcilable can coincide, namely possession of the spirit and yet being in a state of waiting. Here we must not overlook the fact that Paul for his part also starts from the presuppositions of Hellenistic enthusiasm. For the theme of the section 8.1–11 is formulated in ch. 9: to be a Christian means to have the spirit. The exposition in chs. 12 to 16 is even more pointed, and states that the condition of sonship is manifested and actuated by the spirit and is differentiated from slavery by that very thing.

The apostle's anti-Jewish polemic must not be primarily interpreted from the angle of the internal Jewish-Christian conflict. Paul, the Jewish Christian, came into conflict with those who belonged to the Palestinian tradition because he had become the champion of the enthusiastic Hellenistic churches which were growing up free of the Law. But his greatness lies in the fact that he did not throw himself without reservation into the arms of the new ideas which he had helped to produce and that he countered their excesses by means of his Jewish-Christian heritage. That is nowhere more evident than when he opposes to the 'realized eschatology' of the Hellenists, who were proud of their possession of the spirit, the spirit as the pledge and power of hope. In so doing he was by no means breaking new ground. It was in exactly this way that the Jewish-Christian community had already understood the spirit when they allowed it to proclaim, and in a representative sense to anticipate, the future *basileia*. The only new thing is the thematic unfolding of what was already implicit in the formula about the 'spirit of hope', in contrast to a sacramentally based insistence on the possession of the spirit. The extraordinary boldness with which Paul polemically heightens traditional views shows itself particularly in his characterization of hope in our text. The object of hope is the revelation of the glorious liberty of the children of God. It is noteworthy that the apostle describes the parousia, not as the manifestation of Christ but as the manifestation of Christians. The nearest parallel would seem to be II Peter 1.11, according to which the entry of believers into the *basileia* forms the close of world history. What is really parallel in the two cases is admittedly only hope's anthropological alignment. For whereas II Peter sees salvation in the fact that the saints are finally taken out of the world, Paul sees it in the world's realization, through the children of God, that salvation is eschatological liberty.

When once the matter is so formulated, it becomes clear why Paul here argues anthropologically in this way. For it is not enough simply to explain this on the grounds of the importance of anthropology in Pauline theology. It is true that this really is the most important distinction between his theology and both earlier and later theological schemes. On the other hand, anthropology is only the spear-head of Pauline theology, not its central subject or its goal. Like ecclesiology, anthropology is rather the earthly projection of Christology. The struggle for the world-wide kingdom of Christ takes place in the church's missionary activity and in the preservation of the Christian community and its members. Thus far the Christian life appears as an eschatological phenomenon, 'in the spirit' and being tempted belong indissolubly together, and the result in Paul is the dialectic of 'now already' and 'not yet', of the indicative and the imperative. In our passage, anthropology moves so strangely into the centre even of the parousia, because in every Christian life it is Christ's sovereignty which is in question, sovereignty which does not realize itself in any other way than in the establishment of Christ's victory in the situation which meets us on each several occasion and in what results from that situation. The new world is the world under the insignia of the liberty of the children of God, because it is the world under the insignia of the lordship of the Son. The struggle for that world is fought as the struggle for true liberty. It is precisely that which will one day be revealed in the parousia and hence determines the course of world history, a fact concealed from the world but of which even today the church is well aware.

From this starting point the second fact which characterizes our text is to be explained as well. Here, with an emphasis hardly excelled in the New Testament, the solidarity of the Christian community with the unredeemed world is brought out. This solidarity (and that means community in the face of tension) rests in the fact that church and world are together waiting expectantly for the manifestation of the liberty of the children of God. The church does so in clear knowledge of the goal, the world on the contrary out of the deep unrest which stems from the continual experience of fixed limits, unavoidable guilt and unattained peace. The meaningless of life which thereby becomes evident is unbearable without hope. At the same time, however, hope is again prevented by the meaninglessness perceived. Thus the world is constantly in exodus, without finding the way out to salvation. On the other hand, in the Christian sense its unrest may be interpreted, as Paul suggests here, as the shadow of the hope which is granted even to the world, though not that hope's reality. To the church which lives from the promise, as the reverse side of the gospel, and is hence the bearer of a certain hope, the unrest of the world appears to be significant as a path through the world where hope is still concealed.

But what has all this to do with the spirit? Verses 26 and 27, which form the peak of the whole of the apostle's argument, answer with an astonishing thesis which we must now elucidate.

3. THE INTERCESSION OF THE SPIRIT

There is hardly anything comparable with these verses in the New Testament. The question of the right way to pray, the hearing of prayer and the certainty of that hearing are indeed thematically handled from time to time and are even more frequently touched on. But nowhere else do we find the statement that we as Christians do not know how to pray as we ought. It is therefore understandable that attempts should have been made to weaken the sentence by relating the καθὸ δεῖ to οὐκ οἴδαμεν and interpreting: we do not know sufficiently how to pray.[1] It is also a softening when one quietly makes a πῶς out of the τί, as if the point were the method of correct prayer and not its content.[2] The express question of the τί and the parallelism of κατὰ θεόν 'according to the will of God' and αθὸ κεῖ forbid

---

[1] T. Zahn, *Der Brief des Paulus an die Römer*, ³1925, p. 412; E. Kühl, *Der Brief des Paulus an die Römer*, 1913, p. 298.

[2] See, for example, M.-J. Lagrange, *Saint Paul Épitre aux Romains*, 1950, pp. 211 f.; Kühl, *op. cit.*, p. 298.

these ways of escape. Only the spirit knows and comprehends God's will. It must therefore, like the Paraclete of the Fourth Gospel, support our weakness. It does this by offering vicarious intercession for the saints. This at least would not be necessary if the ἀσθένεια which is observed of us were anything other than a real incapacity for right prayer.[3] We do not do justice to the radical nature of the statement, either, if we assume that an occasional experience of Paul's is here being translated into generalized terms.[4] Nor is it any help to point out that the history of religion shows that the ancient world had strayed into devotional crises and doubts through syncretism and enlightenment.[5] In Paul there is simply no sign of this at all, and only a few, at most, of his formulations can be so influenced. Finally, we must not, like Luther and Calvin before us, alter the problem as if the theme were the hearing of prayer.[6] It is only when all these ways out have been barred that the singularity and surprisingness of Paul's statement becomes thoroughly evident. The whole of the New Testament encourages us to pray in trust and cheerfulness. Vigorously though it resists misuse, it none the less opens the way to prayer for everything heavenly and earthly of which man has need. Prayer, intercession, thanksgiving and adoring praise are frequently heard in it to an exemplary degree. Paul nowhere shows himself to have any reservations whatsoever,[7] and it is in general the case that every prayer in the name of Jesus and prayed from a state of sonship is pleasing to God.

Contrary to the general practice,[8] it is not useful to start from what is supposed to be the fundamental element in our text, if what it says is to be understandable. For Paul does not merely say 'We do not know'. Nor does he merely contrast this with our hopes and wishes. He rather speaks quite definitely, and indeed legalistically, about the

---

[3] J. Schniewind, *Das Seufzen des Geistes, Nachgelassene Reden und Aufsätze*, 1952, pp. 81f., rightly opposes the assumption of exceptional states of *accidie*; cf. N. Q. Hamilton, 'The Holy Spirit and Eschatology in Paul', *SJT Occasional Papers* 6, 1967, p. 36; for another view see, for example, A. Dietzel, 'Beten im Geist', *ThZ* 13, 1957, p. 28.

[4] E.g. H. Greeven, *Gebet und Eschatologie im Neuen Testament*, 1931, p. 153.

[5] G. Harder, *Paulus und das Gebet*, 1936, pp. 130–62.

[6] This has continued to have influence down to, for example, O. Michel, *Der Brief an die Römer*, [12]1963, p. 207.

[7] This is the view also taken by Greeven, *op. cit.*, p. 153; Harder, *op. cit.*, p. 162.

[8] Characteristically in W. Bieder, 'Gebetswirklichkeit und Gebetsmöglichkeit bei Paulus', *ThZ* 4, 1948, p. 31; A. Nygren, *Commentary on Romans*, 1952, pp. 329ff.; O. Bauernfeind, *RGG*[3] II, col. 1219.

spirit's intercession,[9] which manifests itself on earth in the στεναγμοὶ ἀλάλητοι of believers.[10] The best course would seem to be to start from this latter fact, because it is from there that the preceding statement that we do not know what right prayer is, which sounds so fundamental, is illuminated and confirmed. The στεναγμοὶ ἀλάλητοι with their peculiar character show that even Christians do not know by virtue of their humanity what it is fitting to pray for and what God really wants of us. Otherwise these signs would not exist – nor would there be any reason for their existence. Our not knowing is for Paul both the real ground and the logical consequence of the actual happening he has in mind. That is why it is not simply stated by him in general terms, but deduced from this happening. Only in the light of that happening can a statement such as we have here be deduced, a statement which is unique in the New Testament and which by no means represents the apostle's general attitude. If that is the case, however, light falls on the event itself as well. The sighs must be highly noticeable phenomena, which as such attract our attention. This means, further, that what is in question here is not primarily, and perhaps not at all, practices of private prayer, which are not in general open to observation and cause no stir. The place of these sighs must rather be viewed as the church's assembly for worship.[11]

For the same reason, it is no help to think of the wordless sighs[12] which are familiar from contemporary devotional practice. As Schniewind rightly says,[13] 'prayer in Paul is never wordless'. Thus Paul would no doubt view this wordless sighing as a merely human possibility, whereas what he finds important is the phenomenon

[9] This idea is reinstated by Schniewind, *op. cit.*, pp. 83, 92, and, for example, by J. Murray, *The Epistle to the Romans*, 1960, pp. 311f.; on the theme of intercession cf. the unpublished Göttingen dissertation by R. Zorn, *Die Fürbitte im Spätjudentum und im Neuen Testament*, 1957. Curiously enough, however, the facts are held not to apply to our particular passage because only Christ and not the spirit is intercessor, and intercession can only take place in heaven, not on earth in the prayer of the spirit (p. 117). The terminological use of ὑπερεντυγχάνειν, however, tells against this view.

[10] For the relation of the 'sighs too deep for words' to the intercession of the spirit, see below.

[11] The view already taken by Ed. Frhr. v.d. Goltz, *Das Gebet in der ältesten Christenheit*, 1901, p. 112; P. Althaus, *Der Brief an die Römer*, [9]1959, p. 84; it is rejected by G. Delling, *Der Gottesdienst im Neuen Testament*, 1952, pp. 32, 24; Michel, *op. cit.*, p. 208.

[12] Contrary to A. Schlatter, *Gottes Gerechtigkeit*, 1935, p. 279; C. H. Dodd, *The Epistle of Paul to the Romans*, 1941, p. 135; V. Taylor, *The Epistle to the Romans*, 1955, p. 55; Nygren, *op. cit.*, p. 336; Greeven, *op. cit.*, p. 153.

[13] *Op. cit.*, p. 86, 1.

brought about by the spirit; and it is a question whether he would have been able to conceive of a wordless intercession at all. After all, αὐτὸ τὸ πνεῦμα is stated with emphasis, attention being thus drawn to the spirit who is to be distinguished from the human spirit and also from the spirit of the individual Christian. The frequently recognized parallel in 8.15f., insufficiently applied hitherto, confirms this interpretation: like the acclamatory cry 'Abba'[14], the συμμαρτυρεῖν τῷ πνεύματι mentioned here undoubtedly also takes place during worship. It comes about once more through αὐτὸ τὸ πνεῦμα which, as against all the individuations of the spirit, means the power which fills the whole assembly. In ecstatic acclamations and cries of prayer, which counted in the primitive church as directly God-inspired and were binding on the church as sacred law, the spirit enters the service of worship in a way which is positively objective compared with our own spiritual experiences, and does so by no means word-lessly but with the cries of the enthusiasts. This makes the meaning of στεναγμοὶ ἀλάλητοι clearer.

Illegitimate though it is simply to identify these with the cry 'Abba', they nevertheless belong together. In both cases we are deal-ing with ecstatic expressions, and in both cases the intention is the same, i.e., the manifestation of sonship. But what does ἀλάλητος mean if it is not to be translated by 'wordless'? This can be discovered from those ἄρρητα ῥήματα which Paul experienced when he was caught up into heaven, according to II Cor. 12.4. The words that he is talking about are not unspoken but unspeakable; they are not directly reproducible and shroud mysteries in heavenly language. ἀλάλητος undoubtedly means just this, if it really refers to ecstatic prayer, which cannot be disputed in view of the whole context.[15] The phenomenon of 'praying in the spirit', not yet attested rabbinically but clearly presupposed in the Qumran hodayot,[16] appears in the New Testament in passages as different as I Cor. 14.13ff.; Eph. 6.18; Jude 20; Rev. 22.17; always in the sense that the spirit puts into man's mouth what he should pray for. Whereas, however, the non-Pauline passages, in accordance with Palestinian tradition, do not permit reason to be thereby dispensed with, Paul follows the tradition

[14] Cf. my article in RGG[3] II, col. 994.

[15] Contrary to Dietzel, op. cit., pp. 29, 32, who is only prepared to call those practices ecstatic in which man's responsibility is excluded; again wrongly, he interprets Paul in our context on the basis of Jubilees 25 and the Qumran hodayot.

[16] On this point see Billerbeck, Kommentar zum Neuen Testament aus Talmud und Midrasch, II, 1924, p. 243; Harder, op. cit., p. 167; Dietzel, op. cit., pp. 24ff.

represented by Philo in particular, according to which inspiration uses man as instrument without his will, as I Cor. 14.13ff. shows.[17] There spiritual prayer is incomprehensible in so far as it means the possibility of speaking with tongues. I Cor. 14.7–12, 22 and the value placed on the gift of tongues in Corinth shows the stir made by this charisma. I Cor. 14 and 11.5, 13 make it clear that it had its fixed place in primitive Christian worship. When once that is established, it is a natural conclusion that the 'sighs too deep for words' of our passage are also simply glossolalic utterances.[18] Although Schlatter[19] opposes this interpretation with especial vigour, his arguments are not convincing. He disputes the glossolalic character of the sighs by contrasting a wordless happening with the one which is to be interpreted (out of a wrong interpretation of ἀλάλητος); and secondly, ascribes the sighing of our text to every Christian and thus distinguishes it from the charisma of glossolalia.[20] But this is only allowable if one thinks it necessary to maintain as a principle that Christian prayer never really knows anything about God's will or what its own content ought to be. This assertion, edifying though it sounds, is simply absurd, and contradicts everything that the New Testament has otherwise to say on the subject, for it would take away from prayer its meaning and assurance. One can only be surprised that interpretation in general fails to experience the problem at a deep enough level and hence inevitably misses the solution: for what in Paul seems to be stated in such fundamental terms is not a general experience at all, but an unusually audacious conclusion which the apostle draws from highly unusual – that is to say ecstatic – happenings in primitive Christian worship, a conclusion which he uses as the basis for one of his boldest theologoumena. We are decisively blocking access to this insight if we fail to understand the sighs of our passage charismatically and in the context of glossolalic prayer. For it is only from that point of view that Paul could conceivably have said 'we do not know'. Schlatter's argument would, indeed, be untenable even apart from this. For it fails to realize that it is the situation of the worshipping

[17] Like Dietzel, Bieder (p. 40) also fails to see this distinction.

[18] Already realized by Zahn, op. cit., p.413; Hamilton, op. cit., p.36; H. Delafosse, L'Épitre aux Romains, 1926, p.58; recognized as a possibility by G. Delling, TWNT I, p.376; viewed as improbable by C. K. Barrett, A Commentary on the Epistle to the Romans, 1957, p.168; rejected by Greeven, op. cit., p.153; Michel, op. cit., p.208; E. Gaugler, Der Römerbrief, 1945, p.323; J. Huby, Saint Paul, Épitre aux Romains, 1957, p.304.

[19] Op. cit., pp.278, 280.

[20] The view also taken by Schniewind, passim.

assembly which is under consideration. And it is the assembled congregation above all which makes it clear that the charismata do not belong to individual Christians; the individual only avails himself of them representatively, whereas in the common worship of the church they are recognized as the joint possession of the whole congregation. No distinction between the charismatic and the non-charismatic can be made in connection with congregational worship.

Thus Schlatter's mistaken interpretation brings its own penalty in that he now has to go on to say that even the spirit submits to our weakness, which determines his mode and measure.[21] There is nothing about this in the text. Intercession is not adaptation to our weakness, but the representation of a plenipotentiary, which can thus assist our weakness. In exactly the same way, the ecstatic ejaculations of prayer are interpreted, at least by the Pauline congregation, as speaking with heavenly tongues, so that they can by no means be placed as a matter of course on the same level as the groanings of creation in v.22. Nor is creation subject to the ἀσθένεια but to the δουλεία τῆς φθορᾶς, which again is not the same thing. Even vv.23ff. are only a preparation for the ideas of 26f. The parallelisms of 21f., 23ff., and 26f. form concentric circles which narrow down, thereby indicating a sharpening and heightening of the thematic statement. Its peak is reached when in an unmistakably Pauline paradox the apostle describes as sighs what the church considers and praises as the manifestation of heavenly tongues and thus compares them with the sighs of the creature and the sighing for redemption from bodily temptation which is familiar to every Christian. To break up this paradox is to miss the theme of the text.

This theme, however, has a deep-lying association in Pauline theology. In order to recognize this, it is useful to start from I Cor. 14.21f. There the speaking with tongues appears as the fulfilment of the Old Testament promise that in the end-time the language of heaven will be revealed to man. But this is interpreted polemically. Whereas the Corinthians probably (as in I Cor. 13.1) understood the glossolalia as the language of the angels and hence see it as the sign of their being caught up into heaven, Paul stresses its unfruitfulness for believers and merely allows it to be a warning to unbelievers, to show them that the end-time has arrived. The same dialectic with regard to glossolalia shows itself in a different way in our text. Here, too, the idea is that speaking in 'strange tongues' is an eschatological event.

[21] *Op. cit.*, p. 278; cf. also Michel, *op. cit.*, p.208.

But now (unlike I Cor. 14) it serves as a comfort to the congregation, being an indication of the spirit's intercession with God. It is not quite clear how Paul thinks of this in concrete terms. The idea presents a problem in so far as intercession (as in Rom. 8.34) can properly only take place at the right hand of God, whereas the speaking with tongues is an earthly phenomenon. The two do not therefore necessarily coincide,[22] but according to the text they may not be torn apart, either.[23] Paul does not simply establish the existence of the earthly occurrence in order to deduce from it that we are not by ourselves capable of right prayer. He enquires at the same time about the φρόνημα of the spirit, which manifests itself on earth in so strange a way; i.e., he asks about its driving concern.[24] This concern is intercession, so that the earthly occurrence is linked with a heavenly one.[25] Since the spirit itself is acting here and the glossolalia in the prayer of believers is the medium through which it cries to God, the earthly phenomenon is the expression and reflection of a hidden heavenly one. The motif of the *oratio infusa*,[26] widespread in the history of religion, is therefore at the bottom of the apostle's remarks. But here it receives a quite specific function, which also distinguishes it from the 'praying in the spirit' familiar from the Qumran *hodayot*. For in our passage Paul's point is not that only prayer inspired by the spirit is capable of praising God rightly and bestowing on our petitions the certainty of a hearing. He undoubtedly had no intention of disputing that, and himself maintains it elsewhere. But the point here is that only the spirit knows and can express the whole urgency of our need of redemption, and that is why only he must and can intercede for us. The question is not how God can achieve his rights and how we can at the same time be certain of a hearing for our intercession. Paul's answer would, of course, be: only through the spirit. But they already knew that in Qumran, too, at least in some of the *hodayot*. When the saints there call themselves the poor, the needy, the tempted, the *extra nos* of salvation is clearly enough recognized, and there, too, 'praying in the spirit' counts as an eschatological gift which only God

---

[22] F. Godet, *Kommentar zu dem Brief an die Römer* II², 1893, p. 110, explained that the place of intercession was the heart of the believer.

[23] Cf. K. Stalder, *Das Werk des Geistes in der Heiligung bei Paulus*, 1962, p.46.

[24] This is what is meant by φρόνημα, not, as Schniewind thinks (p.83), the 'nature'.

[25] Cf. J. Murray, *op. cit.*, p.312; Bieder, *op. cit.*, p.27.

[26] We are reminded of this by F. Heiler, *Prayer*, 1932, p.239; H. Lietzmann, *An die Römer*, 1933, p.87; Dodd, *op. cit.*, p.136.

himself is able to grant. Here, however, it is not brought out that the
spirit leads us beyond our human weakness and raises us above our
own strength in order to bring us near to God. That would be the
pietist answer, which is generally extracted from our text[27] because
the Pauline paradox has not been grasped.

The apostle argues in precisely the opposite direction: even as
petitioners and in our cry to God, we do not see our own situation as is
needful and fitting. Not even Christians do so. Consequently the
spirit must come to our help, not in order to free us from earthly
things but, as our proxy, to bring our necessities before God with in-
expressible sighs. This is what takes place in the glossolalic cries. They
are not the song of the angels, as the Corinthians suppose. They are
rather the proof that believers still have to join in the choir of the
depths, which can still be heard by unredeemed creation. That
explains the difference between this passage and I Cor. 14; II Cor. 12.
5–10, in which Paul obviously tries to repress the glossolalia and other
ecstatic experiences and to make them a private matter as far as
possible;[28] whereas here, on the other hand, he allows the actual
nature of worship and the assembled congregation to be deeply
influenced by these things. The bridge between the two series of
statements is the motif touched on in II Cor. 12.5ff.: the praise of
weakness, which reaches its peak in the eschatological law of v. 9
that God's power is effective – and only effective – in weakness. Just
as the incarnation of Christ is the beginning not of man's deification
but of his humanity, so the same remains true where it is the spirit
that reigns. Far from understanding ecstasies, and particularly the
speaking with tongues, as a sign that the Christian community has
been translated with Christ into heavenly existence (the view taken
by the Corinthian enthusiasts), the apostle hears in these things the
groans of those who, though called to liberty, still lie tempted and
dying and cry to be born again with the new creation. For it is this
that appears here as the specific work of the spirit and hence as the
hall-mark of Christian worship when it is moved by the spirit.

In his brilliant fragment *Das Seufzen des Geistes*, Schniewind rightly
asserted that 'Prayer is described in Rom. 8.26f. as it is formed from
the δικαιοσύνη θεοῦ'.[29] One might also say, meaning the same thing,

---

[27] Cf. on this point K. Prümm, *Die Botschaft des Römerbriefes*, 1960, pp. 113f.;
H. W. Schmidt, *Der Brief des Paulus an die Römer*, 1962, pp. 149f.
[28] Cf. my essay, 'Die Legitimät des Apostels', *ZNW* 41, 1942, pp. 67ff.
[29] *Op. cit.*, pp. 91ff.

that it is aligned with the first beatitude, according to which only the poor receive salvation.[30] The argument here takes place in the sphere of Paul's doctrine of justification and starts from its presuppositions; it is thus formulated in the paradoxical *sub contrario* manner which was rediscovered by the Reformers. Paul certainly does not say, *simul justus, simul peccator*. But he allows the sons of liberty to be those who die and, as those who cry for redemption, to be at one with unredeemed creation. That must not be softened into the sense that there are still weaknesses even in the inner life of the Christian.[31] Otherwise the antithesis between the weakness of man and the power of the spirit, an antithesis bridged by grace, turns into the progressive steps of a pattern of development, grace – sanctification – perfection, which breaks up the Pauline paradox. We are in danger of precisely the same thing if we extract from the text a confession of our weakness,[32] whereas Paul looks quite objectively at the facts and allows the spirit to act in a way beyond our understanding.

Our verses are linked with their context through the perspective of apocalyptic[33] and are therefore the culmination of the passage, not merely a loosely attached appendix.[34] The introduction to the section (v. 18) says that the sufferings of the present time are not worth comparing with future glory. In the counter-movement to this superscription, however, the whole world is shown (vv. 19–22) as being entangled in this suffering, which is more closely defined as the birth-pangs of the new world. Verses 23–25 explain that Christians are not excepted, either. Their very faith makes them one with unredeemed creation, in so far as faith is in its very nature hope and therefore a looking for the redemption of the body. What applies to the individual Christian in this way reveals itself in the worshipping assembly at the very point when, according to the view of Hellenistic Christianity, the power of the spirit expresses itself at its most immediate and most convincing. Even glossolalia is for Paul nothing other than the cry of the tempted for liberty. The church may under-

---

[30] This is practically speaking the starting point of Karl Barth's argument in *The Epistle to the Romans*, 1933, p. 317; cf. E. Gaugler, *Der Brief an die Römer* (Prophezei) I, 1945, p. 314. (Note added in proof: his essay 'Der Geist und das Gebet der schwachen Gemeinde' *IKZ* 51, 1961, pp. 67–94, reached me too late to be used here; it circles round this paradox and hence touches nearly on my account.)

[31] Contrary to Nygren, *op. cit.*, pp. 336ff.

[32] Bieder, *op. cit.*, p. 31; Michel, *op. cit.*, p. 208.

[33] Schniewind, *op. cit.*, p. 96; Hamilton, *op. cit.*, p. 36.

[34] Contrary to Fuchs' view, *op. cit.*, p. 111.

stand it as adoration and heavenly doxology. The apostle holds the opposite opinion: it is the plea of the groaning, and as such the vehicle of the spirit's intercession. It is impossible to demythologize the *theologia gloriae* into the *theologia viatorum* more thoroughly. It now becomes clear how Paul could say that we do not know how to pray rightly. So little do we know this, that we do not even recognize the true meaning of all doxology and do not even grasp that it is the cry for liberty which is pleasing to God and proper to our situation. Certainly, Paul had only the ecstatic utterances of primitive Christian worship in mind. But from that starting-point he goes on to define the concern of the spirit. It must be asked whether we, too, could not and should not learn something here, especially when liturgical renewal is being striven for and discussed on an ecumenical scale.

Since the apostle (according to Rom. 12.1f.) transfers the true service of God to everyday life,[35] liturgy must on no account remove us from this real, everyday world. The church is not the church at all without the counterpart of the world, even in its worship, and thus ceases to be pleasing to God. Paul allows Christian worship especially to be the manifestation of a deep, even if highly-charged, solidarity between church and world.[36] For if its liturgy is what it should be, worship expresses the fact that the whole world is called with us to the liberty of the children of God and that we, together with the whole world, have to cry out for this liberty. Just as in worship the intercession of the spirit takes place for us, believers, so worship is itself (if it is what it should be) something like the intercession of Christians for the world. Otherwise it could not be the basis for our daily service, nor prepare for that service and dismiss us to it. Otherwise this would be the assembly of Christ, the lord of the cult, and not that of the hidden cosmocrator, who desires to change this world of ours into the sphere of his sovereignty. Otherwise worship would be filled with a faith which would no longer be hope and hence would only be stunted faith. Otherwise the work of the spirit would only be understood as freedom from the world and not at the same time freedom for the world – an interpretation which inevitably turns the church into a

---

[35] See my essay, 'Gottesdienst im Alltag der Welt', *Judentum – Urchristentum – Kirche. Festschrift J. Jeremias*, 1960, pp.165–71.

[36] Fuchs rightly talks about the cosmic significance of corporate worship (p. 112). E. Schweizer (*TWNT* VI, pp.428f.) objects that the spirit does not, as in Gnosticism, sigh under the pressure of matter. But although the stress is different from the Gnostic one, the trend is similar in both, because Gnosticism, too, is aware of the 'slavery of mutability'.

conventicle instead of the beginning of a new world.

Of course only those who suffer and die with unredeemed creation have the right to look for the new world and to say that the sufferings of this present time are not worthy to be compared with the glory that is to be revealed. The man who allows the liberty he has received to be confirmed in the worship of the church will speak and act as *beatus possidens*, but he will not really be able to serve the world as a disciple of the one who was crucified. It was already a danger in the early Christian assemblies that they enthusiastically gave themselves up to a doxology which was remote from earthly reality and personal temptation and proclaimed the church without the world and above it. That is why Paul says in an outrageously radical criticism: we do not know what right prayer is. In saying this he was not saying anything against the troubled and perplexed; he was attacking the pneumatics, illustrating what he had to say from glossolalia. The cry for liberty must deeply determine the prayer which is pleasing to God, as well as true Christian worship; and solidarity with the world must not be forgotten, in that worship above all: that is one of the insights for which we are indebted to Paul and which we have to learn from him again and again.

VII

THE SPIRIT AND THE LETTER

The inclination of earlier times to view Paul as the first Christian dogmatist has swung to the other extreme. He is conceded the honour of being the most important reflective theologian in the New Testament; but it would be generally denied today that he developed a system[1] or possesses a firm methodology.[2] Both these opinions may be correct. But that does not mean that the dominating centre of Paul's theology must be denied as well. Although he composed no *Summa Theologica*, it would probably be going too far to set in its place a collection of interrelated ideas about the encounter between God and man, with at most a general thesis about 'judgment and grace'.[3] Such statements are so general that they no longer allow the specific character of Pauline theology to emerge, a character which simply cannot be overlooked and which distinguishes him from all other New Testament writers.

Contrary to the present trend, I should like to maintain the provocative thesis that not only is the apostle undoubtedly upheld in his whole work by a central message, which can even be didactically formulated, but that he also, for the first time in Christian history, developed an approach to a theological hermeneutic.[4] If this last statement is correct, the previous one can no longer be a matter of dispute. The assertion is not so bold as may at first appear. Since the

[1] The view most recently taken by G. Bornkamm, *Paulus*, 1969, pp. 129f.

[2] U. Luz, *Das Geschichtsverständnis des Paulus*, 1968, pp. 107f.; P. Vielhauer, 'Paulus und das Alte Testament' (*Studien zur Geschichte und Theologie der Reformation, Festschrift E. Bizer*, 1969, pp. 33–62), p. 41.

[3] G. Bornkamm, *Paulus*, pp. 129f.

[4] Vielhauer reaches the same conclusion (*op. cit.*, pp. 51, 54).

early church,[5] through the Reformation and down to the idealist period, the Pauline antithesis of spirit and letter have been hermeneutically interpreted and evaluated again and again,[6] although for some incomprehensible reason there is no historical study of the interpretation in existence. It looks as if people had also always been content to see the Pauline antithesis as at most an important hermeneutical possibility, but never applied it explicitly and exclusively to the Christian interpretation of the Old Testament and never brought it to bear at all on the interpretation of the New Testament canon.[7] Much would already have been achieved if this problem were taken up and discussed, even if the result turned out to be negative.

It must be admitted from the very beginning that the textual basis in Paul for the task set here is extremely slight, being confined to the passages Rom. 2.27–29; Rom. 7.6; II Cor. 3.6 and their contexts. That fact alone may make my postulate seem foolish, if one considers its magnitude. On the other hand, these few passages have had such an effect on theology and the history of thought that one is at least not alone in one's foolishness if one reminds people of the problem. On the contrary, the tables can be turned. It is not because clarity has been achieved that exegesis (apart from rare historical surveys[8] and philosophical comments[9]) only deals in commentaries with the verses in question as in duty bound; it is clearly the result of a dilemma. Exegetes have no longer been certain how to deal with these passages since the liberal-idealist tradition came to an end. This tradition started from its concept of the spirit as the power of being aware of oneself and of being able to penetrate understandably the world which one encounters. Fastening on the doubtful and misleading translation *littera* for the Pauline word *gramma*, this tradition then understood the letter as the remaining external, contingent, arbitrary factor, as what cannot be ultimately assimilated into the spiritual life, as what is withdrawn from 'inwardness' and the moral life. This interpretation broke down when it became unavoidably clear that primitive Christianity understood by 'spirit' the divine energy of miracle and ecstasy and that by 'letter' Paul meant one of the func-

[5] On this point cf. B. Schneider, 'The Meaning of St. Paul's thesis "The Letter and the Spirit"', *CBQ* 15, 1953, pp. 163–207.
[6] G. Ebeling, 'Geist und Buchstabe', *RGG*[3] II, cols. 1290–1296.
[7] Even Ebeling, col. 1291, denies this possibility.
[8] Besides those mentioned, R. M. Grant, *The Letter and the Spirit*, 1957.
[9] B. Cohen, 'Note on Letter and Spirit in the New Testament', *HTR* 47, 1954, pp. 197–203; H. Liese, *'De spiritu et littera'*, V.D.11, 1931, pp. 225–29.

tions of the Mosaic law. It is not much help to establish historical facts of this kind or to fit faded fragments from the history of thought hastily and shamefacedly into their appropriate exegetical place. The meaning of the antithesis, and even more its consequences for the apostle's theology, almost always remain undiscussed or shadowy. Virtually the only steps taken have been to extend the Pauline theme to the contrast between Christ and the law, or to the gospel and the Mosaic tradition, to defend the Old Testament from a possible verdict and at most to offer a number of reflections about Paul's ambivalent relation to tradition.

I. THE EVIDENCE

In view of these facts, the Pauline texts must once again be subjected to an exegetical analysis. Rom. 2.25–29 argues that circumcision has no power to justify unless it is joined with the keeping of the law. As a counter position, Paul states that uncircumcision which observes the dictates of the law counts before God as circumcision. Verses 27ff. draw the logical conclusion: 'Then those who are physically uncircumcised but keep the law will condemn you who have the written code and circumcision but break the law. For he is not a real Jew who is one outwardly, nor is true circumcision something external and physical. He is a Jew who is one inwardly, and real circumcision is a matter of the heart, spiritual and not literal (AV: in the spirit and not in the letter)'. In form the text is rabbinically compressed, in content it is polemical, and in its antithesis it is paradoxical. It is particularly important to note that Paul has already said the same thing basically in 2.13f., even if not in this rhetorical form, with its fixed formulae and paradoxical exaggeration. We must consider the point of this repetition at the end of the argument.

Paul is presupposing that the Jew does not in actual fact keep the law and that consequently circumcision does him no good. The two themes – the circumcision of the heart and the real Jew – move into the centre of the discussion. The first of them, deriving from Old Testament prophecy, was only hesitatingly taken over by the Palestinian rabbis, but understandably assumed considerable importance in Qumran and even more in Philo. It is going beyond the limits of what was possible and endurable for any Jew, however, when Paul in v.26 does not even adhere to circumcision in a spiritual sense, but declares it to be irrelevant compared with the circumcision of the heart. As in Gal. 6.13, it is, practically speaking, the mark of the Jewish transgressor against the law. As an initiation rite it can only have the meaning of calling the Jew to obedience. For all others it is superfluous. These statements make it clear that no real dialogue between Christians and Jews is being carried on here, for the premises given offer no basis for such a discussion. The question in v.26b is simply part of the style of the diatribe. But in that case the possibility entertained for the Gentiles is fictitious as well. The Gentiles cannot, being uncircumcised, fulfil the whole Torah at all. Finally, the Gentile Christians ought not to be introduced into the discussion prematurely, either.[10] For the formula about 'keeping the precepts of the law' is simply not the mark of Christian obedience. The argument is therefore a hypothetical one to begin with.

On the other hand, the fact that our statements refer back to and heighten what is said in v.13ff. now becomes important. Paul was undoubtedly not speaking hypothetically when he conceded that the conscience of the Gentiles stood in a practical relation to the Jewish law in so far as it recognized the demands of the Mosaic law (at least to a certain extent and chiefly, apparently, in the moral realm), and even caused these demands to be fulfilled. It is essential to keep this remarkable progression from vv.13ff. to vv.25ff. clearly in mind in order to grasp effectively the problem which is raised with the key phrase about the circumcision of the heart, 'in the spirit, and not in the letter'. For a circumcision of this kind is certainly no fiction for the apostle. There is the presence of the spirit and the rule of the letter; and there is the irreconcilable contrast between the two. There are also Christians in whom the spirit has fulfilled its task through that very circumcision of the heart. We see, therefore, that Paul advances from what was in the first place a hypothetical case towards the description of an actually existing fact. This is the point of the otherwise superfluous repetition and heightening of v.13ff. at the end of the chapter – to bring out the fact that Christians are the recipients and manifestations of the circumcision of the heart.

The apostle finds the transition from the hypothetical case to the exhibiting of the existing reality by introducing the second dominating motif of the true Jew. In his important essay 'Der wahre Jude und sein Lob',[11] A. Fridrichsen failed to recognize this progression from

---

[10] T. Zahn, *Der Brief des Paulus an die Römer*, ³1925, p.146; R. Bultmann, *Theology* I, p.261.

[11] *Symbolae Arctoae* I, 1927, pp.39–49; for this particular point see p.43.

the one theme to the other. He therefore solved the difficulties of our verse by the assertion that Paul, carried away by his polemics, idealized the picture of the Gentile to an unjustifiable degree and then paralleled it with the picture of the ideal Jew, freed for entire manhood from his limitations. He was not disturbed by the fact that no Jew ever wanted to be freed for manhood through the ignoring of the Torah and that the apostle never demanded that he should. All the more striking, however, is Fridrichsen's demonstration that in the Stoa the question of the true man of Greek tradition became acute once more, that the concept of political liberty was existentially deepened and that on this level the difference between being and seeming, the inward and the outward, took on significance once more. For it must be supposed that Paul, if he was not actually directly influenced by such questions, at least raised the theme of the true Jew against this religio-historical background. Admittedly, v.27 already shows that he translated this tradition into eschatological terms. The rabbinic conviction[12] that at the Last Judgment a man will be measured against other men is here no longer expressed prophetically (unlike Matt. 12.41), but in a dogmatic statement, though this is paradoxically heightened. The beginning of the sentence is set in sharp antithesis to the end, and this antithesis is even heightened throughout the verse. The man who is 'physically' uncircumcised fulfils the law. The man who can produce scripture and circumcision shows himself to be a transgressor against the law. The conclusion then follows: the Gentiles will judge the Jews – a blasphemous conclusion for Jewish ears and one which picks up the early Christian message of the eschatological re-valuation of all earthly values. Now the word which we generally translate by 'letter' crops up for the first time. The context is important: it occurs in an eschatological pronouncement and in close association with circumcision, which Paul as a Christian does not allow to have any significance for salvation. From now on he always uses 'letter' in this depreciatory, negative way and always as something which is obsolete for the Christian because it belongs to the old aeon.

On the other hand, it is quite clear that Paul bases what he says on the Mosaic Torah, in so far as this exists in fixed written form and is claimed by the Jews, like circumcision, as a saving privilege. The 'letter' is therefore, practically speaking, the Old Testament in the

[12] Cf. P. Billerbeck, *Kommentar zum Neuen Testament aus Talmud und Midrasch*, III, 1926, p. 124.

aspect which was of decisive importance for the Israelites, an aspect which was transferred from the most important section to the whole. That applies in exactly the same way to the Pauline concept of the law, which can also describe the Mosaic Torah, its individual precepts, or the Old Testament as a whole. 'Letter' and 'law' are therefore in Paul interchangeable, with the single difference that the word 'law' is not only used in a depreciatory sense. It must, of course, be added that 'letter' stresses particularly the existence in fixed written form, so that the relation to 'scripture' is similar to the relation to 'law'. Here, too (and it is completely in accord with what has been said about the law), the apostle does not talk depreciatingly about the Old Testament scriptures; on the contrary, he speaks entirely positively, quite unlike his way of talking even about the law. His scriptural proofs show that beyond any doubt.

We have now arrived at the first result of our investigation: what we call 'letter' is for Paul the Mosaic Torah in its written documentation, which is claimed by the Jews as saving privilege and which for Paul (as the essential portion and aspect of the Old Testament) is identical with scripture as a whole. From this perspective it is understandable that a singular verbal form should be given to the corpus which was originally described by the phrase ἱερὰ γράμματα. We cannot definitely assert that the singular was terminologically used by the apostle for the first time, as is generally assumed. But it is very likely, because in this way Paul arrived at an antithesis to the term pneuma and because he also prefers to talk about the *nomos* in the singular. Later we shall see that the singular usage makes it easier to talk about the 'letter' as a power, which also would seem indicated by the Jewish understanding of the Torah. This may perhaps clarify the meaning of the word sufficiently, but a particular Pauline characteristic still remains to be mentioned: the word only occurs in eschatological declarations whose religio-historical background is the Jewish doctrine of the two successive or antithetical aeons. Consequently the word is always assigned by the apostle to the old aeon. The introductory preposition in v. 27 would seem not to be meant instrumentally[13] but to describe the accompanying circumstance[14] and to have here even an antithetical sense: transgressors against the law in spite of letter and circumcision.

In vv. 28f. Paul is not repeating vv. 25–27 but drawing the con-

---

[13] Schrenk, *TWNT* I, p. 765; A. Schlatter, *Gottes Gerechtigkeit*, 1935, p. 110.
[14] H. Lietzmann, *An die Römer*, ⁴1933, p. 44.

clusion.[15] In elaborate rhetoric, 'Jew' in v.28 is interpreted as an honourable predicate, just as 'circumcision' is a predicative noun, but is used in v.29, in an emphatic chiasmus, as subject. Verse 29c brings a coda of a kind not unusual in Pauline rhetoric. We must not view this in the modern way as mere stylistic elegance. In Paul, rhetoric is always the handmaid of his subject. Here it represents the peak of the antithesis, in that it brings out the theme that was already heralded in v.26. Paul is not content to brush aside the problem of circumcision. It has brought him to the theme of the real Jew, and this theme now leads up to a provocative thesis: the only true Jew is the Christian.

But this interpretation demands proof. It may be useful to start again from Fridrichsen's remarks about the question of the real Stoic, which was raised by Epictetus,[16] for example. Here apparent existence, which is dependent on the attitude of the observer, is contrasted with inner and true existence, which is found in harmony with God and the universe. Probably a variation of this view reached Paul through the synagogues of the diaspora. Even if this were not the case, he would have taken up the theme himself in modified form. For Paul the phrases ἐν τῷ φανερῷ – ἐν τῷ κρυπτῷ are not precisely the same as what we call 'outward' and 'inward'.[17] As in I Peter 3.4, for the apostle it is not merely the 'inward' things which are 'hidden'; it is human existence itself, whose secret is only revealed eschatologically. On the other hand, piety can also belong to the visible things. Further stipulations therefore secure the first antithesis. 'In the flesh' (AV) points to the realm of what is to hand physically[18] as the crystallization of the visible, which is contrasted with the circumcision of the heart. The nature of the latter is finally described in the mysterious phrase, 'in the spirit, and not in the letter' (AV: RSV: 'spiritual and not literal'), which presents us with our real problem of interpretation.

It has frequently been suggested that the meaning of this phrase can be arrived at if one calls to mind the Greek motif of the 'unwritten law'. But that ends in a cul-de-sac. People ran up against the difficult expression 'letter', interpreted 'spirit' in the idealist sense mentioned above, and were able to combine the two all the more easily in the light of the tradition of the 'unwritten law' since the earlier antitheses

---

[15] Contrary to O. Kuss, *Der Römerbrief*, 1957, pp. 90f.
[16] *Op. cit.*, pp. 44f.
[17] Contrary to P. Althaus, *Der Brief an die Römer*, [10]1966, p. 28.
[18] E. Schweizer, *TWNT* VII, p. 128.

THE SPIRIT AND THE LETTER

'outward-inward', 'flesh-heart' seemed to stress something spiritual.[19] The apostle then gives precedence to what is effected by the spirit and cannot be pinned down in written form, in contrast to fixed precepts; i.e., he puts forward a kind of 'unwritten law'. It is curious that these exegetes hardly ever gave any thought to the fact that the Jew simply could not brush aside the law as easily as this;[20] and Paul, even as Christian, still remained Jewish enough to make the law one of the central problems of his theology, instead of viewing it as something entirely negligible. Moreover, the main stream of Greek tradition by no means set up the 'unwritten law' in a contradictory counter-position to the laws of man, but rather saw it as the origin of the latter and as at most their measuring rod.[21] The harsh Pauline antithesis is, therefore, not to be explained in this light, and we would do well to start from his position rather than from its negation.

Although the motif of the circumcision of the heart was largely used in a moral sense in Philo's allegories, in the Qumran writings (e.g., I QS 5,5; 1Qp Hab. 11.13; 1QH 2.18; 18.20), its keynote is dualistic and eschatological, whereas Jub. 1.23 associates it expressly with the promise of the Holy Spirit: 'I will circumcise . . . the fore-skin of their hearts and will create for them a holy spirit.' In the Odes of Solomon it is related hymnically to a redeemed present, as 11.1f. shows: 'My heart was circumcised . . . For the Most High circumcised me through his holy spirit . . .; thus the circumcision became my redemption.' Finally, Col. 2.11ff. also belongs in this context, baptism being described as the circumcision of Christ made without hands, which brings about freedom from the body of the flesh, translation to heavenly existence and a liberating of the church from the rule of principalities and powers. There is no question but that our passage must be understood in this light. The context is an eschatological one and the writer is talking here about a real and not 'spiritualized' circumcision performed by the spirit, which leaves behind the sphere of the letter, with its validity and power, and is contrasted with it – and even contradicts it – being 'made without

[19] Cf. R. M. Grant, op. cit., p.51: 'This spirit gives exegetical freedom. He destroys the tyranny of words.' The Christian understanding of Scripture is 'intuitive rather than based on words'.

[20] H. Koester, 'Νόμος Φύσεως, The Concept of Natural Law in Greek Thought' (Religions in Antiquity. Essays in Memory of E. R. Goodenough, ed. J. Neussner, 1968, pp.521–41, p.535, shows most convincingly that in Philo the Greek motif of the unwritten law has been transferred to the Torah (which was as yet unfixed) as the divine legislation.

[21] Cf. Kleinknecht, TWNT IV, pp. 1017ff.

hands'. Whether one interprets ἐν instrumentally[22] or rather locally ('in the sphere of power') is relatively unimportant. In any case, the writer is not talking about de-nationalized Jews, raised to pure manhood,[23] and the praise in v.29c confirms that the field of mere possibilities and hypothesis has given place to eschatological reality. The Torah no longer exercises any compulsion over those who have received the Holy Spirit – which for Paul means Christians. The phenomenon of the true Jew (for which Billerbeck is significantly unable to produce any evidence) is eschatologically realized in the Christian who has freed himself from Judaism, as from a characteristic of the old aeon and its piety.[24]

Rom. 7.6 does not essentially go beyond what we have concluded from 2.27–29, but is as perfect a confirmation of it as one could wish for. Here, too, the antithesis between spirit and letter is primarily related to anthropology. What was painstakingly reconstructed in the case of 2.27ff. is now unambiguously expressed: the contradictory contrast can be meaningfully applied to Christian existence alone. The baptismal terminology which we also find in Rom. 6.11ff., with the blunt antithesis of 'once' and 'now', as well as the parallelism of 'flesh' and 'letter' in 7.5f., mark the eschatological contrast of the two aeons, which is heightened to an eminent degree through the use of the substantives καινότης and παλαιότης, clearly overreaching possible adjectives.[25] The context cogently displays the identity of the 'letter' and the Mosaic Torah, which according to v.5 is viewed as the sum of its individual demands. On the other hand, vv.7ff. bring out that the Pauline concept of the law possesses a dialectic which is not transferable to the 'letter'. The law in its origin and intention is the sacred will of God, which calls men to obedience and to that degree is, according to Rom. 3.21, a witness to the gospel of God's righteousness and the *nova oboedientia* which is based on it, but could yet be perverted by Judaism into a demand for good works. It is only

[22] The view taken by Zahn and Kuss in their commentaries on this passage.

[23] Contrary to N. A. Dahl, *Das Volk Gottes*, reprint, 1963, p.238. Where does Paul concede that the Jew stands in the inner movement of joyous surrender (Althaus on this passage), in the order of the spirit (M.-J. Lagrange, *St. Paul, Épitre aux Romains*, [6]1950, p.57), or in a spiritual way (C. K. Barrett, *A Commentary on the Epistle to the Romans*, 1957, p.60)?

[24] R. Meyer, *TWNT* VI, p.82.

[25] Luz constantly tries (e.g., pp.93f.) to weaken the contrast in the interests of salvation history. Accordingly, he defines the spirit as the power which helps human impotence, and calls the power of the letter the fulfilling of the law 'in a human way' (p.126).

in this perversion, under which the original intention was lost (having to be rediscovered through the gospel) that the law and the letter are identical. They are not identical fundamentally,[26] but are so *de facto* because the Jewish reality as Paul sees it is dominated by the reality of the perverted law, in this way becoming a part of fallen humanity, which lives in a perverted creation. To this extent, the term 'letter' registers a relationship to the idea of tradition: the letter is what Jewish interpretation and tradition have made out of the divine will in its different intention. It is, that is to say, the law, which in its demand for 'works' perverts the relation between God and the devout Jew, which drives men into transgression and hybris, which causes sin and death – the law, that is, which we have in codified form in the Mosaic Torah, with the sum of its individual demands.[27]

It is surely no over-subtlety of interpretation to extract a relation of this kind between letter and Jewish tradition from the relative clause in 7.6: 'which held us captive'. Here attention is drawn to the permanent captivity which only baptism could abolish, captivity which does not merely apply to individual existence and each several situation, but is already given in salvation history, or rather in its opposite. At the same time, here we have the meaning of that highly controversial passage, Gal. 3.24, in the apostle's own unequivocal interpretation, a fact which will be important for us later: the Mosaic Torah, with its demand for works, is 'our custodian until Christ came', in that it keeps us in custody, like prisoners, blocking our way to freedom. The most prominent characteristic of the letter, according to our text, is ultimately the character of power. It forced us into slavery and was able to kill the original creation. According to v.4, we have to belong to another, namely the one who is risen, and be drawn through baptism into his death, so that we may escape death under the letter and be separated from it even eschatologically.[28] Hence the contradictory contrast between spirit and letter is crystallized in the fact that the understanding of 'spirit' is christologically determined, i.e., as participation in the Christ event.

Having established this, it is an easy transition to the textual

---

[26] E. Kamlah's view in 'Buchstabe und Geist. Die Bedeutung dieser Antithese für die alttestamentliche Exegese des Apostels Paulus', *EvTh* 14, 1954, p.278: the claims of the legal code represent the principle of the old covenant.

[27] Cf. Schrenk, *TWNT* I, pp.747, 765ff.; O. Michel, *Paulus und seine Bibel*, 1929, pp.174ff., 241.

[28] That is the justifiable kernel of Kamlah's attempts to base the antithesis on the cross of Jesus (pp.280f.).

problems of II Cor. 3.6. It must again be stressed that the antithesis
is in the first place the mark of Christian existence, i.e., it has anthropological bearings. But the context obviously goes further than this,
ecclesiology entering the field in 3.2f. and the interpretation of the
Old Testament in 3.7ff. Accordingly, the contrast of spirit and letter
now coincides with the contrast between the old and new covenants,
the sphere of jurisdiction of the two (which are presented as powers
even more clearly than in Rom. 7.6) takes on universal dimensions.
These shifts of emphasis are caused by the fact that the antithesis,
without losing its anthropological relationship to Christian existence,
is now no longer applied to Christians in general, but to the apostle in
particular, as the bearer of the gospel. Paul now has to consider the
contrast between the gospel and the law thematically, and he
broadens out his previous perspective so that it takes in salvation
history.

It is characteristic of Paul's method of argument that the question
of credentials should lead immediately to fundamentals, and it is no
less characteristic of it for the ideas to tumble over one another and
for very different motifs to be loosely linked up by a process of association. The apostle needs no additional legitimation in Corinth. The
church itself is the letter which he can produce, and that not as an
object detachable from himself: his existence is in its inmost being
stamped by this, so that his mission is already thereby legitimized.
This is not, however, due to his own merits. He carries his metaphorical style further by describing the church (in a motif familiar
from the 'letters' in Revelation) as a heavenly epistle[29] addressed to
himself and revealed through his service which is recognizable to
everyone in its eschatological significance. Finally, because it is an
eschatological event that is taking place, Paul is able to establish the
fulfilment of the prophecy of Jer. 38.31ff. LXX.[30] He does so first by
placing the tradition of the stone tables written by the finger of God
(Ex. 31.18; Deut. 9.10) in the antithetical context of Ezek. 11.19;
36.26, according to which Israel's stony heart is to be replaced by a
heart of flesh. Through this manipulation[31] he arrives at a contradictory contrast which is presupposed and adhered to in what

[29] Most recently D. Georgi, *Die Gegner des Paulus im 2. Korintherbrief*, 1964, p.
253.
[30] Cf. H. Windisch, *Der Zweite Korintherbrief*, ⁹1924, p. 110; Schrenk, *TWNT* I,
p. 767.
[31] Vielhauer, *op. cit.*, p. 47, talks about a conscious reinterpretation of the Old
Testament text. That is already the case here.

follows. For him, the hearts of the Israelites are not just hardened (as for Ezekiel), so that they have to be turned back into human hearts again and made capable of hearing. Rather, the stone tables of the law have been replaced through the action of the divine Spirit. Their place is taken by tablets represented by human hearts. The Christian church with its members is the eschatological charter[32] which replaces the Mosaic Torah.

The formulation of the last sentence seems exaggerated. But our concern is to do justice to the emphasis of what is laid down in written form in our verses, which (although suggested by the opening theme) does not represent the link between the various statements merely by chance.[33] We are not justified in contrasting the work of the spirit, as the 'empirical datum' which appeals to and forms the inner nature of man, with what is 'merely written',[34] again reading the motif of the 'unwritten law' into our text.[35] This is to block access to what follows, in which the theme of the two covenants is expressly linked with the question of the interpretation of the Old Testament scriptures. We must at least establish that here Paul also allows the spirit to take on objective form in the church, visible to all the world, and does so in phraseology which speaks of written documentation. It is not plausible that he is here making use of his opponents' slogans and reversing their opinions,[36] even if II Cor. 3.7 onwards picks up a pre-Pauline Midrash on Ex. 34.30ff. or is a variation on it. There may be a leap from one motif to the next, but the associations which lead to this leap are not absurd in themselves. The interest, or perhaps even the bearing, of vv. 2f. lies in the fact that the spirit, though certainly taking the place of the stone tablets in importance, has in its turn found visible expression in the community which bears its hall-mark as well as in the person of the apostle. In this it is parallel to the Mosaic Torah, to which it otherwise stands in sharp contrast.

Verses 4–6 now, however, emphasize the contradictory contrast of the two. Here the apostle refers back to v.2. There the danger already existed that his work for the church might be misunderstood

---

[32] *Urkunde* is Windisch's translation (p. 109) of the term *diatheke*.
[33] Cf. A. Schlatter, *Paulus, der Bote Jesu*, 1934, pp. 505f.; Luz, *op. cit.*, p. 123.
[34] Contrary to I. Hermann, *Kyrios und Pneuma*, 1961, pp. 28f.
[35] Windisch, *op. cit.*, p. 111.
[36] Contrary to Georgi, *op. cit.*, pp. 252f. His thesis that Paul's opponents directly linked spirit and letter (p. 272) and understood the Old Testament as the 'archives of the spirit' (p. 268) becomes improbable alone through the fact that the antithesis of letter and spirit in the Epistle to the Romans appears independent of this.

as being due to his own merits, i.e., as being his own achievement. This is warded off in v. 3a by the idea that the church is the heavenly epistle addressed to, and made known by, him. Verses 5–6a heighten this observation by stressing in a highly paradoxical way the basic incapacity of the instrument chosen by God for the service assigned to it and which it performs. The salient point of the statement is that God himself enters the stage where his work is being done and that he then constantly reveals himself as the creator out of nothing and the raiser of the dead. When he uses a tool, he always works with instruments which are in themselves incapable of serving him and which only become usable through his spirit. This view obviously picks up the message of the justification of the ungodly and is a development of it: even the apostles, as bearers of the gospel, are incapable of fulfilling their task unless grace gives them the power. That is no doubt the reason why Paul took over Ezekiel's phrase about the 'hearts of flesh' in v. 3. God works on, and with unusable material, in both creation and redemption. Just as II Cor. 4.7ff. talks about earthen vessels, the imperfect, the outcast and the dying; just as II Cor. 12.9 speaks of those in need of grace; just as all the catalogues of tribulation call those tempted in every way the tools of the victorious gospel – so here, too, those who are in themselves powerless are the eschatological manifestations of the spirit in his earthly activity.

This prepares for the antithesis of spirit and letter, as well as indicating its centre. The basic condition of the eschatological new redemptive order expresses itself, as in I Cor. 1.26ff., in the revolutionary reversal of worldly standards. This also applies to the sphere of piety. Wherever the law rules, works are demanded of which only the strong are capable: hybris and despair in transgression and self-righteousness are here unavoidable and the God who gives and calls for the verification of his gift is transformed into an idol who is only capable of acting as the referee of man's struggle with himself and the world. Spiritual and physical death then have the last word. The letter kills because it forces man into the service of his own righteousness (even when it does so in the name of God), understands the law (like IV Esdras 5.23ff.) as the document and guarantee of election, and possesses supernatural glory and power. Everything which forces us back on our own strength, ability and piety kills because it snatches the creature out of his creatureliness and thus away from the almighty power of grace, of which we are in constant need. Just as the law is perverted when it is turned into the demand for works, so it perverts the man who falls in with this demand, and delivers him up to the power of death by setting him at a distance from the creator who gives and receives.

It is a remarkable fact that even if Paul was here provoked by his Jewish opponents and was actually involved in anti-Jewish polemics, he talks about the spirit and the letter against a world-wide background. They appear as cosmic forces, and death and life, with which all men have to do, issue from them accordingly. This view was prepared for by Judaism. There too, as Qumran shows, the cosmic order was included in the Torah and every creature was deemed subject to at least the Noachic law; Philo associated the Greek doctrine of the unwritten law with the Torah[37], which he (and the Wisdom writings) identified with the divine, world-pervading *sophia*; and the echo of the Sinaitic law was held to be perceptible throughout the earth, even if it was not taken up.[38] Paul also makes use of the same motif when in Gal. 4.9f. he traces bondage to the stars to the preaching of the law. Finally, we must remember that the synagogues of the diaspora maintained the same world-wide validity for the Torah in their mission that primitive Christianity claimed for the Gospel.

Of course, this only shows the historical background of our statement, and not yet its theological meaning. In order to discover that, one must go deeper than we can do here into the relationship between the Jewish law and the religious practice of paganism, a relationship which the apostle himself hardly explained sufficiently. In the course of investigation two discoveries, at least, would be made, both relevant to the text under discussion: on the one hand, Paul shares the Jewish view that the will of God, universally attested in creation, was expressed through its fixation in the Torah with a clarity which distinguishes Israel as the bearer of revelation above all other nations. The possession of the scriptures raises Israel above the world of other religions because a specific promise is associated with it, a promise with which the Christian faith cannot dispense either. Salvation history is the sphere of this promise. On the other hand, in Judaism this promise has been interpreted as a demand for good works and has been perverted into a privilege which is a restriction of the divine grace. By this, Israel has placed itself in the same domain as other

---

[37] Cf. Koester's essay mentioned above.
[38] Cf. E. Haenchen, *Die Apostelgeschichte*, [13]1961, p. 138, which is indebted to G. Kretschmar, 'Himmelfahrt und Pfingsten', *ZKG* 66, 1954–55, pp. 209ff.

religions, from which it wished to shield itself through the bulwark of the law. Where the demand for a righteousness of one's own encroaches, the will of God is disregarded, the promise is unrecognized and the fall described in Rom. 1.20ff. repeats itself; Rom. 7.7ff. deals with this thematically. To this degree Israel illustrates in exemplary fashion the temptation which is bound up with all piety, to misuse the gift of God as the means to one's own glory. Israel now becomes the representative of the fate of human religiosity in general, so that the contradictory contrast of spirit and letter characterizes with incomparable rigour the struggle of faith and superstition, and the domain of salvation history paradoxically makes clear the reality of its opposite. For it is the promise which makes the fall possible and places man under constant attack. The spirit and the law are counterparts, but not unrelated counterparts.

It is not for nothing that Paul reminds his readers of scripture when he talks about the law as *gramma*, i.e., the Torah laid down in the Old Testament; and by spirit he does not understand, like the enthusiasts, an uncontrolled ecstatic force. He defines *pneuma* Christologically, allowing it to be the power which sets man in the presence of the exalted Lord on earth. It can only be this if it frees us from striving after our own righteousness and calls us back to the condition of the creature described in v.5. Elsewhere there may be fantasy heavens and piety which strives for self-transcendence; but there is not the earthly presence of Christ. The spirit and the letter therefore part company under the insignia of the message of justification. This is the criterion which divides the principalities and powers. In its light, the old and new covenants diverge[39], as well as those who serve them. For the apostle is not acquainted with the idea of the renewed covenant with Israel, which Jewish Christianity used for a time in order to show its continuity with Judaism and to prove that it was the eschatological fulfilment of the prophetic promise of the gathering of the scattered tribes. In Paul the idea of the covenant is drawn into the conflict of law and gospel,[40] so that here, too, he arrives at a contra-

[39] In view of Rom. 7.6, one ought not like Conzelmann to diagnose a 'timeless conceptuality of letter and spirit' (*Outline*, p. 170). Luz is correct in opposing this (p. 126).

[40] This means a fundamental contradiction of H. J. Schoeps, *Paulus*, 1959, pp. 210, 225ff. Paul by no means tears law and covenant apart, as our particular context shows, nor does he reduce the Torah to an ethical law, like later Christendom. But he does interpret the old covenant dialectically in the light of the antithesis between promise and law, instead of using the idea of the covenant to paralyse the Jewish demand for works.

dictory antithesis, in the sense of the two contrasting aeons.[41] It is actually the case that the sphere of salvation history cannot exist without the reality of its opposite. Christianity looks back to this reality as to something that is past, but without forgetting that the 'old things' are its own past and that it is in constant danger of reverting to them. The universal mission of the law still exists in various forms to which not only the heathen but even the church's own members are susceptible. Its faith proves itself in a ceaseless renunciation of superstition, and this struggle finds its centre in the dispute with those who in the name of the law and its glory spread round them death (according to v.7), condemnation (according to v.9), and the overcoming of perishability (according to v.11).

Contemporary theology has forgotten, generally speaking, that its true opponent is not unbelief, which is in any case probably more or less a fiction. For a man to take an unbelieving attitude towards the Christian message by no means implies that he is completely unbelieving. Unbelief is a manifestation of superstition, whether religious or secularized, and the Christian church is only the company of believers when it is and remains at the same time the central battlefield for the conflict with the superstition in its own midst. In view of the frankness with which ecclesiology in its various variations is made on all sides the decisive criterion of theology, it is worth giving critical attention to the question of whether superstition has not contributed more to the continuity of church history, theology and Christian institutions than faith. For faith can hardly be inherited, and the man who keeps his eyes fixed on unbelief as its real opponent easily forgets that superstition (at least in the domain of the church) easily disguises itself as faith, and may even really believe itself to be faith. Demythologizing is one of the tasks of historical criticism, and it is true that a very much better understanding of the Christian message can be achieved with its help. But faith does not spring from a better historical understanding, which can *per se* easily be a substitute for faith. There are plenty of orthodox and liberal theologians who use evidently true or sham history as the substitute for faith and view the spirit completely undialectically as the new law, permitting it to be an instrument for the preservation and passing on of ecclesiastical tradition.[42]

[41] At the same time the Christian modification of the Jewish system becomes evident here. The coming aeon is already present.
[42] Contrary to I. Hermann, *op. cit.*, p. 104.

Wherever the relationship of spirit and letter is discussed, the problem of tradition is bound to arise. Our passage confirms this. It is not by chance that from v. 7 onwards the contrast between the old and new covenants merges into the question of the meaning and right interpretation of the Old Testament as holy scripture. Paul does not abolish the idea of the covenant when he draws it into the conflict of law and gospel. Nor does he fundamentally identify the letter with the law, but defines it as the actual, ruling perversion of the documented will of God, and even in this form still allows it to possess divine glory. In v. 14 he speaks of the reading of the old *diatheke*, with which as a matter of course the theme of the old covenant is taken up via the theme of Old Testament scripture.[43] Paul was a Jew, and remained one even as a Christian, in that he still allowed the Torah to be the kernel of the Old Testament and was consequently able to give the same name to both and to bind them indissolubly together through the motif of the covenant. He did not solve the problems of the law and the Old Testament radically by denying the divine gift and intention of the former and by abolishing the latter altogether, as if he had been the first Marcionite. Nor did he ethicize and spiritualize the law, like the later Gentile church, so that the gospel might be viewed as the *nova lex*. His view of salvation history, with its eschatological determination, made both courses impossible. Anyone who disregards this will inevitably fall a victim to the Scylla or Charybdis of these later attempts at a solution, and in so doing will surrender a decisive part of the apostle's dialectic and miss his understanding of the relation between spirit and letter.

The problem of the spirit and the letter arises because the law and its perversion in the letter presuppose the recognition of scripture, but on the other hand Paul's recognition of scripture as being given beforehand does not legitimate the Jewish understanding of the Torah as a demand for good works. Starting from these premises, he has to decide between the old and new covenants, instead of seeing both as a historical continuity in the light of the concept of the renewed covenant. From this angle he has to contrast the stone tablets of Moses with the 'epistle of Christ' (AV) which was written by the spirit in the hearts of Christians. Here two scriptures diverge, and it is significant that the second was not fixed in ink. This means that it does not draw its authority from particular words, which could be taken possession of once and for all by an exegetical and dogmatic

---

[43] Luz's general comments on pp. 92ff. must be revised from this angle.

tradition. On the other hand, it was exactly that which happened to the Old Testament in Judaism. For that very reason, Jer. 38.31ff. could not find its fulfilment here. This leads to the Midrashic and allegorical interpretation of Ex. 34.30ff., which is apparently directed polemically against the Jewish (and perhaps also Jewish-Christian) interpretation of the text and, with its intention, violates the possibilities of rabbinic exegesis, which knows itself to be bound to the literal meaning.[44]

Since Sinai, a veil has lain over the Old Testament which is not lifted even when it is read and heard in worship. On the contrary, this very Judaic usage draws the veil over the hearts of reader and hearer, in that they hear the words and interpret them out of their own exegetical and dogmatic tradition, namely from the law's demand for good works as the kernel and meaning of scripture. This veil is lifted for the first time through Christ – is raised for those who do not listen to Moses, but are converted to the Lord who leads men into the liberty given by the spirit and who allows his eschatological glory to shine out in the place of the passing glory of Moses. The scripture must be read in the light of Christ and as a preparation for him; then even the law regains its original divine intention and becomes a promise of the new, eschatological obedience. Here the spirit takes on a hermeneutical function. Like the letter, it has a bearing on scripture in its character as something given beforehand, a character which we are bound to recognize. Where, however, the exalted Christ enters the earthly stage in the spirit, the ways part, even as regards the scriptures. For then the two possibilities diverge – either to see the Old Testament under the veil of the Torah in its misunderstood character as a demand for good works; or to understand it in the light of the lifting of that veil through Christ, which is to say, practically speaking, from the angle of the message of justification. The Christology that is interpreted through the doctrine of justification is the criterion which decides between spirit and letter, both of which can be derived from the scriptures.

2. ROMANS 10.5–13 AS A TEST CASE

Having arrived at these conclusions in principle, we must go on to test them against particular cases. All the texts which reflect Paul's interpretation of the Old Testament must confirm our results if we

[44] Cf. Vielhauer, *op. cit.*, p. 51.

want to be sure that they are correct. This is impossible within the framework of an essay. Without our having to turn back to Rom. 4, Rom. 10.5–13 offers itself as a particularly useful test case.[45] The passage is a scriptural proof of the thesis put forward in Rom. 10.4. For that reason alone this verse ought not, as is common practice, to be linked up with what follows. On the other hand, it is so controversial that we must establish its meaning, at least briefly. In view of what we have said about Rom. 7.6 and Gal. 3.24, as well as in the light of the verse's context, it is impossible to avoid the conclusion that Christ is here being described as the end of the law, although systematists particularly, in contrast to most exegetes, play with what is, philologically speaking, an entirely possible translation 'goal', 'meaning', 'fulfilment'. The contradictory contrast of letter and spirit (which interprets the spirit as the earthly manifestation of the exalted Lord, and the letter as the Jewish perversion of the established will of God) also presupposes a chronological end to the rule of law in the Christian church.[46] Seeking for one's own righteousness, which is the mark of the ancient people of God according to 10.3, no longer has any place. The righteousness of God does not presuppose our obedience; it creates it. Christ and Moses are just as exclusively contrasted with one another as Christ and Adam in Rom. 5.12ff. Salvation history, which here too draws anthropology into its shadow, is characterized by the breach mentioned in 3.21; 5.20; 7.1–6; 8.2f. and 9.31ff. Israel's path does not reach its goal because, caught up in the illusion that works are demanded. it fails to recognize the true will of God, which is only revealed anew by the spirit and, according to 13.10, can be fulfilled through love.

For Christians, the Mosaic Torah is replaced by the word of the gospel, which is near to us. That is the theme of our text, with which we shall preface our analysis: 'Moses writes: the man who practises the righteousness which is based on the law shall live by it. But the righteousness based on faith says, Do not say in your heart, "Who will ascend into heaven?" (that is, to bring Christ down) or "Who will descend into the abyss?" (that is, to bring Christ up from the dead). But what does it say? The word is near you, on your lips and in your heart (that is, the word of faith which we preach); because, if you confess with your lips that Jesus is Lord and believe in your heart that God raised him from the dead, you will be justified (RSV:

---

[45] Cf. also Vielhauer, *op. cit.*, p. 54; Kamlah, *op. cit.*, p. 281.
[46] Contrary to Luz's view, *op. cit.*, p. 157.

saved). For man believes with his heart and so is justified, and he confesses with his lips and so is saved. The scripture says, "No one who believes in him will be put to shame". For there is no distinction between Jew and Greek; the same Lord is Lord of all and bestows his riches upon all who call upon him. For, "every one who calls upon the name of the Lord will be saved".'

The two quotations from Lev. 18.5 and Deut. 30.11–14 are sharply contrasted.[47] Moreover, in the first Paul omits the Old Testament antecedent and in the second everything which is concerned with commandments and works. In place of this, three interpretations are introduced. On the basis of these alterations the quotation-character of the second passage particularly has been disputed ever since Calvin, and the passages have been assumed to be merely rhetorical paraphrases.[48] But the three-fold 'that is' in vv. 6–8 only makes sense if a genuine exegesis is being presented.[49] What we have here is a *pesher* interpretation (familiar to us today from Qumran) which is characterized by its tendency to actualize and by the insertion of extensive interpretative sections, as well as interpretations linked on to catchwords or aphorisms. The whole is divided up by scriptural sayings in vv. 8, 11 and 13, which round the argument off. Whereas the subject of vv. 6–8 is promise, vv. 9–13 deal with its eschatological fulfilment, which manifests itself in the confession of faith according to vv. 9–11 and, according to vv. 12–13, in calling upon the Lord.

It is a matter of dispute whether vv. 5 and 6 are in contradictory contrast. If one denies the polemical character of the passage[50] and considers that v. 4 is talking about the goal of the law, then the obedience of faith must be understood as the fulfilling of the law, and the latter as being a promise pointing forward to the righteousness of faith (as in 3.21).[51] But Paul is employing harsh antithesis down to the actual details of his formulation. As the law-giver with his demand for works, Moses stands over against the righteousness conferred by faith, which expresses itself in the acceptance of the

---

[47] Vielhauer, p. 49f.

[48] Cf. the commentaries on this passage by Zahn, Billerbeck and Barrett; H. Ulonska, *Paulus und das Alte Testament*, 1964, p. 191.

[49] Cf. the commentaries on this passage by E. Kühl, *Der Brief des Paulus an die Römer*, 1913; Lietzmann; O. Michel, *Der Brief an die Römer*, [12]1963; J. Munck, *Christus und Israel*, 1957, p. 67; Kamlah, *op. cit.*, p. 281; Luz, *op. cit.*, pp. 91f.

[50] Luz, *op. cit.*, p. 92.

[51] P. Bläser, *Das Gesetz bei Paulus*, 1941, pp. 179f.; F. Flükkiger, 'Christus, des Gesetzes Telos', *ThZ* 11, 1955, p. 155f.

divine promise. This manifests itself, he writes, in the *viva vox evangelii*;[52] here too, therefore, there is an allusion to the relation between letter and spirit. The diatribe offers a profusion of parallels, of interest to form critics,[53] for the personification of the righteousness of faith. It has theological relevance for the understanding of Paul's concept of the righteousness of God,[54] because in the righteousness of faith the power of the spirit becomes visible – the power, that is to say, of the Christ who shows himself to be present and of the new aeon brought about by him. This tallies with the statement in 10.3, where the equally personified righteousness of God demands our obedience through our acceptance of the Gospel. In this way the theme of the nearness of the Word emerges. Because the synagogue resisted this Word, the church has assumed precedence over it, receiving a prerogative which manifests itself in the end of the law and in the apostolic mission. It is the turning point of the aeon.

The importance which Lev. 18.5 had for the apostle is shown by his accurate rendering of the Septuagint text in Gal. 3.12, his paraphrased summing-up of it in Rom. 2.13, and by the way in which, in v. 5, he puts the decisive phrase first, for the sake of antithesis. The righteousness of the law demands works, and promises temporal and eternal life only to the man who performs these works.[55] According to Rom. 2.17–3.19 and Gal. 3.10–12, Paul was certain that no one can or should achieve righteousness in this way. The lawgiver Moses himself pointed this out in warning tones. The introduction to v.6 clearly suggests that to interpret the text in this sense is to violate the meaning of Scripture. For the statement in Deut. 30 cited here is taken from the very same Moses who is quoted in v.5. The apostle apparently sees in this no problem. The Word which is near to us and which as promise points forward to the gospel is in contradiction to Moses to the extent in which he embodies the 'letter'. In content, therefore, Lev. 18.5 and Deut. 30.11ff. must be distinguished, although both passages belong to the Torah. Never, perhaps, did Paul

---

[52] Luz, p.92, is unwilling to stress the antithesis because there is no direct mention of the Spirit.

[53] R. Bultmann, *Der Stil der paulinischen Predigt und die kynisch-stoische Diatribe*, 1910, pp. 87f.; H. Thyen, *Der Stil der jüdisch-hellenistischen Homilie*, 1955, p. 42, n. 25.

[54] Contrary to H. Conzelmann, 'Paulus und die Weisheit', *NTS* 12, 1966, p. 242. Personification as a 'conventional stylistic expedient' does not remove the question of whether in any given case a mythological background is present, and whether personification in our passage and in the context of the relation between spirit and letter is theologically significant.

[55] Cf. Billerbeck on this passage.

show more clearly that, as a matter of course, he drew a dividing line even through Scripture; and the criterion he applies is the difference between promise and law or – to put it in even stronger terms – the message of justification. It is this which forces him to deal dialectically even with the concept of the law.

This point must be carried even further. The apostle also takes Deut. 30.11ff. from the fixed, written Old Testament tradition. We must therefore realize (contrary to the idealist tradition) that a thing does not become 'letter' because it is moulded by a tradition deposited in written documents. It can 'speak' to us through this very form, in so far as it is the promise of grace. The antithesis between spirit and letter therefore by no means coincides with the antithesis between spirit and tradition; the two overlap. As well as the law, Christ also ends the tradition which ministered to the demand for works. Because this is true even of the scriptures, large parts of the Old Testament have become meaningless for Paul. On the other hand, the spirit again and again takes up tradition – not only original Christian material but also tradition in the form of scriptural evidence. Then it begins to 'speak'.[56] Unlike Philo, the apostle did not spiritualize scripture, so that it would be permissible to make the greater 'inwardness' of Deut. 30.11ff. the reason for Paul's approval of this quotation.[57] Still less does his interpretation content itself with saying 'it is written'. The dialectical handling of the Old Testament which is obvious here fundamentally implies a critical interpretation of scripture and of all tradition in general, even if Paul did not discuss this theoretically. What was fore-given here was the tendency – a tendency which was already dominating Judaism – to interpret the Old Testament eschatologically. The apostle took over this just as he took over many rabbinic methods of exegesis. But he did not simply give it an extra messianic emphasis, as Judaism was also frequently able to do. Breaking away from Jewish methods and intention, he exploited the tendency critically, playing it off even against scripture and tradition, by making the doctrine of justification the essential and criterion of the 'near' Word. In that light he was forced to set

[56] Curiously enough Luz (p. 92) thinks that Paul is hardly aware of the problem of the gap between exegesis and text; he believes that the question of the proper use of Scripture is not in dispute (p. 110); and does not even recognize the Spirit as being the voice of the Scriptures (p. 133). Yet on p. 135 he denies the existence of a hermeneutical system which theologically masters the Old Testament as a whole.

[57] C. H. Dodd's view in *The Epistle of Paul to the Romans*, [8]1941, pp. 165f.

scripture against scripture, tradition against tradition, the law as promise against the Torah as a demand for works; and so, as a result of this proceeding, even Christology, eschatology and anthropology adopt their criterion from this starting point – as is the case, for example, in the dispute with the Corinthian enthusiasts. Although Paul did not develop any systematic dogmatic system, he was yet well aware of an *articulus stantis et cadentis ecclesiae* and clung to it through-out the whole of his theology with an extreme systematic boldness and clarity.

It is only in the light of this insight that we can do justice to the details of Paul's interpretation. The introduction to v.6b, which no doubt derives from Deut. 9.4, underlines the perplexity behind the question which follows. In v.7 the text of Deut. 30.13, which could not be applied Christologically and which spoke of a fruitless voyage, is replaced by a reminiscence of Ps. 107.26. The phraseology used there about ascending into heaven and descending into the abyss is a proverbial way of describing superhuman efforts directed towards some impossible goal.[58] The Christological interpretation reads into it the sense of Ps. 70.20 LXX and Wisdom 16.13, and relates it to the Christological creed. For the first time in the New Testament the ascension is paralleled not, say, by the incarnation[59] but by the descent into the kingdom of the dead.[60] The questions, therefore, now have a meaning which only Christians can understand and affirm. They no longer characterize utter perplexity but the convic-tion that help can be obtained from Christ alone. They do so, how-ever, not merely in rhetorical emphasis but with a plain theological concern: we are to be shown in what way this help is to be achieved.

The Pauline argument has a past history which can be elucidated by the history of tradition and which can hardly be understood with-out. Deut. 30.11–14 was already frequently quoted by the rabbis in order to show how easily one might partake of the divine Word in the Torah, in Israel and in the schools.[61] In Bar. 3.29f., Deut. 30.13 was

---

[58] Cf. Billerbeck on this passage; Luz, *op. cit.*, p.92.

[59] Cf. A. Nygren, *Commentary on Romans*, 1952, p.381; Barrett, commentary on this passage.

[60] Traub, *TWNT* V, p.526; W. Bieder, *Die Vorstellung von der Höllenfahrt Jesu Christi*, 1949, p.72; E. Schweizer, 'Zur Herkunft der Praeexistenzvorstellung bei Paulus', *EvTh* 19, 1959, pp.67f.

[61] Billerbeck on this passage; cf. the legend (mentioned by Kamlah, *op. cit.*, p.276, and cited by Billerbeck, IV, p.314f.) telling of the banishment of R. Eliezer ben Hyrcanus.

applied to Sophia:[62] 'Who hath gone up into heaven, and taken her; And brought her down from the clouds? Who hath gone over the sea, and found her?' The answer which Bar. 3.36f. gives is: 'He hath found out all the way of Knowledge, And hath given it unto Jacob his servant, And to Israel that is beloved of him.' Whereas the original text depicted the needlessness of a long seeking after the Word of God in rhetorical-antithetical terms, this has now become a mythological statement about the heavenly concealment of Wisdom, to which only revelation put an end. Here, too, it is a question of preserving Wisdom, in so far as this is identical with the Torah. But the aspect which is being particularly stressed here is the divine gift as something of which Israel has become the sole partaker and which is the hall-mark of the Jewish community. Most remarkable of all is the mythologizing of the Deuteronomy text, which takes the form of the personification of the divine Word in the figure of the Sophia. The tendency towards a personification of this kind is also to be found in a fragmentary Targum, which too touches on the 'abyss' motif which was so important for Paul:[63] 'Had we but someone like the prophet Jonah, who descended into the depths of the sea.' 'Had we but someone like the prophet Moses, who ascended into heaven. . . . Had we but someone like the prophet Jonah, who descended into the depths of the sea.'

Rom. 10.6ff. has its roots in this tradition. It is by no means rare for Paul to take over motifs from the Sophia myth, especially from Jewish homilies,[64] and the trend was already in existence among Jewish Christians (as I Cor. 2.9 and 10.4 perhaps show). The connection with Phil. 2.8f. ought not to be overestimated.[65] But at the same time we have here the pattern of the humiliation and exaltation of the redeemer, which is bound up with the acknowledgment of the kyrios – a scheme which the apostle preserves hymnally and liturgically but which he otherwise replaces by his own characteristic pattern of cross and resurrection. What is more important is the combination of Christ's ascension and descent as this is presented by John 1.51; 3.13 and, analogously, 6.62. The notion of the ascent into heaven and descent into Hades, which is otherwise alien to Paul, is expressly expounded in·I Peter 3.19, but is already reflected in the quotation

[62] Cf. the commentaries by Lagrange, Lietzmann, Barrett; F. W. Maier, *Israel in der Heilsgeschichte nach* Rom. 9–11, 1929, p. 76; Luz, p. 92.
[63] On this point see Luz, pp. 92f.
[64] Cf. H. Schlier, *Der Brief an die Epheser*, 1957, pp. 160f.
[65] Contrary to Munck, *Christus*, pp. 68f.

in Eph. 4.8. In the latter passage the two motifs are associated, as they are in Rom. 10.6f., in a Midrash-like interpretation of an Old Testament text, with the same purpose of justifying the cosmic rule of Christ and the introduction of the charismatic proclamation of the Word in the church. We must above all realize that the apparently rhetorical questions in Rom. 10.6f. which are strongly emphasized by Paul's interpretation of the Christ event, take on concrete meaning in the light of this tradition. We meet in them the same problem which is familiar to us from the farewell discourses in the Gospel of John: how can a man 'remain' with the redeemer after he has gone away? Where and how is he present? Where and how can those he has left behind obtain salvation, help and comfort? It would be not only impossible, it would also be foolish, to want to fetch Christ back to earth from the realm of the dead. For he is no longer there. But it is equally impossible and unnecessary to call back the exalted one to earth again; for that would deprive him of his present dignity. Both Paul and John reply that from now on the exalted one is near his own earth in the Word of the Gospel. In a way our passage anticipates a piece of Johannine theology and thereby gives a suggestion of the situation in which this theology grew up, as well as the Jewish-Christian background to it, as this is indicated by the motifs of the Sophia myth.

What did the apostle do with this tradition, which already lay ready to his hand? The most significant thing of all is the polemical tendency of our verses. This expresses itself in two ways. By transferring the Sophia myth to Christ, the pre-Pauline tradition established that in Christ God had come close to the church. Over against this Paul energetically draws his readers back to the text of the Old Testament, stressing Deut. 30.14. The exalted Lord is only present in the Word. The righteousness of faith forbids us to seek him anywhere else. Contrary to every theology of the 'facts of redemption', it is established here that the incarnation of Christ does not need to be prolonged or restored. As I Cor. 1.18ff.; II Cor. 2.14ff.; 4.5f. bring out, the gospel is now the mode of his earthly presence and hence (according to Rom. 1.16) the power of God. The whole key of the passage is therefore derived from v.8, which is therefore elucidated in what follows.

At the same time the apostle sets himself apart from the synagogue. It is only acceptance of the gospel which saves. Consequently he does not mention that Deut. 30.14 talked about action and a man's hands as being the tools with which to achieve salvation. The contrast with v. 5 cannot be expressed more clearly.[66] It is also shown by the fact that the original meaning of the phrase which Paul preserves 'with your mouth and in your heart', has been completely altered. The point is no longer to be ready to serve God with the whole person and all one's members; the essential thing now is preaching and confession of faith. The interpretation 'the word of faith' brings this out. What Paul means by this is the Word which precedes us as *fides quae creditur*, i.e., the gospel in the form of homology.[67] Verse 9 makes this clear. Even the order of 'confess' and 'believe', which at first seems odd, is not meaningless. The proclamation of the lordship of Christ in the worship of the church brings about faith in his resurrection.[68] The verse has the structure of one of the precepts of the sacred law, describing the precondition for eschatological salvation. Very probably what we have here is a pre-Pauline formulation[69] into which Paul introduced the allusions to Deut. 30. 14.The introductory ὅτι would then have a recitative sense, and the placing of 'confessing' before 'believing' would thus be more understandable. In v. 9a there is a call to the familiar acclamation, 'Jesus is Lord', the succeeding phrase justifying this on the basis of Christ's resurrection: it is only the one who is risen who is the *Kyrios* of the church and (as v. 12 brings out) of the world. In putting an end to the piety of works, he also ends the despair which searches for salvation without finding it. In v. 10 the apostle's own voice is heard once more. The whole context shows that his concern is to stress faith, which he therefore puts before confession. This order also has good reason behind it. For although it is generally assumed that the verse is talking here mainly about the faith of the heart, it really means the dogmatic belief which the confession of faith preserves and which is a summary of the gospel, as in I Cor. 15.3f. He is not primarily speaking in anthropological terms; he is talking about the relation between church and synagogue. Thus the endorsing quotation from Isa. 28.16 in v. 9–10 reverts to 9.33b.

Whereas the preceding verses bring out the exclusiveness of the salvation which is bound up with faith in justification, vv. 12f. stress its universality, which is expressed in the frequent use of the word πᾶς

---

[66] Luz, *op. cit.*, p. 90.
[67] Bultmann, *TWNT* VI, p. 210; *Theology* I, p. 317; Luz, *op. cit.*, p. 93.
[68] Barrett, commentary on this passage.
[69] E. Dinkler, 'Prädestination bei Paulus', *Festschrift für G. Dehn*, 1957, p. 89.

and, even more clearly, in the abolition of the distinction between Jew and Greek in salvation history. As in Acts 10.36, the 'Lord of all' is the cosmocrator, although in true Pauline fashion his universal rule is initially manifested in believers. The following participial clause has the same meaning. The eschatological fullness of grace, with which Christ is able to enrich the whole world, is to be seen in the church. By 'calling upon', Paul is not merely thinking of prayer but also of acclamation and the proclamation of divine intercession, so that besides the preaching of v.8 and the homology of vv.9f. the event of worship now moves into the foreground. The people who are 'calling upon' the Lord are those who are assembled for worship, described in traditional terms. The 'near' Word has its fixed earthly place and its specific earthly bearer. The promise in Joel 3.5 LXX was fulfilled in the Christian church, which, according to the following section, asserted its Lord's claim to the world through the apostolic mission. The Old Testament had already pointed towards this and in this way appears as chief witness to the fact that the synagogue with its piety of works has been succeeded by the church, which represents the righteousness of faith.

The significance of our passage lies in the fact that it combines the various facets which exercise us under the theme 'letter and spirit'. The antithesis describes in anthropological terms the state of the Christian, divides the church from the synagogue ecclesiologically and is of eschatological and cosmic moment in so far as it asserts Christ's claim to universal rule. Its decisive criterion is belief in justification. In so far it can also become the hermeneutical key to Paul's understanding of the Old Testament, as is the case both in our passage and in Rom. 4 and II Cor. 3.7ff. Paul developed no fixed exegetical method and no self-contained dogmatic system. But he did have a theme which dominates the whole of his theology: the doctrine of justification. This did not only provide him with a 'hermeneutical approach'[70]; it consistently determined his interpretation of Scripture and, from the perspective of the antithesis between law and gospel,[71] gave it a critical determination.[72] In this way he arrived at a curious dialectic, which is already evident in connection with the concept of

[70] Vielhauer, *op. cit.*, p. 54.
[71] Contrary to Luz (p. 108), according to whom 'the voice of the individual biblical word itself shows itself to be the word of God, without any presuppositions at all'. Contrary to the statement on p. 135, Paul in fact limited freedom of interpretation.
[72] Vielhauer, *op. cit.*, p. 57.

the law, which further leads to the varying evaluation of Abraham and Moses, and finally permits him to play off scripture against scripture. It would hardly be going too far to talk in epigrammatic terms about a canon within the canon.[73]

We must not, of course, go on to conclude from this that Paul's Old Testament hermeneutics, which are so characteristic of him, grow out of soteriology, not out of Christology.[74] If this statement means that the contrast of law and gospel – i.e., the doctrine of justification – is its main characteristic, this is entirely correct. But if this is exaggerated into an antithesis, it may certainly ward off a traditional, over-simplified view which appeals to the Reformed slogan 'what presents Christ' and uses this as starting point for the comfortable scheme of promise and fulfilment. The critical function of Paul's hermeneutics must not under any circumstances be passed over apologetically and positivistically, as is almost always the case today. But at the same time an antithesis between Christology and soteriology is not to the purpose and involves the danger of moving a Christian anthropology into the centre of the apostle's theology, so that this theology is understood from the perspective of faith in justification instead of in the light of the righteousness of faith. This would be to make the theme 'spirit and letter' the code for Pauline hermeneutics, not their key. We should then no longer be sufficiently expressing the fact that Christian faith is based not only on the kerygma which brings it about, but also on the scriptures already given, in which the pre-eminence of the gospel over every form of ecclesiology is documented in the most emphatic way possible. We should also be failing to recognize that for the apostle, the spirit constitutes not only the earthly presence of Christ but also his lordship, and that to a universal degree. Pauline soteriology simply means the presence and lordship of Christ and therefore the justification of the ungodly. Only the Christ who draws near to us in the Word of the gospel and rules through that Word preserves our faith from becoming a Christian ideology. Because Jesus allies himself with the ungodly in the name of God, the Spirit permits the justification of the ungodly to be proclaimed and believed, the exalted one remains, in him, identical with that same Jesus and is present among us on earth, and the work of Jesus goes forth to the ends of the earth. The Pauline doctrine of justification is inseparably anchored in Christology, just

[73] *Ibid.*, p. 54.
[74] Contrary to Vielhauer, *op. cit.*, p. 43.

as, conversely, it interprets this Christology so that the *Kyrios* does not simply become one religious hero among others. The theme 'the spirit and the letter' is accordingly incorporated in the antithesis of gospel and law. It preserves, however, the primacy of Christology in theology. The Spirit is the Lord who becomes present on earth through the Word, and who may not simply be remembered in a theology of the facts of redemption or replaced by a creed.

This has consequences for hermeneutics as well. The Old Testament is a document to which both Judaism and Christianity appeal. It is a misuse of that Old Testament if we forget this fact for a single moment. When the Gentile church simply took away the Old Testament from the Jews, it had to pay for this by only being capable of interpreting it allegorically or morally, or in the light of a scheme of a salvation-historical development from promise to fulfilment. It forgot that Paul had been able to term the Old Testament the 'letter', or misunderstood this as being a call to spiritual or historical-critical interpretation. As a result the Christianity of the Gentiles generally followed in Philo's footsteps or ended up with Marcion. Paul would have been in a position to warn the church against both. He spurned neither scripture nor tradition, but recognized both as the 'speaking Word' – the documentation of the spirit. But at the same time he made the binding nature of scripture and tradition in the Christian church depend on their being interpreted in the light of the spirit and on their capacity for being so interpreted. Because, however, he was compelled to define the spirit Christologically in the dispute with the Jews and the enthusiasts, he was bound to put the critical question: where in the Old Testament was the voice of the righteousness of faith to be heard, and where that other voice which spoke of the piety of works? He could only do this by forbidding the righteousness of faith to be considered as one kind of piety among others, and by calling it instead the work and the lordship of that Christ who, both before and after his exaltation, joined himself to the ungodly.

INDEXES

INDEX OF BIBLICAL REFERENCES

169

INDEX OF MODERN SCHOLARS